INDIA AND HER NEIGHBOURS

INDIA AND HER NEIGHBOURS.

BY

W. P. ANDREW

GYAN

Published by

Gyan Publishing House
5, Ansari Road
Daryaganj, New Delhi-110002
Phone: 011-47034999, 9811692060
E-mail: books@gyanbooks.com

Distribution Network
gyanbooks.com
India, USA, Canada, UK, Australia

ISBN: 978-93-6208-043-1 (PB)
First Published, 1878

2nd Impression 2024

Printed at: Gyan Press, Delhi.

INDIA AND HER NEIGHBOURS
Author: W. P. ANDREW

INDIA AND HER NEIGHBOURS.

BY

W. P. ANDREW,

AUTHOR OF THE INDUS AND ITS PROVINCES, A MEMOIR ON THE EUPHRATES,
&c., &c., &c.

WITH

MAPS AND APPENDIX.

LONDON:

WM H. ALLEN & CO., 13, WATERLOO PLACE,
PALL MALL, S.W.
1878.

PREFACE.

All eyes in the East, as in the West, have long expected the struggle for supremacy between England and Russia. That struggle, if for a season deferred, still appears to be inevitable.

Every act in the great drama of war between Russia and Turkey has most powerfully affected the nations of Central Asia and agitated our north-west frontier in India. While in our peaceable and well-ordered possessions the call to arms against the Czar has excited the utmost enthusiasm.

The Seikh and the Gourka, the fiercest soldiers in Asia, to whom the din of battle is as the breath of their nostrils, vie in ardour with the Mussulman, who burns to avenge the wrongs of the Head of his faith. Even the Hindostanee, forgetting his caste restraints and prejudices, longs to strike a blow for those whose salt he and his fathers have eaten in contentment and peace.

In Northern India, the Punjaub and the border lands beyond, we have an inexhaustible field for recruiting men of fine physique whose trade is war, and accustomed to arms from childhood.

"There never was put forward a greater fallacy or an error more likely to be mischievous, than, that the Turkish question was of no importance in an Indian point of view." The grand problem now in course of solution in Turkey must affect in its results, whatever they may be, in the most immediate and powerful manner, our prestige and prosperity in India. Even during the Crimean campaign, the varying fortunes of the field elicited either the apprehension or the applause of the nations of the East, from the shepherd in his solitude to the warrior chief in his stronghold, while thousands of Moolahs prayed Allah to bless the arms of the "Sooltan of Room."

When the fall of Sebastopol was announced at Dera Ismael Khan, on the Upper Indus, the news was received with the greatest enthusiasm by all classes. The bazaars of the city were brilliantly illuminated, every wealthy shopkeeper displaying from 1,000 to 1,200 lamps.

The native soldiers of India have not only fought the battles of the Empire in Persia, China and Abyssinia, but the Sepoy of Bengal and Madras crossed bayonets with honour with the French in the Mauritius, while their brethren of Bombay were sent under Sir David Baird to encounter the same gallant enemy in Egypt, by Lord Wellesley, a Governor-General of India whose eagle-eyed and bold conceptions were at the time as much decried and cavilled at by lesser men as now we see decried and maligned the manly and good old English policy of the present Government in upholding the honour of the country and in protecting the rights of nations confirmed by treaties.

The policy of the Empire at this moment is resisted even by those whose experience and knowledge might have taught them that in the gravest crises of our time loyalty to the throne and love of country would be best evinced by a noble forbearance, if not a generous support, to Her Majesty's servants under such momentous circumstances.

It is in vain to say India is not threatened, that the Suez Canal is safe. The canal—glorious work as it is—can be easily injured, or even for a time destroyed. We want an alternative route to India, and, after having ignored for years the warnings of our leading statesmen and soldiers, are we to be told from Vienna that the best alternative route is not only threatened but that if Russia gets possession of "Batoum, which, in relation to the Upper Euphrates valley forms the first stage from a political, military and commercial point of view down to Mesopotamia and the Persian Gulf,"* the command of the best route to our Indian possessions would be in the hands of our rival for empire in the East?

It is certain if we decline to connect the Mediterranean with the Persian Gulf, Russia will connect the Black Sea with the Persian Gulf. The nation desires peace, but the strong man must be armed to hold his goods in peace!

Is it too much to say that had the Persian Gulf been united with a port on the Mediterranean by the Euphrates Railway the Russo-Turkish war would not have occurred? When peace is restored, it is to be hoped that our Government will come to an agreement with the Porte as to the Euphrates Railway on the basis recommended by the Select Committee of the House of Commons, presided over by Sir Stafford Northcote in 1872, and for the Euphrates telegraph, terms for which were arranged with Her Majesty's Government in 1857. The Porte however preferred a line through Asia Minor.

I cannot refrain from again calling attention

* *Vienna Correspondent of Times*, 8th May, 1878.

to the opinion of the Austrian War Minister, who, after the battle of Sadowa, re-organised the army and brought it to its present state of efficiency.

So long ago as 1858 Field-Marshal-Lieutenant Baron Kuhn von Kuhnenfeld predicted that Russia would in future probably try to satisfy her craving for an open sea-board by operating through Asia.

'"She will not," says this distinguished authority, "reach the shores of the Persian Gulf in one stride, or by means of one great war. But taking advantage of continental complications, when the attention and energy of European States are engaged in contests more nearly concerning them, she will endeavour to reach the Persian Gulf step by step, by annexing separate districts of Armenia. . . . .

'"Whatever the commercial value of the Suez Canal to Central Europe, there is no doubt that it is secondary in importance to the Euphrates Railway, which affords the only means of stemming Russian advances in Central Asia, and which directly covers the Suez Canal.'"*

At this moment when great events in Europe are being watched by our distant fellow-subjects in India and by the tribes and nations which

* *Vide* Appendix E. 368.

dwell between us; when the first Mahomedan power in the world is held in the deadly grasp of the Czar; when England, this time not "the unready" is slowly but resolutely putting her native legions in motion, and their dusky brothers in India are hurrying to arms at the call of their common sovereign; at this moment some account of the past and present history of India and Her Neighbours may not be deemed inopportune.

Among the more important considerations presented to the reader of this volume, the following appear to merit special remark—

That England is not only a great Eastern Power, but that she possesses more Mahomedan subjects than the Sultan and the Shah together;—

That the standing armies of the feudatory princes of India number over 300,000 men with more than 5,000 guns;—

And that it is urgent to have improved and additional means of communication between England and India.

In order further to interest the general reader I have made prominent as central figures, the heroes and heroines of Indian history, surrounded by the dramatic incidents of their careers, leaving in shadow the minor actors, and passing over altogether, or but briefly alluding to, events of secondary importance; giving, in short, a series of word-pictures of the more remarkable characters, occurrences, and places.

I have to thank kind friends for valuable advice and assistance, and to Mr. Edwyn Sandys Dawes I am specially indebted for that which relates to commerce and finance.

W. P. A.

CONTENTS.

PAGE

CHAPTER XII.

THE REMARKABLE WOMEN OF INDIA—*continued.*

CHAPTER XIII.

THE REMARKABLE WOMEN OF INDIA—*continued.*

CHAPTER XIV.

THE REMARKABLE WOMEN OF INDIA—*continued.*

CHAPTER XV.

THE REMARKABLE WOMEN OF INDIA—*continued.*

CHAPTER XVI.

THE REMARKABLE WOMEN OF INDIA—*concluded.*

CHAPTER XVII.

ORIGIN AND PROGRESS OF BRITISH RULE IN INDIA.
BOMBAY PRESIDENCY.

CHAPTER XVIII.

ORIGIN AND PROGRESS OF BRITISH RULE IN INDIA—*continued.*
MADRAS PRESIDENCY AND BRITISH BURMAH.

PAGE

CHAPTER XXXII.

COMMERCE OF INDIA.

CHAPTER XXXIII.

COMMERCE OF INDIA—*continued.*

CHAPTER XXXIV.

INTERNAL COMMUNICATIONS.

CHAPTER XXXV.

EXTERNAL COMMUNICATIONS.

CHAPTER XXXVI.

FINANCE.

CHAPTER XXXVII.

OUR NEIGHBOURS.

CHAPTER XXXVIII.

OUR NEIGHBOURS—*continued.*

CHAPTER XXXIX.

OUR NEIGHBOURS—*continued.*

CHAPTER XL.

OUR NEIGHBOURS—*concluded.*

APPENDIX.

APPENDIX A.

APPENDIX B.

APPENDIX C.

APPENDIX D.

APPENDIX E.

GENERAL INDEX TO CONTENTS.

CHAPTER I.

GENERAL PHYSICAL FEATURES.

Boundaries—Extent—Himalaya Range and minor Hills—Valleys—Principal Rivers and Sources—Ports.

Boundaries.—India, includes not only the great peninsula stretching southward, like a vast triangle, from the Himálayas to Cape Comorin, but also a long strip of seaboard on the eastern side of the Bay of Bengal, from Chittagong to the tenth parallel of northern latitude. The base of this pyramid is formed by the long mountain ranges of the Himálayas—the "Abode of Snow," answering to the Imaus of Greek geographers—which divide all upper India from Turkistan and Tibet, bearing away south-eastwards from Cashmere to the eastern corner of Assam. The natural barrier thus formed between India and the outer world, is carried on southwards by the hills which separate the Punjab and Scinde from Afghánistán and Beluchistan. From Assam, at the eastern end, a like hill-barrier marks off British territory from Burmah and Siam. The whole length of India's land-boundary is nearly 4,500 miles; the seaboard from Kurrachee on the west, to the southernmost point of Tenasserim on the east, being about 4,000 miles.

Extent.—Some idea of the size of our Indian Empire may be gathered from the fact that Peshawur and Cape Comorin are more than 1,800 miles apart, while the distance from Kurrachee to Rangoon is nearly 1,900 miles, or nearly thrice the distance of the Land's End from John o' Groat's. Even in Southern India, it is 900 miles across from Bombay to Point Palmyras on the Orissa coast. India, in short, covers an area of more than 1,500,000 square miles, or as much ground as all Europe, without Russia.* Of this area, three-fifths, or more than 900,000 square miles, are ruled directly by us: the remainder, consisting chiefly of Native States, owning in different degrees a certain vassalage to the Paramount Power, which has supplanted alike the Mahratta and the Mogul. The French and Portuguese still retain the rights of Sovereignty over limited territories.

General Physical Features.—The vast and sparsely wooded plains watered by the Ganges and the Jumna, and stretching for many hundred miles from Umballa to Rájmahál, show broad tracts of level well-cultivated ground, interspersed with sandy waste. In Bengal a vast alluvial plain yields an increase elsewhere unknown. In parts of the Punjáb and Rajpootana, in Central India, and Guzerat, the surface of the ground is broken into frequent hills and valleys, more or less wooded. In Southern India and the Central Provinces, there are no plains of any magnitude, if we except the strip of coast overlooked by the Eastern and Western Ghauts. Indeed, nearly the whole of Southern India, or the Deccan, is a rugged table-land, girdled with a chain of hills varying in height from 1,500 to 7,000 feet.

Hills.—Hindustan, or the land of the Hindoos, is,

* From this reckoning the Island of Ceylon is, of course, omitted, as forming politically no part of India in the present day.

strictly speaking, the country between the Himálayas and the Vindhya Hills, with the Indus for its western and the Ganges for its eastern boundary ; the southern half of India being more correctly styled the Deccan, or Southern Land. The great mountain mass of the Himalayas, some 1,500 miles long by 150 broad, is at once the largest and loftiest in the world. Its snowy peaks tower with solemn majesty from twenty to twenty-nine thousand feet above the sea, while the passes across it are often 17,000 feet high, only a thousand feet below the line of perpetual snow—2,000 feet above the summit of Mont Blanc. The glaciers in these mountains far surpass in extent those of the Alps. For rugged grandeur nothing can approach the higher ranges, while the lower and outer, on which stand Simla, Kasaulee, Mussoorie, Nainee-Tal with its beautiful lake, Almora, and Darjeeling, at heights varying from 6,000 to 8,000 feet, have the softer beauty of steep hill sides clothed with oak and fir, and noble rhododendrons. From some of these hill-stations, you may look over a billowing sea of hills to the great Snowy Range some fifty or sixty miles away, yet in certain seasons seeming quite close at hand. In these mountains, with the exception of Kangra, and the Dhoon, there are few valleys of any great extent, the hills usually rising steeply up from hollows many hundred feet, and the villages climbing with difficulty up the slopes. From the plains to Simla and other hill stations there are good roads, but in the interior of these regions the road is usually but a few feet wide, with a rocky wall on one side, and a precipice going sheer down from the other. Here and there, through a deep narrow gorge or yawning chasm, winds a swift stream, only to be crossed by a hanging bridge of rope, swaying with every movement, or the trunk of a mighty pine. One charm of mountain scenery is wanting here. Except in the rainy season, when every dry watercourse becomes a torrent, there is a general absence of water, especially in the form of lakes.

"The advantages of the Neilgherry Hills have yet to be fully utilized for European settlements. The climate, configuration, soil and water supply of these hills are all favourable; and the range is easily accessible. In establishing new stations there, however, or in enlarging existing stations, it will be well to keep in mind the mistakes of plan and the neglect of sanitary precautions which have brought so many hill stations into disrepute, and which some years ago, in like manner, affected the reputation of Ootacamund as a place of residence."*

Valleys.—The Kangra and smaller valleys of the Himalayas are of great fertility. In them we see the astonishing spectacle of the productions of the temperate and torrid zones growing side by side, the creeping rose intertwining its branches with the bamboo, and the wild violet and tulip flowering round the roots of the plantain. Further in the interior there are inexhaustible forests of pine growing in a rich vegetable loam, on which all the fruits and vegetables of Europe will thrive in perfection. In Kanawur, the vine unpruned, uncultivated, growing like a bramble in the hedges, yields a grape unequalled in the world. Water power, as we have seen, is not

* Indian Public Opinion.

wanting at certain seasons. The wool trade might be increased to any extent. At the confluence of certain streams gold dust is found. The Kulu valley, in the Kangra district of the Punjab, is very rich in minerals, one of the most valuable of which is galena or lead ore, often containing large percentages of silver. Still more valuable than gold or silver—iron exists in the hills in extraordinary abundance, though coal is wanting. Following the lead of the Government, European enterprise has already made great progress in the cultivation of the tea plant in the hilly regions of India.

Rivers.—From the heart of these mountains spring the great rivers of Northern India, the Indus, the Sutlej, the Jumna, the Ganges, and the Brahmapootra, which after gladdening and fertilising the plains below, find their way by many mouths to the Arabian Sea and the Bay of Bengal. The longest of these rivers is the Indus, which after receiving the other rivers of the Punjab, reaches the Arabian sea some 1,800 miles from its source. The Ganges, with a total length of 1,500 miles, having its turbid volume swollen at Allahabad by the blue waters of the Jumna, debouches in the Bay of Bengal. At one time the country through which these rivers now flow, was the sandy bed of a broad sea rolling between the Himálayas and the Vindhya Range. In those days, many parts of the Deccan must have been under water. Some curious fossils have been found in the Sewalik Hills, a low range outlying the Himálayas.

The Suliman Hills which form the western boundary

of the Punjab overlook the course of the Indus for some 350 miles, from a height almost of 11,000 feet. Much lower than these, but with a savage grandeur of their own, are the Aravulli Hills, from whose southern spurs the Vindhyas stretch away across the peninsula at a height seldom exceeding 2,000 feet. Their northern ridges slope down to the table-land of Málwa. Between them and the bolder line of the Satpoora Hills, flows the Nerbudda along its rocky bed through 800 miles of winding cliffs and dark forest down to its outlet in the Gulf of Cambay. Into the same gulf below Surat falls the Táptee.

From the western end of the Satpooras a long chain of hills passes near the seaboard down to Cape Comórin, their height varying from 1,000 to 4,700 feet at Mahabuleshwar, the summer retreat of the Bombay Government, to 7,000 near Coorg. At this point the Western Ghauts or "Stairs" meet the loftier Neilgherry or Blue Mountains, and these again stretching eastward join the Eastern Ghauts, a lower range which runs up the Madras Coast northward to melt into the highlands of Orissa. The country enclosed by these ranges forms a broad and rolling table-land, watered by many rivers and broken towards the south into craggy hills. Of these rivers the chief is the Godavery, which rising in the Western Ghauts near Nassick bends south-eastward to cross the Nizam's dominions, and receiving the drainage of the Satpooras cleaves its way, after a course of 900 miles, through the Eastern Ghauts into the Bay of Bengal near Kokonáda. Next in length comes the Kistna, which also rises in the Western Ghauts, and after a devious course reaches the Coromandel Coast near Masulipatam. In the north-eastern corner of the Bay of Bengal lies the Delta of the Brahmapootra, one of the greatest of Indian rivers, which under the name of the Sanpoo flows for many hundred miles along Tibet, until turning the eastern corner of the Himalayas it rolls westward through the broad Assam valley, past Goalpára, into Lower Bengal. Another large river, the Irawaddy, descends from its Himálayan cradle through Upper Burmah southward into Pegu, and after a course of nearly 1,100 miles reaches the sea by several mouths between Cape Negrais and Rangoon.

Ports.—For all its length of coast-line India possesses but few good harbours. That of Bombay however is one of the noblest in the world. Kurrachee, the European port of India, is destined to be to the Indus and its tributaries what Calcutta is to the Ganges and its tributaries. Moulmein and Rangoon carry on a thriving trade, and, in spite of some dangerous shoals in the Hoogly, the port of Calcutta is the seat of a sea borne trade worth more than £50,000,000 sterling. Goa, a good harbour on the western coast, belongs to Portugal. Carwar, Cochin, and Viziadroog might be made more useful at no great cost, and the harbour now making at Madras on the skilful plan of Mr. William Parkes, consulting engineer to the Secretary of State for India, will turn an open roadstead into a welcome and sheltered haven.

CHAPTER II.

CLIMATE.

Seasons in Hills and Plains.

Climate.—India in its hills and plains may be said to possess every variety of climate and temperature.

The seasons are three ; the hot, the rainy and the cold seasons. These vary much in different localities, but as a rule the hot season generally may be said to prevail from the middle of March to the middle of June.

In the plains of India, during the hot weather, the moist heat of Bengal and the dry heat of the hot winds of North-Western India and the Punjab, rising to 120° in the shade, differ from each other much as a vapour bath does from the mild blast of a furnace.

Along the coast line the sea breezes are very refreshing and serve to temper the heat. At Simla and other hill stations the summer is delightful.

About the middle of June the rains commence and continue with little intermission till the end of September. The rainfall varies greatly. In the North-West Provinces and Guzerat it ranges from 15 to 30 inches, most of it falling in three months. In the Khasia Hills 600 inches of rain have been measured in the year. This is also the season of inundation from the melting of the snow in the mountains, causing the rivers to overflow their banks.

November December and January constitute the winter months or cold season which is preceded and followed by short periods of moderate heat. During the winter months in the N.W. Provinces and the Punjab there is invigorating cold weather, when water is frozen in the shallow pools during the night and there is hoar-frost in the morning, the comfortable warmth and glow of a fire reminding the English sojourner of home. Even in Lower Bengal and Southern India, the temperature is moderate, and life something more than enjoyable from the buoyancy of the air under a cloudless sky.

At the hill stations, such as Simla and Mussoorie, the cold is intense during this period, and the fall of snow prolonged.

So recent is our acquaintance with those portions of our widely extended dominions best adapted for the residence of Europeans, that at the neighbouring stations of Bareilly, Moradabad, and Shajuhanpore, the existence of the beautiful lake at Nainee Tal was as much a mystery, 30 years ago, as the sources of the Niger.

The Himalayan and Inter-Himalayan regions are wonderfully adapted for the European constitution. They are as salubrious, and generally cooler than a great portion of Australia. Europeans can, if they choose, work in the open air, in proof of which it is stated that the strongest built house at one of the hill stations was constructed entirely by European soldiers, without any native aid whatever.

The offspring of pure European parents brought up in the hills does not degenerate. East Indians or Eurasians rather improve than otherwise in those elevated regions.

This being so, one would ask why military settlements have not been made in the Himâlayas of time-expired or pensioned European soldiers, whose sons could succeed their fathers in the ranks. A small colony of Europeans in the hills with railways in the plains would have been a sheet anchor during the mutiny and might have prevented it. *

Now that railways are being extended in all directions it is to be hoped that fitting stations may be found in the hills, for the majority of the European troops in India. This would promote health and efficiency, saving many valuable lives and much expenditure.

* *Vide* Colonization in India and Australia, compared by the Author.

CHAPTER III.

FLORA AND FAUNA.

Flora.—The broad belt of marshy jungle deadly to human life which divides the Himálayas from the adjacent plains, affords, in wood and some other materials, the means, to a limited extent, of smelting the abundant iron ore found on the lower slopes. Many parts of India are rich in forest trees suited to almost every purpose of use or ornament. The teak tree abounds in British Burmah, the Godavery valley, and Malabar; the bamboo in Kamaun, Bengal, and Southern India. Pines and deodars luxuriate in the Himálayas; saul, ebony, and satin-wood, in Central India; the sandal, iron, and blackwood in Coorg, and Mysore; oak and walnut-wood in Sikkim; the India rubber-tree in Assam; and the palm-trees of the tropics, in Bengal.

The noble mango-groves of Hindústán give welcome shade to the traveller weary with marching over miles of sun-burnt plain, and the banyan-tree of Bengal grows into a forest by throwing out new roots from its spreading branches. Cottages are thatched with palm-leaves, and houses built with the help of scaffolding made of bamboo. Cocoa-nut fibre makes excellent rigging, and cocoa-nut oil is highly prized for lamps. Bamboo fibre serves for mats and baskets; a bamboo stem makes the best of lance-shafts, while one of its joints will do duty for a bottle. From the sap of the palm-tree is brewed the taree or toddy, a favourite drink among the lower classes. Another kind of palm yields the betel-nut, which natives of every class and both sexes delight to chew. The saul and deodar are largely used for railway sleepers, and in districts where coal is dear, forest timber serves as fuel for steamers and railway trains.

All over India there are two harvests yearly; in some places three. Bájra,* jowár,† rice, and some other grains are sown at the beginning and reaped at the end of the rainy season. The cold weather crops, such as wheat, barley, some other kinds of grain, and various pulses, are reaped in the spring. It is a mistake to suppose that the people of India live entirely on rice. Rice is grown mainly in some parts of Lower Bengal, in British Burmah, the Concan, and Malabar. In Hindústán and the Punjab the staple food is wheat and millet; in the Deccan a poor kind of grain called ragee.‡ Berár, Khándesh, and Guzerat yield large crops of cotton, while the sugar-cane abounds in Rohilcund and Madras. The poppy-fields of Málwa and Bengal yield the opium which forms a main source of Indian revenue. Indigo and jute are raised in Bengal. Coffee has become the staple product of the hill districts in Coorg, Wainad, and the Neilgherries. The tea-gardens of Assam, Cachár, Sylhet, and the southern slopes of the Himálayas from Kangra to Darjeeling furnish ever-increasing supplies of good tea. The quinine-yielding chinchona is grown in forests yearly

* Holcus Spicatus.—A small round grain, very nourishing.
† Holcus Sorgum.—Common in Levant, Greece, and Italy.
‡ Cynosurus coroianus.

increasing on the Neilgherry and Darjeeling Hills. Another medicinal plant of great value, the ipecacuanha, seems to thrive in the Sikkim Terai. Cardamoms and pepper abound along the Western Ghauts, hemp and linseed are largely exported, and tobacco is widely grown throughout India.

Of fruit and vegetables there are many kinds. Mangoes, melons, pumpkins, guavas, custard-apples, plaintains, oranges, limes, citrons, and pomegranates, abound everywhere; figs, dates, peaches, strawberries, and grapes thrive well in many places; apricots, apples, and black currants grow wild in the hills, as the pine-apple does in British Burmah. Cucumbers, yams, tomatoes, sweet potatoes, and many vegetables grown in England, are raised abundantly for general use. "Flowers of every shape and hue, and often of the richest scent, from the rose and jasmine to the oleander and the water-lily, spangle the plains, cover the surfaces of lakes and ponds, or glimmer in climbing beauty among the woods. The rhododendrons of the Himálayas grow like forest trees, and crown the hill-side in April and May with far-spreading masses of crimson blossoms. From the rose-gardens of Gházipúr is extracted the attar, a few drops of which contain the gathered fragrance of a thousand flowers.*"

Fauna.—The jungles are alive with elephants, bears, wild buffaloes, tigers, leopards, panthers, and hyænas. Wolves and jackals prowl among the ravines in quest of deer and other prey. The lion, inferior in size and courage to his African brother, is chiefly to be found in the wilds of Rajpootana and Guzerat; the camel in the

* Trotter's "History of India."—Introduction.

sandy regions of the North West; the one-horned rhinoceros among the swamps of the Ganges. Deer of many kinds abound everywhere. Snakes, poisonous and harmless, haunt the jungles and glide among the ruins of old cities. Wild boars are common in Bengal and Western India. Monkeys abound in most parts of the country. The rivers swarm with fish, and alligators bask like huge lizards along their banks. Horses and ponies of divers breeds are used chiefly for riding, while the fields are ploughed and the carts and carriages of the country are drawn by bullocks of the Brahmini or humped species. In many parts of India oxen still serve as carriers of merchandise. Buffaloes are generally kept for milk and ploughing. Sheep and goats are very common, and the goat of Thibet supplies the soft *pashmína* of which Indian shawls and other articles of clothing are made.

The woods re-echo with the harsh cry of the peacock and the lively chattering of parrots, woodpeckers, and other birds of gay plumage; to say nothing of those which are common to India and the West. Eagles and falcons are found in some places; kites, vultures, and crows may be seen everywhere. The great adjutant stork of Bengal with much gravity does scavenger's duty in the most populous cities. Pheasants, partridges, ortolans, quail, snipe, wild-geese and ducks in great variety and abundance tempt the sportsman. The sparrow has followed the Englishman into the Himálayas. It is worth remarking however that song-birds are almost as rare in India as snakes in Ireland.*

* *Vide* Appendix A "Life in the Jungle;" or, "The Sportsman's Paradise."

CHAPTER IV.

MINERALS.

Precious Stones—Coal—Iron—Mineral Oil—Tin.

Precious Stones.—Of mineral wealth India possesses her fair share. It is true her once renowned wealth in diamonds and other gems has disappeared and the famous mines of Golconda have ceased to yield their former treasures; but opals, amethysts and garnets, jasper and carnelians are still found in various places, and gold is washed in small quantities from her streams. More useful minerals are now however the most diligently sought for.

Coal.—India possesses extensive coal fields, and of late years, and notably during the scarcity of this fuel in England in 1871 and 1875 much capital has been invested in opening up collieries. At Raneegunge near Calcutta several mines have been worked for the past twenty years with more or less success, and on the East Indian and Great Indian Peninsular Railways native coal is chiefly used. The low prices, however, at which English and Australian coal is now being delivered at the seaports of India operates against the development of this branch of native industry.

Iron.—Iron is also known to exist in many parts, but more particularly in the sub-Himalayan districts of Kemaon and Gurwal and in the Madras Presidency. It is very pure and abundant, but the absence of coal in the immediate vicinity of the ironstone prevents it being worked. Sooner or later, probably, arrangements will be made to convey the iron ore to the Bengal coal fields, and coal from Bengal to the iron-producing districts; and a trade will spring up similar to that now so extensively and profitably conducted between ports on the Spanish coast and our own great iron towns on the east coast of England, or in the progress of chemical science ere long means may be found for extracting the metal from the ore by some more economical process than the present costly system of smelting, with its excessive consumption of fuel.

Mineral Oils.—In Burmah there is a considerable and growing production of mineral oils.

Tin.—In the Malay peninsula the rich mines of tin are beginning to be worked; but both of these industries are yet capable of great extension.

CHAPTER V.

THE PEOPLE.

Population — Government — Races—Languages—Religions—Mahomedanism—Brahminism—Budism—Parsees—Religion of the Seiks.

Population.—According to the latest census returns, British India, as apart from the purely Native States, is now peopled by 190 million souls; a number largely in excess of all former estimates. Add to this the 50 millions roughly reckoned for the Native States, and a quarter of a million for French possessions, and half a million for those of Portugal, and we get a total of 240¾ millions for all India. Of this vast number, the Province of Bengal was found to contain 64¾ millions within its area of 212,451 square miles, or an average of 305 to the square mile. But now that the thinly-peopled tracts of Assam and Kachar have been formed into a separate province, Bengal may be said to yield an average population of 380 to the square mile, or a total of 60½ millions. Without Orissa the average would be 430, and in some districts or shires, such as Burdwan or Patna, exceeding 550 to the square mile.

In the North-Western Provinces—the "Doáb," or "country of two rivers," to wit, the Jumna and the Ganges—there are 30¾ millions of people over an area of 81,000 square miles. This means an average of 380 souls to the square mile in a province nearly as large as

England, Wales, and Ireland together, and little less populous than England herself. The grain producing country of Oude, lying between the Ganges and the Nepaulese Hills, covers an area of 24,000 square miles, equal to Holland and Belgium, with $11\frac{1}{4}$ million souls, or an average of 469 to the square mile. In the Panjab, exclusive of Cashmere and other tributary States, there are nearly 18 millions of people, or 171 to the square mile. In British Burmah, about $2\frac{3}{4}$ millions, or only 31 to the square mile, are scattered over an area larger than the North-western Provinces. Madras contains about $30\frac{1}{4}$ million people, in an area of 124,500 square miles, or 243 to the square mile, which is a good deal larger than the British Islands. Bombay and Scinde, with an area little less than that of Madras, number only $16\frac{1}{3}$ million souls, or 131 to the square mile. The Central Provinces, though nearly as large as the North-Western, appear to have only $8\frac{1}{5}$ million, or an average of 96 to the square mile. This is about half the average of Mysore, and but little higher than that of the small hill-province of Coorg. In Ajmeer, the English portion of Rajpootana, the average is reckoned at 115, and in Bérar at 126 to the square mile.*

Government.—All these provinces, except Mysore, now held by us in trust for its future sovereign, the descendant of the old Hindoo dynasty displaced by Hyder Ali, and Berár, still nominally governed for the Nizam of Hyderabad, make up the empire directly ruled by the British crown. Subject to the general con-

* Statistical Abstract of British India from 1865 to 1875; presented to Parliament.

trol of the Home Government, the Viceroy and Governor-General in Council may be said to govern as well as reign over the widely extended Empire of British India.

The Presidencies of Bombay and Madras are ruled by Governors appointed from England, with legislative and Executive Councils. Bengal is presided over by a Lieutenant-Governor, aided by a Legislative Council. The North-Western Provinces and the Punjab have each a Lieutenant-Governor without a council. The latter is still a "Non-Regulation Province," so far as its government is not conducted by civil officers alone, and according to the old regulations of the Company. To the same class belong Oude,* the Central Provinces, Assam, Berár, and British Burmah, which are governed each by a Chief Commissioner, with a staff of officers, civil and military, who dispense justice, look after the revenue, and preserve the peace in districts larger than a good-sized English county.

Races.—The people of India may be classified in three ways, according to race, language, or religion. First in order come the aboriginal races, now scattered among the hills and jungles throughout the country to the number of about twelve millions. Under the name of Sántháls, Bheels, Coles, Mairs, Gonds, &c., they all seem to belong to the same Papuan or Australoid type; short of stature, dark skinned, with high cheek bones, flattish noses, large jaws, wide mouths, very little beards, and long coarse hair. They eat all kinds of food, drink fermented liquors, ignore clothes, worship their own gods, speak a language and follow customs unlike those of their more

* Now merged in the N.W. Provinces.

civilised neighbours. Their weapons are bows, arrows, and spears, useful alike in hunting and in war. In parts of Southern India, as in Australia, the boomerang is also used.

Of a kindred, but seemingly higher type, are the Dravidian races of Southern India, who number about thirty millions; whose languages, the Támil, Telugú, and Canarese, have a literature more than a thousand years old, and whose early civilisation dates back some way beyond the Christian era. To the old Dravidian settlers, whencesoever they came, may perhaps be ascribed the dolmans, cromlechs, cairns, flint tools, iron spear-heads, and other relics of a remote past, similar to those which have been found in various parts of Europe. In the hills that border Assam, Bengal, and Upper India, we meet with races of Indo-Chinese or Mongolic stock, akin to those which inhabit Burmah, Thibet, and Siam. They all speak dialects of the same language, and show their common origin in their short but sturdy frames, small eyes, high cheek bones, scanty beards, thin lips, flattened noses, and yellowish or copper-coloured skins.

By far the most numerous of Indian peoples are the Hindoos themselves, whose language and physical traits alike proclaim them sprung from the same Aryan stem as the Persians, the ancient Greeks, the Celts, and nearly all the nations of modern Europe. Their Sanskrit-speaking forefathers seem to have gradually made their way from the regions of the Hindoo Koosh, across the Indus, into the plains of the Punjab and Sirhind, or the country between the Sutlej and the Ganges. Their first settlements were probably made about 1500 B.C., if not before. Their earliest literature, the Vedic hymns, written in a language far older than the Greek of Homer, stamps them as already a cultivated and progressive race, of high religious instincts, varied mental power, and much capacity for social and political growth. Their oldest epic, the Rámáyan, older than the Iliad, or even the Pentateuch, teems with pictures of every domestic virtue, with passages of pure moral beauty and keen poetic insight, with tokens of far reaching philosophy, lofty religious yearnings, and refined enjoyment of all good things in Art and Nature. In many of the arts and sciences these old Hindoos were in advance of nearly all the more civilised nations, Aryan, Semitic, or Turanian, of their day. They had learned to till the ground, to trade, to build tanks and temples, to weave muslin, to produce cunning work in iron, gold, silver, earthenware, ivory and precious stones, ages before Rome was founded or Hezekiah reigned in Judæa. In their village communities and caste-rules of the present day, we have still at work the principles of a system of law and self-government which appears, from the famous Code of Menu, to have been firmly established many centuries before the Christian era. For breadth and subtlety their old philosophers have never been surpassed by the boldest thinkers of any age or country. In short, the Aryan forefathers of the modern Hindoo were a race whom the most civilised nations in modern Europe might be proud to claim as kin.

As the early Aryan settlers gained the mastery in Hindustan, they drove before them most of the older races into the hills and forests, much as the Saxons served the Britons, while the remainder, held in a kind of serfage, made up the lowest of the four castes or classes into which the new social system of their conquerors was divided. Great Hindoo kingdoms, which lasted for many centuries, covered the country north of the Nerbudda. In due time Bengal itself was peopled by an Aryan race, and finally the whole of Southern India passed under the sway of Hindoo princes, though there the process of absorbing or exterminating the subject races was never carried so far as in the north. Among the later Aryan settlers in India were the Yavans, probably Ionian Greeks, who founded a dynasty in Orissa, and the followers of Alexander have left their mark in the Punjab. Of Hindoos by race, the actual number for all India may now be reckoned at 150 millions, who differ from each other in as many ways as an Englishman differs from a Frenchman, a Spaniard or a Greek. But all alike, from the fair-skinned fiery Rajpoot and the broad-shouldered Seik of the north, to the lithe little Mahratta in the west and the dark-skinned, peace-loving trader or peasant of Bengal, are remarkable as a rule for handsome faces, delicate features, slenderly graceful figures, and well shaped limbs.

Of kindred race to the Hindoos are the Parsees. In the eighth century, not long after the Arab conquest of Persia, and the establishment of Islám in the room of the old national sun-worship, the Parsees, a small remnant of the unconverted race were driven by steady persecution, from their retreats in Khorásán to the isle of Ormuz, in the Persian Gulf. Their ill-fortune still following them, they took shelter, first at Diú, in the Gulf of Cambay, and some years later in Guzerát. Here under certain conditions they were allowed to dwell, to erect their towers of silence for the departed, and to build the temples which held the sacred flame kept ever burning in honour of their god—the pure and bright Ormuzd. From Guzerát they gradually made their way over Western India, until at last a new Parsee settlement sprang up in Bombay itself, where the Parsees have since taken the lead in every field of commercial enterprise and social progress.

The Patans, or Afgháns, on the other hand, who inhabit the Punjab frontier, parts of Rohilkund, and much of Hyderabad, belong to that Semitic race which furnished Mahomet with his first converts, and India with her earliest Mahommedan rulers. Far more numerous are the Moguls, a Turkish race, whose forefathers followed the genial, daring and chivalrous Báber into Hindustan. They number more than thirty millions in all, peopling mainly the Punjab, the country around Delhi, and Bengal.

Languages.—The languages or dialects spoken in different provinces, exceed in number those of all Europe. Of those derived from Sanskrit there are at least a dozen of which Hindí, the language of North-Western and Central India, is the most purely Aryan, and Urdú, the language of the official classes, is the most largely mixed with foreign elements, Persian, Arabic, and even English. Each great province, sometimes each district, has its own dialect, differing from the others much as English differs from German, or as both differ from Italian or French. In Southern India the Dravidian languages, such as Támil and Telugú, have the widest prevalence, except in Máhárashtra the country of the Mahrattas, who speak a dialect resembling Hindí. Assam and Nepaul are Aryan by language, while Bootan, British Burmah, and Manikpoor belong in language as well as race to the Turanian family.

Religions.—Classified according to their religious creeds, the people of India might be broadly divided into Mahommedans and Hindoos. In Bengal alone the followers of the Arab Prophet exceed 20 millions. Of the remaining 21 millions, more than 13½ are to be found in the Punjab and N.W. Provinces, and ¼ million in the Central Provinces. In Hyderabad, also, and Cashmere, the Mahommedans muster strong. If language is not always a sure clue to race, neither is religion. While the Patans and Moguls of India speak a language mainly of Aryan birth, millions of Mussulmans in Bengal, and nearly all the Mussulmans in Cashmere, are Hindoos by race, whose forefathers adopted the creed of their Moslem conquerors. The Hindoos in their turn have made a large number of converts in the lowest caste from the people whom they originally subdued. Most of the Indian Mahommedans profess the Sunee or Turkish form of Islám, but the Shea sect, who like the Persians, pay special homage to Ali, the prophet's son-in-law, and to Ali's two sons, Hassein and Hossan, as his lawful successors in the Califate, are to be found chiefly in Cashmere and the Deccan. The differences between them correspond to those between different sects of Christians. In spite of quarrels on minor points, they agree in revering the Korán as the word of God delivered through his prophet Mahomet, the great fountain of moral, social, and civil law for all true believers.

A third form of Islám is the Wahábee, which has lately made some way among the Mahommedans of Behar. These Puritans of their faith are followers of Abdul Wahàb, whose son, in the latter half of the eighteenth century, began to preach a religious revival among his countrymen in Nejed. In India the movement was taken up by Seyed Ahmad of Roi-Bareily, who, exchanging the life of a freebooter for that of a fanatic, took to studying divinity at Delhi, made a pilgrimage to Mecca, and after preaching his new doctrines in Calcutta and Bombay, set out for the Punjab to proclaim a jehad, or holy war, against the Seikhs. His death in battle in 1831 brought his mission to an early close. But his influence survived him, and a Wahábee colony in Swát beyond the Indus, became the centre of a movement in which the Mahommedans of Patna have since borne a leading part. During the great mutiny they plotted freely against their Christian rulers; but the punishment inflicted on their leaders taught them a lesson which they will not soon forget.

The Hindoos by religion outnumber the Mahommedans by about four to one. Their creeds, however varied, resolve themselves into one common essence. Whether they worship the Supreme Being under the form of Brahma, Vishnu, or Siva, or bow down to all the minor gods of the Hindoo Pantheon, to say nothing of the sprites, demons, stocks, and serpents, borrowed from surrounding races, they all alike profess their belief in the Shástras or holy books, as expounded and enforced by their Brahmin teachers. From the Védas, the Puránas, and other Sanskrit writings, these Indian Priests and Levites have built up a religious system which has held its ground through all the political changes of three thousand years. The inroads of Budhism, Islám, and Christianity, have made but little impression on a creed so wonderfully adapted to all shades of Hindoo thought and feeling. In its purest form, as represented by the Vedantists, who accept the teaching of the Védas only, it is a Theism of a high order. Under the guise adopted by the Brahma Samáj, the new eclectic school of Rámohan Roy and Kesháb Chunder Sen, with a lofty conception of the all pervading power of the Deity, it emulates the beneficent spirit of Christianity, but the seal is wanting—the belief in the Great Atonement. It is among the higher and more cultivated classes that Brahminism in its more spiritual forms may chiefly be found. With the multitude it degenerates into mere idol worship and the mechanical observance of the rites and practices enjoined by their spiritual guides, whose principle of action—"populus vult decipi, decipiatur"—is not unknown in countries boasting a purer creed.

From the older Brahminism sprang the Budhist reform of which Sákya Múni, a prince of Kápila to the north of Oude, was the real or traditional author in the sixth century before Christ. Budha, or the Sage, as he was afterwards called, denounced the Brahmin priesthood of his day in much the same spirit as the early Christian teachers inveighed against the Pharisees. He taught that faith and pure living were better than sacrifices and formal penances, that the path to happiness lay in love, forgiveness of injuries, self-control, and doing good. Rebelling against the tyranny of caste, he declared that men were equal in God's eyes, and that a Brahmin had no more claim to special sanctity than a Sudra or a Pariah. The new doctrine gradually spread over many parts of India, and in due time won its way into Ceylon, Burmah, Thibet, and China. But Brahminism fought hard for life; in the course of centuries it supplanted its younger rival; and in the tenth century of our era Budhism in India was fairly trampled out. The only traces of it now visible there, besides the temples, halls, and other buildings which mark its former sway, may be discovered in the Jains, of whom a few hundred thousand dwell in Western and Central India, retaining some of the old Budhist usages mixed up with those of the Brahminic school. Budhism as such is now confined to British Burmah and the hills bordering on Cashmere.

Another revolt from Brahminism was proclaimed in the 15th century by Nának Shah in the Punjab, who learned from his master Kabír, that lesson of spiritual brotherhood which he afterwards strove to practise in his own way. His chief aim was to establish a religious system embracing alike Hindoo and Mahommedan. But his followers, the Seikhs, as they were called, found so little favour with the Mahommedans, that after many years of persecution they took up arms under Guru Govind, a successor of Nának, and maintained a long and furious struggle which finally left them for half-a-century masters of the Punjab. Their fiery prowess must have made up for their numerical weakness, for at this moment the true Seikhs in the Punjab number little more than a million, as compared with over 16 millions Mahommedans, and Jats and others.*

* Parliamentary Paper.

The native Christians of India are supposed to number about a million, most of whom are to be found in Malabar, Travancore, Tinnevelly, and other parts of Southern India. In the North there are only a few thousands, representing the scanty outcome of many years of missionary work. Of the southern Christians the great bulk belong to the Romish or the Syrian Church. Tradition assigns the origin of the latter to the preaching of the Apostle Thomas. Be that as it may, a Christian community appears to have flourished in Malabar since the second century of our era, and in the tenth century many converts were made by Syrian missionaries in Travancore. In the middle of the 16th century the zealous St. Francis Xavier gathered the first converts into the Romish fold. Swartz, the Danish missionary, did the like service two centuries later for Protestant Christianity in Southern India. Some fifty years elapsed before the first English missionaries set foot in Bengal;—amongst the most zealous and distinguished of whom were Carey, Marshman and Ward, Henry Martin, and Archdeacon Corrie the friend of Heber; and in more recent times, Dr. Duff and other eloquent and devoted men have worthily followed in their steps.

The Mogul Empire lost its power in India in a great degree by interfering with the religion of the people. The decline of the Portuguese dominion was also accelerated by the same cause. From that error we as a government wisely abstain.

CHAPTER VI.

THE PEOPLE—*continued.*

Caste—Character of the people—Hindoos—Mahommedans, &c.

Caste.—In the social and religious life of the Hindoos the caste system has always played an important part.* The four castes or "colours" of the old village communities, as described in the Code of Menu, were marked off sharply from each other by rules and restrictions of the most binding character. First in order came the Brahmins, the favourites of the Gods, the privileged expounders of the holy books, to kill one of whom was the worst of crimes, while even to insult one was a wrong almost inexpiable. The Cahutriya or warrior caste ranked next. To this belonged most of the old Indian princes, and its purest living representatives are perhaps to be found in the Rajpoots of Central India. In the third rank came the Vaísyas, who concerned themselves in law, medicine, trade, and agriculture.

These three classes embraced all men of pure Aryan

* "The first impression is, that caste is a thing positively unique; there is nothing in any country with whose history we are familiar, ancient or modern, with which it can be compared; it has a social element, but it is not a social distinction; it has a religious element, but it is hardly a religious institution; it finds its sanction in a religious idea, inasmuch as Brahma is said to have been its author, but it lives on irrespective of religious faith or observance."—"The Trident, the Crescent, and the Cross," by the Rev. James Vaughan. Longmans and Co., 1876.

blood; all the "twice-born," as they proudly called themselves, who alone had the right to wear the sacred thread that distinguished them from men of low or non-Aryan birth. To the fourth or Sudra caste were relegated all the "low-born" and converts, who served as hewers of wood and drawers of water for the conquering race. They might follow only such trades and callings as were forbidden to the three higher castes. In order to keep them in their proper place, they were shut out from every privilege enjoyed by the twice-born. No Sudra for instance might dare to read the Védas, to eat or intermarry with a member of a higher caste, to sit on the same mat with a Brahmin, or even to amass property for his own use.

In course of time however, these distinctions tended to melt away or reappear under new aspects in ever-increasing numbers. Caste still seems to bind Hindoo society together, but under conditions very different from those of Menu's day. Instead of four castes there are now some hundreds, most of which represent particular trades, callings, or creeds, and so answer to the guilds, trade-unions, and sects, of mediæval and modern Europe. Even the Brahmins no longer form one caste, or refrain from pursuits once forbidden to their priestly forefathers. In the struggle for life they and the Sudras have often changed places, and a Brahmin now thinks it no shame to be a soldier, or a clerk in a public or merchant's office, or to fulfil still more humble duties. The very Pariahs and dregs of Indian society, scavengers, leather-dressers, conjurors, thieves, and so forth, have formed themselves into castes, each fenced round by strict rules. In one shape or another, caste has made its way among the Jains, the Seikhs, and even the Mahommedans, numbers of whom indeed retain little of Mahomet's religion beyond the name. As a means of holding society together, of keeping men under some kind of moral discipline, the caste system, in its present shape, must be regarded as a power for good rather than evil, whatever fault may be found with it as a hindrance to the spread of Western influences and the free play of individual energies.

Character of the People.—In mental as in bodily traits, there are certain broad differences between the Hindoos and the Mahommedans. The latter, as a rule, are bolder in speech and bearing; more truthful, energetic, self-asserting; less refined in their tastes, less supple-witted, less patient of steady toil, less slow to move along new paths. Of the "mild Hindoo," we heard more perhaps twenty years ago than we do now; and remembering how he behaved during the Mutiny, one is tempted to think of Byron's Lambro, "the mildest-mannered man that ever cut a throat." Still, in a subject race, mildness of manner, if coupled with other good qualities, has an undoubted charm; and the Hindoos strongly resemble the Italians, alike in their worse and better traits. If they are more or less prone to crooked and cunning ways, if they are slow to forgive an enemy, and generally careless about speaking the truth, they are also, in the main, temperate, courteous, self-controlled, cheerful, industrious, keen-witted, religious, and kind-hearted. In short, according to Professor Monier Williams, as he lately told us, there are "no people in Europe more religious, none more patiently persevering in common duties, none more docile and amenable to authority, none more courteous or respectful towards age and learning, none more dutiful to parents, none more intelligent." As for the vices and defects he found among them, these abound to no greater extent than they do "among those merely nominal Christians who, after all, constitute the real mass of the people in Europe."

Those who have mixed most freely with the Hindoos, Mountstuart Elphinstone, for instance, and Colonel Meadows Taylor, bear witness to the same effect. Both describe them also as honest in their transactions with each other; and Elphinstone, who had a clear eye for both sides of their character, declares with much truth, not only that those who have known them the longest have always judged them most favourably, but that "all persons who have retired from India think better of the people they have left after comparing them with others, even of the most justly-admired nations." Lord Northbrook spoke on a recent occasion under similar impressions. "Taking India altogether, those millions of Indians are a people who commend themselves most entirely to the affections of those who govern them. I do not think there exists a more contented people, a people more ready to obey to the letter and feel confidence and trust in those put over them. All do their duty to their relations and friends in times of difficulty, and all live peaceably one with another. There is no man, I venture to say, who has had charge of a district of India, and has had to deal with the natives of that country, who will not say the same as I am saying now —no man who has had charge of a district who does not go away with a feeling of affection for the natives of India—a feeling which remains with him during his life."

The Hindoos are humane by nature, and believing as they do in the transmigration of souls are, especially in the South, careful of animal life, lest in destroying a beast of prey, or a noxious reptile or insect, they may have injured a remote ancestor or deceased friend.

But it is hardly possible to give a perfectly fair and sound estimate of the general character of a people divided into so many castes and classes, loosely held together by certain affinities of race, language and religion. What is true for instance of the modern Bengálee, as painted for us in Macaulay's memorable portrait of Nand-Kumár, would be far from true if applied to the average Hindoo of the North-West Provinces, or even to the Mahrattas of Western and Central India, and would in no way be applicable to the Seikhs. Differences of climate and passing circumstances must have played their part in moulding for good or ill the different types of native character, mental as well as physical. Consider, too, the difficulty of passing a fair judgment on people with whom we can never come into close social contact. As the moon always shows the same side of her body to our earth, so it is obvious that our native Indian subjects show but a part of their true nature to their foreign lords. That very courtesy which leads them to say pleasant things to our faces, enhances the difficulty of judging them aright. If it is hard for an average Englishman to understand an Irishman or a Frenchman, how very much harder for him to take the true measure of a people whose ways, thoughts, feelings, interests, are widely distinct from ours; whose social leaders will not even eat or drink with us, with whose wives and daughters no man is permitted to talk face to face, and whose self-esteem is continually wounded by the proofs of their subjection to a strange, unyielding, though far from oppressive rule.

Giving every consideration to the many good qualities possessed by the natives of India, it must be admitted by those who know them best that they are not a people formed to govern, but rather to yield obedience to a stronger will, their ability to pass competitive examinations, notwithstanding.

Of course there are numerous individual exceptions to the above, especially in the northern and western provinces of India, but as for the acute and subtle genuine Bengalees, "there never, perhaps, existed a people so thoroughly fitted by nature and by habit for a foreign yoke."*

* Lord Macaulay's Critical and Historical Essays.

CHAPTER VII.

EARLY HISTORY OF INDIA.

Complication of early Indian History—Alexander's Invasion of the Punjaub, B.C. 327—First Authentic Information—Commencement of Continuous History, A.D. 1000—Rule of Rajpoot Princes—First Mahommedan Invasion by Mahmoud of Guzni—189 Years after his Death his Dynasty was exterminated by Mamoud, of Ghor.

HAVING described the extent and physical characteristics of the country, and having given some account of the various races which inhabit it, a brief glance at the early history of India appears desirable before adverting to the origin and progress of British rule in that country.

That complicated record of countries and dynasties, which we include under the comprehensive title of the history of India, presents great difficulties alike to the student, and to the historian. The vastness of the subject would seem to exact detail, yet the amount of details, which interrupted civilisation, continual warfare, the history of vast territories, complex constitutions, and quickly changing dynasties afford, seems almost to defy a comprehensive treatment of the subject. Little or nothing is known of the history of India before the time of Alexander's invasion. The Vedas date about 1400 B.C., the code of Menu from 900 to 300, the Ramyana and the Mahabarata somewhat later. But these sacred books give us a picture of the religious and social condition of India, rather than of its political history.

It is to the officers of Alexander's army, that we owe our knowledge of ancient India. The accounts they wrote, condensed and verified by Diodorus, Strabo, Pliny, Arrian, and Athenæus, dating from the invasion of the Punjab, B.C. 327, are our earliest authentic sources of information, and it is not until the year A.D. 1000, that we have anything like a continuous history of India.

That date marks the era when Mahmoud of Ghuzni invaded the country of the Hindoos, and Sanscrit, the ancient language of poetry, philosophy, and science gave way, before the rougher language of the camp. From the earliest records, we learn that India had always been divided into large provinces, or kingdoms, and that these were ruled by rajahs, or kings, supported by a council of Brahmins or priests, who were entitled to sit on the right of the throne, while the Cahutriyas, or warriors, occupied the left. The Brahmins had supreme power. They could condemn a king, if they saw fit, but no provocation on their part would have been recognised as an excuse for that sovereign, who should dare to take the life of one of these holy men. It is believed that from very early ages, the provinces, west of the Indus, were tributary to the kings of Persia. Alexander the Great claimed India through Persia, and 800 years after Alexander's time, we find that the Shah of Persia still styled himself king of India. There was however no paramount sovereign of India at the time of Mahmoud's invasion. The rajahs were united for defence, under the rajah or king of Canouje, to whom as Protector all tributary princes paid allegiance. The Rajpoot race was dominant, and Hindostan, at that time divided into four great kingdoms, *i.e.* Dehli, Canouje, Mewar, and Guzerat. The first, second and last-named had magnificent capitals. Subuctugi, the father of Mahmoud, from a slave had risen to sovereignty, and at the time of his death Mahmoud was absent in Khorassan. His brother Ismael seized the empire, and attempted by bribery and corruption to secure his position on the usurped throne. Mahmoud first tried persuasion upon his treacherous brother, but soon had to reconquer his crown and capital at the point of the sword, and was clemently satisfied, to confine his mischievous relative for life in the luxurious fortress of Georghan. At the age of twenty-eight [A.D 997] Mahmoud's supremacy was acknowledged from the frontiers of Persia, to the banks of the Indus, from Balkh to the Arabian Sea. He reigned without a rival in the East. He was no less a scholar than a warrior, delighting in the liberal arts, building gorgeous palaces, and laying out exquisite gardens; a prince, splendid and magnificent, even in the land of splendour itself. Besides these more civilised tastes, the lust of conquest and the fanaticism of the "true believer" possessed him. His avarice was largely tempted, by what, during his father's life-time, had become known to him of the riches of India, and had he needed it, the warrant of the Prophet was not wanting to encourage him in a war of extermination against all unbelievers. "The sword" says Mahomet, is the key of paradise, whoever falls in battle, his sins are forgiven." The comparatively effeminate Hindoos must have seemed a pleasant and easy prey to these fierce fanatics from the North, whose swiftness to shed blood, desolated during 300 years the Eastern world. During a period of twenty-four years Mahmoud made twelve expeditions against the cities and temples of India. Every object of Hindoo worship was ruthlessly destroyed; the plunder brought back to Ghuzni from the ravaged lands was fabulous alike in quantity and quality. The Rajpoot king of Lahore, on being taken prisoner in battle, collected a funeral pile, to which he set fire with his own hand, and so died, but not before ten necklaces had been taken from his neck, one of which alone was valued at £82,000. It is however to be borne in mind that the quantity and value of jewels and gold taken from the Princes and temples of India owe much to the oriental imagination. After this victory Mahmoud established a Mahommedan governor in the Punjaub, and returned to Ghuzni. He annexed Moultan and the whole of the Peshawur Valley, and the greater part of Scinde, and exacted tribute from every sovereign from Cashmere to the mouths of the Indus. One of his expeditions was directed against the temple and fort of Binné, a structure said to have been roofed and paved with gold, and the enterprise of its conquerors was rewarded by incredible amounts of gold, silver and jewels.*

Andipal, king of Lahore, entreated the conqueror to spare the temple of Tannassar, the most holy of their sacred places; the Mecca of the Hindoos. Mahmoud replied that "the followers of Mahomet were vowed to root out idolatry." The shrine of the god was pillaged, and the image of Jug-Soom smashed into a thousand

* Sir Edward Sullivan's "Princes of India."

atoms, which were sent to pave the streets of Ghuzni, Mecca, and Bagdad. After plundering Dehli, Mahmoud returned to Ghuzni laden with treasure, and accompanied by 40,000 male and female captives. In the year 1013 he turned his destructive steps towards Cashmere, the paradise of Persian poets. This happy valley was devastated by his troops, and in the year 1018, after settling some little difficulties with his northern neighbours, the kings of Bokhara and Charism, he marched on Canouje the capital of Hindostan. His Afghan and Tartar bands struck terror into the hearts of the inhabitants of the capital, and they fled in all directions, whilst the craven prince Korra, Maharajah of Canouje, after paying an enormous ransom, embraced the Mahommedan faith, and three years later was with his whole family put to death for his apostacy, by neighbouring Hindoo princes. But this submission on his part did not save Muttra, the fabled birth-place of the divine Krishna, from devastation. For 20 days it was given up to plunder and massacre, and 63,000 Hindoo devotees to the shrine, were slain in cold blood. The wealth acquired by Mahmoud was enormous. Great idols of pure gold, with eyes of rubies and adorned with sapphires were among the spoils borne homewards on 350 elephants, followed by 50,000 captives. With the accumulated plunder of eight expeditions Mahmoud now proceeded to beautify his Alpine capital. Ghuzni, built on a rock 300 feet above the surrounding plains, soon became a city of groves, temples, and palaces, the beauty of which was unrivalled in Asia. It would be impossible to follow the insatiable and rapacious

Mahmoud through the twelve expeditions, which mark his ambitious and cruel progress. His last raid was on Anhulwarra, the capital of Guzerat, the third and most wealthy of the kingdoms of Hindostan. After occupying Anhulwarra he proceeded to Somnauth "the Dwelling of the Deity," where for forty centuries had stood the temple of the Hindoo god Soma, "The Lord of the Moon." From the extreme confines of Balkh and Persia, from the uttermost regions of the Carnatic and Bengal, millions of credulous pilgrims had from time immemorial wended their way hither, to lay their offerings at the feet of the Hindoo Pluto. Fabulous accounts of the riches of this shrine had reached Mahmoud's ears, and he resolved to make its treasures his own. His troops however, at the last moment, wavered, and could not penetrate beyond the outworks of the sacred portions of the holy city. Then the grey-haired warrior, rising in his stirrups called aloud on the name of Allah, and taking his favourite general by the hand, shouted to all true sons of the Prophet to follow him. The troops rallied; a final charge was made, and the prize which he had come 2,000 miles to conquer, lay at length at his feet. The Brahmins offered enormous sums to save their God, but in vain. Amidst the groans of an agonised multitude Mahmoud, raising his mace, struck the desecrated idol a blow on the face, and his soldiery speedily concluded the work their sovereign had begun. The idol was hollow. Piles of diamonds and sapphires, a ruby of enormous size, and a quantity of pure gold were extracted from the shrine.

The last days of Mahmoud were overshadowed by the

consciousness, that his successes notwithstanding, the empire of Ghuzni was already tottering to its fall. The very Tartar hordes that had proved such valuable adjuncts in his victorious hands, threatened to become his most dangerous enemies. The size of the empire constituted its chief danger. A few days before his death, he entered his treasury; then bursting into tears, closed the doors in silence, on the vast wealth which it contained. A day later he reviewed his troops, and as legion after legion passed before him, he again wept bitterly; then retiring in silent anguish to his "Palace of Delights," raised with the plunder of numberless Hindoo shrines and cities, after thirty-four years of adventure and success, he breathed out a saddened soul at last. It is now just thirty-four years ago, since British arms bore back in triumph to the capital of Hindostan those world-renowned sandal-wood gates, which Mahmoud tore from the temple of Somnauth, and which his successors raised in remembrance and glorification of that act above his tomb. Equally successful in war and in peace, Mahmoud was not without some of the milder virtues. Mussulman historians depict him as a benefactor of the human race, and to this day Moslem priests read the Koran, over the tomb of this true son of the Prophet, Hindoos describe him as a consuming firebrand, whose claim to immortality lies in the magnitude of his crimes. But little of his private life is known. He is said to have been just, and anecdotes are told in confirmation of the assertion. His favourite wife, the daughter of his treacherous foe, the king of Cashgar, was called the "Sun of Beauties," but as a rule, harem life is totally devoid of interest in its details, and it is enough to know the fair Haramnour had many rivals. Mahmoud was the only great sovereign of his race, and in 189 years after his death, his dynasty became extinct. He had already foreseen the disruption of his empire, when the growing power of the Turkoman race had made itself apparent to him before the close of his reign, but its final ruin was caused quite as much by internal weakness and treachery, as by the attacks of external foes.

Mahmoud left two sons who repeated in their own persons the history of their father's accession and their uncle's treachery. The younger, Mahommed, usurped the elder Musuad's throne, but was soon deposed, and branded across the pupil of his eyes with a red-hot iron. Five years later the blind Mahommed restored to liberty and sovereign power, returned with interest the treatment he had received. He degraded and imprisoned Musuad and raised his own son to the throne. This prince, Ahmad I., at once slew his uncle Musuad, and though Mahommed the blind king wrote to his nephew Modoad disclaiming all complicity with the deed, Modoad did not hesitate to avenge his father's murder. He took Ahmad prisoner, and slew every member of his uncle's family. His brother Musdoad now made war against him, but some unknown hand assassinated the rebel and his general, and Modoad returned to reign at Ghuzni.

Modoad had died at Ghuzni and was succeeded by his infant son, who was murdered after six days by his uncle Ali. Ali reigned two years and was deposed by Resehed, a son of Mahmoud who after forty days was assassinated by his omrahs, and Feroch Zaad, a son of Musdoad chosen by lot to succeed him. Feroch reigned six years and was succeeded by his brother Ibrahim, a prince who delighted in learning and the arts of peace. He reigned thirty-one years, and was succeeded by his son Musaod II., who walked in the steps of his father. Musaod was succeeded by his son Shere, who was almost immediately assassinated by his brother Arsilla. Byram, a younger brother defeated Arsilla under the walls of Ghuzni, and seated himself on the throne, but after a disastrous reign of thirty-five years, Byram was obliged to fly to India, where he died in the year 1152. Chusero, the son of Byram, retired to Lahore and ruled there for seven years, when he was succeeded by his son Chusero II. Chusero and all his family were betrayed and put to death by Mahmoud, brother of Yaas, king of Ghor, and with them the Ghuznite dynasty became extinct. *

* Keene's "Fall of the Mogul Empire."

CHAPTER VIII.

EARLY HISTORY OF INDIA—*continued.*

Hindoo Princes resolve to throw off Mussulman yoke—Mahomed of Ghor invades India and is defeated—Pithowra king of Delhi carries off the daughter of Jye-Chund Ray of Canouje—Mahomed Ghor invades India again—Takes Delhi and Canouje—Death of their Kings and final overthrow of Rajpoots—Mahomed returns to Ghuzni—Made nine Expeditions to India—Was succeeded by the Slave Kings for 81 years—Genghis Khan, with his Scythian and Tartar hordes—St. Louis and his Crusade—Timour the Lame—Triumphs over Bajazet—Returns to Samarcand laden with spoil—His Death.

THE time had now come when, perceiving the family quarrels, the revolt of its governors and the encroachments of the Turkomans imperilling the Ghuznite empire, the Hindoo princes of India resolved to make a combined effort to throw off the Mussulman yoke.

Mahomed of Ghor, an Afghan warrior, coming presently to the throne, proceeded to invade Hindostan, and singling out Pithowra, king of Delhi, engaged him in single combat, but his gallantry was in vain. His army was scattered and he himself carried almost insensible to Lahore. Pithowra king of Delhi, after quarrelling with his ally Jye-Chund Ray king of Canouje, bore off the daughter of the latter, and, defended in his retreat by the pick of India's chivalry, succeeded in gaining his capital with a lovely and willing bride, not however at a less cost than that of leaving nearly all his warrior-band dead upon the road. The abduction of this lady led to war between the Rajahs of Canouje and Delhi, which was the cause of their final overthrow and withdrawal from that part of India, but not before Jye-Chund Ray had taken Delhi and Pithowra had expiated his sins against his kingly neighbour by death. Mahomed Gori roused by the news of the conquest of Delhi now equipped himself for a crusade against India. He took and sacked Canouje; and Jye-Chund Ray its king, met with a congenial death in the sacred waters of the Ganges. Jye-Chund Ray of Canouje and Pithowra of Delhi were the last great Hindoo sovereigns of Hindostan (1194), and with the fall of their capitals and the expatriation of the Rajpoots the military spirit of the people was extinguished. After the conquest of Delhi Mahmoud turned his arms against Bengal, where he took the sacred city of Benares, and after pillaging a thousand shrines and temples returned to Ghuzni at the head of his victorious army followed by 4,000 camels laden with the spoils of his conquests. Mahomed Ghor made nine expeditions to India, and left a treasure, the amount of which sounds incredible in western ears. He was at last assassinated, and left only one daughter. After his death the empire was divided amongst his slaves. The so-called dynasty of the slave kings lasted for eighty-one years. It presents the usual features of crime and assassination, since it numbered ten sovereigns, only three of whom died natural deaths.

It is not until the year 1227, the year in which St. Louis led his ill-fated crusade to the Holy Land, that Genghis Khan at the head of his Scythian and Tartar hordes arrests the attention of the student of Indian History. Chief of the pastoral millions of central Asia, the career of the Shepherd King was one of unceasing bloodshed. He burst on the kingdoms of Asia with an army never equalled in numbers either before or since. According to Elphinstone, "This irruption of the Moguls was the greatest calamity that has fallen on mankind since the Deluge. They had no religion to teach and no seeds of improvement to sow, nor did they offer an alternative of conversion or tribute; their only object was to slaughter and destroy, and the only trace they left was in the devastation of every country which they visited." *

Knowing no god but his own will, no pleasure but the destruction of his kind (it is said that upwards of 14,000,000 were slaughtered by Genghis during the last twenty years of his life), he scoffed alike at learning and religion, littered his horses with the contents of the grandest library in Asia, burned the Bible, and cast the Koran under his horses feet in the holy mosque of Bokhara. The empire he bequeathed to his son extended 1,800 leagues from east to west, and more than 1,000 from north to south. His was the portentous shadow that heralded the coming event. The Mogul age had fallen on India, and Genghis was only

* "History of India," by the Hon. Mountstuart Elphinstone. Edited by E. B. Cowell, M.A.

paving the way for the invasion of Timour the Tartar 150 years later.*

Genghis Khan was succeeded by Feroze, and he in turn by his sister the beautiful Sultana Rizia, who was put to death soon after her accession. In 1287, Feroze the Benevolent ascended the throne. Alla the Sanguinary carried war into the Deccan, an account of which will be found in a later chapter. From 1321-1387 endless Afghan rulers sat on the throne of Hindostan. Amongst them may be numbered Mubarick, Chusero, Ghaji, Toghlak, Mahomed III. and Feroze the Benevolent.

In 1398, nearly 400 years after the invasion of Mahmoud of Ghuzni, came Timour the Tartar, or Timour Leng, so called from his lameness. During five days this ferocious slayer of men gave up Dehli to rapine and pillage, and every soul above fifteen years of age was ruthlessly butchered by his soldiery. History has no horrors to compare with those of this wholesale slaughter. In less than an hour after the diabolical order was given one hundred thousand human beings had, according to Mussulman historians, been massacred in cold blood. Erecting his standard above this city of shambles, Timour seated himself on the ancient musnud of the Sultans of Dehli, and there received the petitions of fallen kings, and the homage of suppliant sovereigns. Petitioned by the Brahmins to spare their god, "I will break your gods," he ruthlessly replied, "to give them the opportunity of performing a miracle and making themselves whole."

Timour did not remain long in Hindostan. He feared

* Sir Edward Sullivan's "Princes of India."

the effects of its enervating climate on his army, inured to the snow and frosts of Central Asia. At this time the fame of Bajazet's, the Ottoman conqueror's exploits, reached Timour Leng's ears, and he determined to lose no time in picking up the gauntlet for supreme authority, which he conceived Bajazet to have cast down. But though he resolved on quitting Delhi, he was equally determined that his name should not be forgotten. He caused the money of the ancient capital of Hindostan to be stamped with his image and superscription, and his name to be invoked in the mosques (as it was cursed in the Brahminical temples) of Hindostan.

Timour triumphed over Bajazet, and glutted with conquest returned to Samarcand, to hold high festival in celebration of the marriages of his six grandsons. The gardens of the Imperial palace ran with kermiz, hippocrene, brandy, and the choicest wines; several large forests were cut down to supply fuel for the banquets, which lasted two months. The turquoise gates and the porcelain pavilion were open to all comers, whilst the Green Palace which Timour had erected as a convenient place whither to conduct rivals or relatives quietly, and there kill them outright, or, if clemently disposed, apply the terrible "fire-pencil" to their eyes, was closed by royal command. Soon after this pompous celebration of his pride and victories, the king of twenty-eight crowns was summoned to his last account. Calmly stretched upon his bed, as though his life had been one of serene benevolence from his earliest career, he awaited death with the often-repeated Mahomedan formula on his lips: "There is no God but God."

CHAPTER IX.

THE MOGUL OR TARTAR DYNASTY.

Baber founder of Mogul dynasty—Baber's Exploits and Character—Hoomayoon—Contemporary Events and Characters—Flodden Field—Knights of St. John and Solyman—Luther—Francis the First and Bayard—Charles V. and Titian—Michael Angelo—Torquato Tasso—Henry VIII.—Pope Leo—Akbar the Great—His rare Personal Qualities and Enlightened Policy—His reign coincides with that of Elizabeth—His death—Memory, how revered—Jehangire—The beautiful Noor Mahal—Shah Jehan—Built the Taj Mahal and adorned Delhi—Aurungzebe a bad man but a good Sovereign—What he did and how he died—Anarchy—Shah Alam I.—Concessions to Mahrattas—Sivajee—Peishwa—Nadir Shah—Massacre at Delhi—Retires laden with spoil—Peacock Throne—Koh-i-noor—Nadir murders his son and is himself assassinated—Shah Alam II. rescued by Lord Lake in 1803—The last great Mogul dies a convict in a remote province.

Baber Khan of Kokhand, the founder of the Mogul dynasty of Hindostan, 1527, was descended both from Genghis Khan and from Timour. He was well-fitted, alike by birth and nature to take his place amongst the splendid array of contemporary sovereigns who mark the period of the "Renaissance"—The age that witnessed the chivalry of Scotland meet a glorious death on Flodden Field; that saw the Knights of St. John striving hopelessly against Solyman with his army of 140,000 men, and his fleet of 400 ships. It was during this age that the German monk burned the papal bull before the gates of Wittenburg, and Francis the First solicited knighthood after the battle of Marsignano at the hands of Bayard. It was in this age that the Emperor Charles V. stooped at Titian's feet to pick up the brush which had fallen from the great master's hand. Michael Angelo built St. Peter's, and decorated the Sistine Chapel, and Torquato Tasso wrote his "*Gerusalemma Liberata.*" The eighth Henry reigned in England, the first Francis in France, the fifth Charles in Germany and Spain, and Pope Leo X. a Mæcenas amongst Popes.

Before the age of sixteen Baber had twice seized and occupied the great Mogul capital of Samarcand; he took Cabul in 1504; in 1518 he conquered the Punjaub; in 1526 he invaded India, met Ibrahim Lodi, the last Sultan of the Lodi race that reigned in Hindostan, and defeated him at the battle of Paniput, where after the victory, the dead body of the king was found surrounded by 6,000 Afghan nobles, who had fought until their last breath by the side of their sovereign. In the year 1527 the Afghans and Hindoos led on by Sanga Rana of Oudypore, leagued themselves together against Baber, but were utterly routed near Agra, and the capture of Chanderi, 1528, seemed to establish his ascendancy. Yet it was not until his forty-fourth year that Baber seated himself permanently on the throne of Delhi, and established the Mogul dynasty in Hindostan. Thenceforth his energies were devoted to the arts of peace. His memoirs, written in simple language, form one of the most delightful biographies ever given to the world. He was a poet, a musician, and a botanist. Learned in all eastern lore, he united with the theology of Mahomed the abstruse studies of the Moorish doctors, and a thorough knowledge of the Persian poetry and literature of his native Turkestan. Merciful for a Mogul, tolerant for a Mussulman, chivalrous, generous, and brave; an affectionate son and a devoted father, we find in him united all the noblest qualities of the east and of the west. The only blot upon his otherwise noble character was that fatal vice common to his race and lineage, but not even the degrading effects of intemperance could dim the lustre of his fine nature, or overthrow his powerful intellect. His son being ill, Baber was told by the wise men that the only propitiation for his life would be the sacrifice of what he himself most valued. "That must be my own existence" he replied, and in nursing his heir he contracted the illness which was shortly to kill him. By his dying request his remains were taken to Cabul. He met his end calmly and bravely. His last words were the Mahomedan formula "there is no God but God," and with these upon his lips, Mahomed Baber, surnamed the Victorious, passed away from a world where even in that splendid age, few could be said to equal, none to excel him.

Baber dead, his beloved son Hoomayoon ascended the throne, which already began to totter to its foundations. Shere Khan, the foremost man in India, an Afghan chief of great physical and mental power, rebelled and conquered Hoomayoon at Agra. Escaping with his life to Ajmere he was received by its friendly Rajpoot sovereign, and here in the fortress of Ammercote was born his son Mahomed Akbar, destined to become the most enlightened legislator and the greatest monarch that ever ascended an eastern throne. Shere Khan having established himself on the musnud of Hoomayoon, reigned five years and left the throne to his son Selim, who reigned nine years, and followed in the enlightened footsteps of his father. Four princes of the family of Shere Khan sat on the throne of Hindostan, in the two years succeeding Selim's death, when in 1555 Hoomayoon was recalled after a banishment of sixteen years to his capital. The sceptre of empire had now passed for ever from the Afghans, but Hoomayoon did not live to enjoy his restoration. He slipped on the terrace of his palace at Delhi, was taken up insensible and never spoke again. In the tomb of Hoomayoon, near Delhi, the first hereditary Mogul sovereign, the last Mogul Emperor of Delhi was taken prisoner, with three of his sons; the latter were soon afterwards shot on their way to Delhi by Captain Hodson in 1857. Hoomayoon was succeeded by his son, Akbar the Victorious, whose reign coincides with that of Elizabeth of England. He was the first Indian emperor who made no distinction between Hindoos and Mussulmans. He maintained that each creed had an equal claim on his protection and impartiality, and disclaimed both by word and deed all sympathy with the intolerance of his countrymen. He suppressed enforced suttees, and permitted widows to marry again. In accordance with his principles of perfect toleration he allowed the Jesuits to build churches in Agra and Lahore, and to endow colleges. Chivalry offers nothing more striking than his daring deeds of prowess; rejoicing in fighting for fighting's sake, he yet possessed the most conspicuous ability as a great commander, and the most beneficent genius as a wise king. Proud of his personal strength, humane, just, and generous, he stands a splendid and unrivalled figure in the history of

Hindostan. He recovered Delhi and Agra from Hemu Rajah, stormed and took Chitore, reconquered Guzerat, Behar, Bengal, and Orissa from his rebel nobles, and thus crushed out the last remains of Afghan power in Hindostan. Cashmere was conquered in 1587, Scinde in 1592, and Candahar in 1594. Besides his hereditary dominions beyond the Indus, the whole of Hindostan except Oudypore was under his sway. The great mistake of his life was that of attempting to conquer the Mohammadan kingdoms of the Deccan. The successful defence of Ahmednuggur by its noble Queen is celebrated in Indian history. Akbar succeeded, it is true, in annexing Kandeish, and Jehangire, and Aurungzebe followed up these conquests, but they were nevertheless destined to be the ruin of the Mogul Empire. When Akbar's days were drawing to a close, he called his eldest son Selim to his side, and confided his kingdom and faithful servants to the care of his successor, closing his farewell address with the touching words, "my servants and dependents when I am gone forget thou not, neither the afflicted in their hour of need; ponder word for word on all that I have said to thee. Do thou bear all in mind, and again forget me not." And thus on the night of the 10th October, 1605, Akbar Shah, the ornament of the world, the Asylum of the Nations, the King of Kings, the Great, the Fortunate and the Victorious, took leave of the world, and passed to "where beyond these voices there is peace." To this day his memory is held in reverence by the faithful, and pilgrimages are made to his magnificent tomb near Agra.*

* Lord Lake quartered in this vast building a regiment of dragoons with their horses.

Akbar was succeeded by his son Jehangire Selim, surnamed the Conqueror of the World, whose eldest son Chusero rebelled against his father, and was imprisoned for life. His third son Shah Jehan succeeded him, and was in turn succeeded by his third son Aurungzebe, names well known in history. But although the Mogul Empire seemed to grow in outward glory, the race of Baber never produced after Akbar a really great man. Jehangire, an intemperate and vicious prince, owed much to the services of Aiass the good, the father of the celebrated Noor-Mahal, or light of the Harem, a woman who during 20 years ruled Jehanghire and the Empire of Hindostan with a power as absolute as that exercised by Semiramis or Cleopatra. Sir Thomas Roe, the English ambassador sent by James I. to the Court of the great Mogul, gives a most amusing account of his intercourse with, and the life and habits of, this singular sovereign whose frightul habits of intemperance were most disgusting. The Empress Noor-Mahal survived Jehanghire 18 years, and £250,000 a year was paid to her annually as jointure out of the national treasury.

Shah Jehan ascended the Mogul throne in 1628, and inaugurated his reign by indiscriminate slaughter of all his male relatives. He married a niece of the beautiful Nour-mahal and never took any other woman to wife. To her memory a devoted and faithful affection raised the celebrated Taj Mahal, the most perfect specimen of Saracenic architecture in the world. During twenty-two years 20,000 men were employed, and nearly a million sterling was expended upon it. The years 1631-32 were marked by plague, pestilence and famine, which converted the smiling plains into howling wildernesses. Seeing the distress of his people, Shah Jehan did all that he could to relieve their sufferings, but still the hand of the angel of death was not stayed. At length, disgusted by the apathy which sought relief at the shrines of their gods rather than in action and energy, he drew the sword of religious persecution and destroyed temples and gods alike with an unsparing hand. The impolicy of such a line of action soon became apparent to him, for he said he had converted after this fashion thousands to enthusiasm and martyrdom, and observed that "a prince who wishes to have subjects must take them with all the trumpery and trouble of their religion!" Shah Jehan was an able ruler, though his private character was disfigured by many vices. He was boundless in his display and enjoyed a revenue of 40 millions sterling. He beautified Agra with the Taj and immortalised himself by those lovely gardens at Delhi which have inspired all subsequent eastern song and romance, as well as by the fortified palace and other magnificent structures within its walls. Shah Jehan's sons rebelled against him as he had rebelled against his father, and Aurungzebe his third son, who usurped his throne and kept him for the last eight years under restraint, was never mentioned by Shah Jehan without curses. "Fathers have been dethroned by their sons before," it was his custom to observe, "but it was reserved for Aurungzebe to insult the misfortune of a parent." His death made no difference to Aurungzebe who had been for many years the actual Emperor of Hindostan.

Ascetic by nature and ambitious by disposition, Aurungzebe was eminently adapted to carry out a policy of dissimulation. Hypocritical, unforgiving and crafty, suspicious, cold-hearted, and a bigot in religion, he was none the less a skilful ruler. A bad man but a good sovereign, his evil acts were those of nature, his good those of policy. His powerful character declared itself when his father Shah Jehan was first struck with paralysis. He threw his brother Morad, the favourite of the army, into prison, and finally caused him to be beheaded. Dara, his eldest brother fled beyond the Indus, and soon after, losing his only, and passionately loved wife, Dara tore off his imperial turban, cast aside his magnificent robes, and renounced for ever the hopes and pleasures of life. Not long after this he was betrayed to Aurungzebe and carried in ignominy to Delhi, where his brother and sovereign ordered his immediate assassination. Sujah the youngest brother was slain in Arracan, and Soliman the son of Dara, and Sefe his grandson, as well as the child of Morad, having been compelled to drink "poust," the potion prepared from poppy seeds, by which it was customary to remove superfluous princes of the house of Timour, Aurungzebe at length reigned undisturbed, the greatest potentate of the eastern world.

He defeated the Afghans, forced them to re-cross the Indus, and carried fire and sword into the fair valleys of Afghanistan. Notwithstanding religious intolerance, peace marked the history of the central provinces of Hindustan, but the Emperor's contests with the kingdoms of the Deccan and the inroads of Rajpoots, Afghans, Seikhs and Mahrattas show how numerous were the enemies of the Mogul race. A portent of the rapid fall which it would experience whenever the master hand should fail.

From this period the history of Aurungzebe is so involved with that of the history of the Deccan that we must refer our readers to the succeeding chapter for much which belongs properly to the history of Hindustan. It was in the year 1707 at Ahmednuggur in the Deccan, in the fiftieth year of his reign and the ninetieth of his age, that the great message came to Aurungzebe. Vanity of vanities, all is vanity! was like that of Solomon, "the sad and splendid," his farewell cry. He desired to be buried in the simplest manner, and left orders that no splendid mausoleum should be erected to his memory. A bad son, an unjust father, an inhuman brother, he was nevertheless as a ruler nearly as great as Akbar, as a warrior as brave as Baber, and as a sovereign more magnificent than either of those princes. He encouraged learning, science and the arts; developed commerce and agriculture, was indefatigable in business, and moderate in his pleasures.

Some idea of the anarchy that succeeded Aurungzebe's death may be gathered from the fact that during eleven years 1707-1718 five sovereigns sat upon the musnud of the Moguls, two of whom, together with six unsuccessful competitors, were slain in battle or otherwise came to untimely ends. Bahádur Shah the successor of Aurungzebe was forced to make concessions to the Mahrattas, who under Sackojee and the Peishwas had already seized their opportunity. From 1718-1803 they were often supreme at Delhi, but the sight of Rajpoots, Mahrattas, Seikhs and Jats all contending against each other, or united against a nominal sovereign, could not fail to arrest the attention of the conqueror, who was watching the situation with a keenly observant eye and only waiting the opportunity to dash in and seize the prize.

The invasion of Nadir Shah in 1738 completely shattered the empire of the Moguls.

Nadir Shah was a Persian of low origin. He answered all enquiries as to his birth and lineage by the conclusive argument of the pedigree of the sword. His son desiring to marry a princess of the race of Timour, an envoy of the now merely nominal sovereign of Hindostan required that he should prove a male pedigree extending through seven generations. "Go, tell your master," Nadir Shah replied, dismissing the ambassador with contempt, "that my son is the son of Nadir Shah, the son of the sword, the grandson of the sword, and so on until he has a descent of seventy generations instead of seven."*

Nadir Shah after driving the Afghans out of Persia followed them into Hindostan. The Emperor Mahomed made a feeble show of resistance, but quickly retired before the victorious arms of the conqueror. In the massacre he ordered at Delhi the streets ran blood, but during the awful hours of slaughter Nadir Shah, unmoved and calm, remained seated in a mosque in the great Bázár. So terrible was his countenance that none dared approach him. At length Mahomed and his omrahs ventured into his ruthless presence. He asked them what they wanted, and they humbly implored him to spare their city, but he answered not a word, until Mahomed, bathed

* Sir Edward Sullivan.

in tears, prostrated himself on the ground, laying his crown at the conqueror's feet; and on this act of submission, Nadir ordered the massacre to be stayed.

Thirty-seven days Nadir Shah occupied Delhi. Before quitting the city he replaced the humbled Mahomed on the throne. He commenced his return march laden with treasure variously estimated at from 10 to 30 millions sterling. Amongst his spoils were the famous peacock throne* of Shah Jehan, and that historic diamond which excited the admiration of the visitors to the Great Exhibition in 1851, and is now the most precious gem in the regalia of the Empress of India.

Had he chosen to do so, there is no doubt but that Nadir could have established a Persian dynasty on the throne of Delhi, but he was wise enough to see that an empire with two capitals so far apart as Delhi and Ispahan must result in disaster, and naturally preferring the land of his speech and kindred to that of Moguls and Hindoos he returned to Persia. He was assassinated in his tent near Meshed by his own nobles, whose indignation he had excited first by the murder of his own son, and then by the massacre of 50 persons of high rank, because they had not interfered on behalf of his heir.

Mahomed Shah survived the invasion of Delhi nine years, and died in 1748, after a disastrous reign of 30 years. He was succeeded by his son Ahmed Shah, but the days of the Mogul dynasty were numbered, and another Power with advancing standards was in the field, to whom Mogul and Mahratta must alike give

* Valued by Tavernier, a French jeweller, at £6,000,000—an evident exaggeration.

place. The fifteenth great Mogul, Shah Alam II., was rescued by Lord Lake from the Mahrattas in 1803, and the seventeenth and last, a victim or traitor, or both, was taken prisoner after the treacherous outbreak of 1857 and died a convict in a remote corner of the distant province of Pegu in 1863.

Thus ended the once powerful and magnificent dynasty of the great Mogul which in the zenith of its power possessed a revenue of £40,000,000, and a veteran army of 500,000 men, with a mighty artillery under Europeans. The Court of the Emperor, whether he was enthroned in his sumptuous palace at Delhi, or took the field either for pleasure or war, was, under Shah Jehan and Aurungzebe, unequalled for the number of subject kings and princes, and the splendour of its appointments.

Sir Thomas Roe, Bernier and others who accompanied the Mogul in these imperial progresses, describe the grand camp as on a colossal scale, containing within its canvas walls ample accommodation not only for a great army and its countless followers, but every luxury, however superfluous.

In addition to magnificently caparisoned elephants, and horses with hawks, hounds, and hunting tigers for field sports, there was a menagerie of the rarest animals for the amusement of the Emperor and the Court.

There were "Halls of audience for public assemblies and privy councils, with all the courts and cabinets attached to them, each hall magnificently adorned, and having within it a raised seat or throne for the Emperor, surrounded by gilded pillars with canopies of velvet, richly fringed, and superbly embroidered; separate tents, as mosques and oratories; baths; and galleries for archery and gymnastic exercises; a seraglio as remarkable for luxury and privacy as that of Dehli." *

Nothing according to Bernier, can be more royal and magnificent than the seraglio on the line of march. "Stretch imagination to its utmost limits, and you can conceive no exhibition more grand and imposing," the ladies, in curtained canopies, mounted on huge elephants, blazing with gold and azure, surrounded with eunuchs, well mounted and splendidly dressed, with troops of female servants from Tartary and Cashmere, fantastically attired on handsome horses.

No wonder if such a vision inspired the imagination of Indian poets, and made them "represent the elephants as conveying so many goddesses, concealed from the vulgar gaze."

* Sydney Owen, Bernier, &c.

CHAPTER X.

THE DECCAN.

Physical Features—Ancient Splendour of Madura and Beejanuggur—Well-being of the People—First Invasion by Alla the Sanguinary—Arabs—Kingdoms of the Deccan—Mahommedan Kings of Beejapore, Ahmednuggur, Golconda and Baidar league against great Hindoo Kingdom of Beejanuggur—Site of Madras granted to England in 1640—Mysore—Akbar—Beautiful Queen of Gurrah—Aurungzebe—Rise of Mahrattas—Sivajee—Sack of Surat—Raja of Satara—Nizam-ul-Mulk founder of Hydrabad dynasty—The Peishwas—Tara Bhye—Hyder Ali—First Mysore War—Sir Eyre Coote—Second Mysore War—Tippoo Saib—Third Mysore War—Fourth Mysore War—Fall of Seringapatam and Death of Tippoo—Hindoo Dynasty restored—The last of the Peishwas—His odious Administration and Deposition—His adopted son the Nana Sahib, of Bithoor.

THE history of the Deccan, or the south country, is closely interwoven with that of Hindostan, but it has nevertheless a history and fortunes of its own.

Between the 23rd and 25th parallels of latitude the Vendhya range, extending from the north-west of Guzerat to the Ganges, divides the Deccan from Hindostan, although the Mogul Emperors affected to regard the Nerbudda as the boundary of the provinces directly subject to the Imperial Crown.*

* The Mogul Emperors fixed the Nerbudda for the limit of their provinces in those two great divisions, but the division of the nations is made by the Vindhya mountains. It is well remarked by Sir W. Jones and Major Rennell that both banks of rivers in Asia are generally inhabited by the same community. The rule applies to Europe and is as true on the Rhine or the Po as of the Ganges or the Nile. Rivers are precise and convenient limits for artificial divisions, but they are no great obstacles to communication; and to form a natural separation between nations, requires the real obstruction of a mountain chain.—*Mountstuart Elphinstone.*

The Deccan, is, after passing the broad and deep valleys of the Nerbudda and Taptee, for the most part a lofty table land of triangular form, buttressed on all sides by ranges of hills, called the Ghats or Stairs, that on the west being the highest and best known, having a border of low land intervening between them and the sea, possessing in some portions scenery of singular beauty and variety.

The lofty table land has a general inclination, from west to east, from the Malabar to the Coromandel coast the province of Orissa, its eastern border, and merging on the south-west in the large table-land of Mysore. It's chief rivers, having their rise in the Western Ghats, flow across the peninsula in deep channels, little accessible to the cultivator for the irrigation of his fields.

There are vast tracks of forest, having patches of cultivation, with villages few and far between, but the usual aspect of this elevated region is that of billowy downs, covered with verdure, or that of vast plains of waving cotton and corn, without a tree or a farm house to break the monotony; the people choosing as is usual with the agricultural population, especially in Eastern countries, to live together for mutual protection in villages more or less remote. When the crops are gathered and the grass is withered from the heat of the sun, nothing can be more dreary than the general aspect of the country.

"All the traditions and records of the peninsula recognise, in every part of it, a period when the natives were not Hindus."*

Tamil, the language of the most ancient kingdoms of

* Professor Wilson.

the south of the peninsula appears to have preceded the introduction of Sanscrit, and Professor Wilson is of opinion that the civilization of the Deccan preceded our era by many centuries.

Strabo and Arrian on the authority of the companions of Alexander describe the inhabitants of the south as not inferior in refinement to the other nations of India, and the former historian mentions that Pandyon, one of the minor kings of the Deccan, had sent an ambassador to Augustus.

There are five languages spoken in the Deccan which appear to point to a similar number of national divisions.*

Centuries before our era the Pandyon dynasty reigned in Madura, where they have continued to reign until comparatively recent times. The Cholas reigned in Conjeveram and afterwards in Tanjore.

After many revolutions and changes, of which we know little or nothing, these states in 1300, were merged in the vast Hindoo kingdom of Beejanuggur. Madura and Beejanuggur are represented by travellers as having exceeded Delhi and Canouje in splendour and magnitude, whilst the irrigation works, tanks, highly-cultivated country and general well-being of the people proved the Government to have been an enterprising and enlightened one. It was under Alla the Sanguinary, nephew and murderer of the amiable Feroze that the Deccan was first invaded (1294) by a sovereign of Hindustan. During his predecessor's lifetime Alla had been Governor of those districts of which the boundary is the Nerbudda. The fabulous accounts of the temples

* Mountstuart Elphinstone.

and shrines, of the fair cities, and fruitful plains of the countries of the Deccan, tempted Alla on ascending the throne to advance upon the coveted territory. He took and sacked Dowlatabad, and the Agas of the Moslem conqueror were astonished by the undreamed-of glories of Ellora and Ajunta. Encouraged by success, Alla despatched his General Cafoor with orders to penetrate south as far as the kingdoms of the Carnatic and Mysore.

There were few Mahommedans in the Deccan; but a band of enterprising Arabs had established themselves on the coast of Malabar, and with a fierce and untiring vigour, carried on a joint war for the true faith, and in defence of their trading occupations. Whilst Cafoor was ravaging the smiling regions of the south, sacking Hindoo cities and pillaging Hindoo shrines, Alla invaded Guzerat (A.D. 1300), and destroyed the cities of Anhulwarra and Somnauth, rebuilt after the conquest of Mahmoud by a subsequent Jain sovereignty. From thence he led his armies against Rajpootana and other states.

Alla and his general, Cafoor, having ravaged Guzerat, Rajpootana and the fertile kingdoms of the Carnatic, were now called home by the incursions of the Mogul on Delhi; but from the first invasion of the Deccan under Alla the Sanguinary until 1818, when English arms reduced its princes to submission, the Deccan never again knew a moment's peace. In 1347, fifty-two years after Alla the Sanguinary first conquered Dowlatabad, the great revolt of the Deccan Ameers against Mahomed bin Tuglak occurred, when Zuffier Kahn, a successful soldier, was raised to the throne. He founded the Brahmini dynasty, so called in grateful remembrance of his old master and

5

benefactor, who was a Brahmin, which reigned at Kalburga from 1347 to 1526.

In 1526 the kingdom was divided under the Adil Shahis of Beejapore, the Nizam Shahis of Ahmednuggur, the Kutub Shahis of Golconda, the Fuad Shahis of Berar and the Barid Shahis of Baidar. After this rebellion the Mahommedan rulers of Delhi never again crossed the Nerbudda until the reign of Akbar. These Mahommedan kingdoms of the Deccan were at the height of their prosperity when the Portuguese first went to India; and in 1565 the kings of Beejapore, Ahmednuggur, Golconda and Baidar combined against the Hindoo kingdom of Beejanuggur. The aged king, Ram Raja, was slain in cold blood, and his kingdom rent in pieces; and it was from a successor of Ram Raja that the English in 1640 received the grant of the site of Madras. It was then that Mysore became independent. Akbar carried his arms into the Deccan, but was met by heroic opposition from the beautiful Hindoo Queen of Gurrah, Durghetti, who, deserted by her troops and agonised by the loss of her son, preferred death to disgrace, and terminated her own existence.

It was during the wars caused by the endeavours of Akbar's successors to reduce the kingdoms of the Deccan, that the Mahrattas rose to supreme power, both in the Deccan and Hindustan.

The Mahrattas were so called from Maharastra, a land of mountain fastnesses—a Switzerland—on the western margin of the Deccan, a fitting cradle for the future plunderers and conquerors of India.

These mountain rats, as the Great Mogul Aurungzebe contemptuously called them, notwithstanding the want of any literature of their own—their rude and ungainly appearance, the absence of all refinement in manners and social habits and their inferiority in other respects to the other natives of the Deccan, have, from their indomitable perseverance and energy, whether as peaceful tillers of the soil or as marauders or soldiers, achieved an influence and renown, not only beyond all the other nations of the South, but have more nearly accomplished universal dominion in India than any other Hindoo people.*

The Mahrattas early took service in the armies of the Mahommedan kings of Delhi and the Deccan. In 1553 Shajec, of the respectable Bosla family, was commander of a party of horse of the Nizam Shah of Ahmednuggur. He was the father of the famous Sivajee, who was born at the fort of Joonair in 1627. At nineteen he seized the hill fort of Torna, and with the treasures there taken built the fort of Raighur. Soon after he took Surghur and Purundar, and in 1659, when the Beejapore Government attempted to seize him at Pertabghur, he successfully baffled them by the treacherous murder of their general, Afzul Khan, whom whilst pretending to embrace, he ripped open with

* The Mahratta country proper extends from Surat and Nagpur to Bijapur and Goa—a hilly tract bounded by the Satpura Mountains on the north, and the Shyadri range of the Western Ghats, and the maritime belt of the Kohkan on the west, and watered by the Nerbudda, the Tapti, the Godavery, the Bima, and the Kishtna. The cradle of the race lies in the Mawuls of the Deccan, or upland valleys of the mountain sources of the Godavery, Bima, or Kishtna. The Mahratta country, indeed, corresponds with the kingdom of the ancient Rajput dynasty of the Yadavas in Telingana. It is the Cabul of the Deccan—a country abounding in all the resources of war, in which armies can be prepared in perfect secrecy, and descend to sweep the rich plains below without a moment's warning, to which every road affords a safe retreat, and which is unassailable, except by a scientific foe.—*The "Times" Summary.*

steel-hooks "tiger-claws" secreted in his left hand, and then dispatched him with the dagger which he held in his right. He next became master of Kalian and the greater part of the Concan.

When the king of Beejapore sent messengers to Sivajee requiring him to submit, he proudly answered, "What superiority has your master gained over me, that I should consent to your mission? begone speedily, lest I disgrace you!"

Adventurous Hindoos joined his standard from all parts of the Deccan and the Concan, and his plundering bands of wild horsemen became the terror of the inhabitants.

When Aurungzebe, who had been appointed Viceroy of the Deccan by his father Shah Jehan, began to meditate treason, he saw in Sivajee one who could assist him in his unscrupulous projects. He encouraged him to attack the kingdom of Beejapore, and made over two or three forts to him to assist his plans. When later on he was preparing to march towards Agra to dethrone his father, he sent to Sivajee requesting him to join him. But Sivajee treated the prince's messenger with indignity, drove him from his presence, and ordered the missive he had brought to be tied to the tail of a dog.

He next turned his arms on Surat, took the city by *coup de main*, and plundered it for six days. He was content with the spoil of the Mussulman merchants, and, as the city was overflowing with the gold of Persia and Arabia, he left the Dutch and English factories unmolested. Aurungzebe was so delighted with the successful resistance of the English, that to show his gratitude and admiration, he conceded fresh privileges to the East India Company. After this Sivajee submitted to

Aurungzebe and distinguished himself in his service in the invasion of Beejapore. But Aurungzebe never forgave him his former insolence and defiance, and always spoke of him as "the mountain rat." His son Sumbajee became a commander of 500 horse in the Mogul army. In 1666 Sivajee visited Delhi. He was coldly received by Aurungzebe and placed among the inferior omrahs, who at a considerable distance surrounded the throne of the great Mogul. It is said that the proud Mahratta shed tears of rage and indignation at this premeditated insult, and hurled threats and defiance at "the conqueror of the world." Tradition adds that a daughter of Aurungzebe looking through a grated window into the hall of reception was so struck by the bold and undaunted indignation of the Mahratta, that her pleadings and intercession moved the heart of her imperious and relentless parent to mercy. Sivajee escaped from Delhi and rapidly regained his own dominion. In 1668 both Golconda and Beejapore paid him tribute. In 1676 he invaded the Carnatic, and on returning to Raighur died there in 1680. "Born in a fort, his greatness rose from his forts, and in a fort he died." He was fifty-three years old at the time of his death. "He was a great captain," said Aurungzebe, on hearing that his old enemy was no more; "and the only man who has had the power to raise a new kingdom, whilst I have been endeavouring to destroy the ancient sovereignties of India." Sivajee is one of the greatest princes of Hindoo history. Nearly the same age as Aurungzebe, his character had many points of similarity with that of the great Mogul. Both were energetic, crafty and ambitious. Aurungzebe was a Mahommedan bigot, Sivajee was mild and merciful. A devoted worshipper of Brama, he seemed to retaliate on the Moslems the cruel persecution they had inflicted on his race. He styled himself the "Champion of the Gods," and made it his special boast that he protected "Brahmins, kine and cultivators." His daring in action, his craft in council, his lavish generosity, his strength, courage and activity, were the glory and admiration of his race, and long after his death it was the proudest boast of a Mahratta soldier to have seen Sivajee charge hand to hand. Sivajee left immense wealth, and at his death was absolute sovereign of a large territory in the Deccan. In the distant south he possessed the district of Tanjore, equal in extent to many native sovereignties.

The latter years of Aurungzebe were full of great and well-merited anxieties. His children, one after the other, turned against him, and always found in the Mahrattas and Rajpoots allies able and willing to support them. His fourth son, Akbar, had formed an alliance with Sumbajee, the son of Sivajee, and his banner frequently flaunted side by side with that of the Mahratta, on the hard-fought fields of the Deccan. The rebellion of the Deccan was now general. The kings of Beejapore and Golconda united with other Deccanee princes, and directed by Sumbajee, formed a powerful league against the advancing power of the Mogul. Everywhere Aurungzebe's arms were victorious; but it was only for a time. The kings of Golconda and Beejapore submitted; his son Akbar fled in an English ship, whilst Sumbajee, in a state of intoxication, was betrayed into the hands of the Mogul. He was blinded with a red-hot iron, had his tongue torn out, and was beheaded. His minister Kulushi shared a like cruel fate. The king of Golconda was publicly scourged, to extort confession of his wealth, and the monarch of Beejapore was paraded in silver chains before the conqueror. Sumbajee was succeded by his son Sackojee aged six, known in history as Sáho, or "thief," a nickname given him by Aurungzebe. He was kept prisoner, and Ram Raja, his uncle, assumed the leadership of the Mahrattas. In 1700 Aurungzebe took Satara, and Ram Raja dying in the same year, his widow Tara Bhye assumed the command of the Mahrattas in their strife with the Moguls. On Aurungzebe's death (1707) Sackojee was released, the sword of Sivajee and territory of Satara were restored to him, and a grant of a percentage of the revenues of the Mahratta country, on the condition of his maintaining tranquillity. At this time also, the famous Nizam-ul-Mulk, the founder of the dynasty of the Nizams of Hyderabad, was appointed Viceroy of the Deccan by Shah Alam I. Sackojee appointed Balajee Kishwanath, a Brahmin, his Prime Minister, or Peishwa. and from this time the Brahmin Peishwas were the real heads of the Mahratta confederacy. In 1718 Sackojee sent an army to assist the Seyud faction in Delhi, with the history of which city until 1803 the Mahrattas are henceforth closely connected.

When Nizam-ul-Mulk, Viceroy of the Deccan, died in 1748, his son Mizaffir Jung should have succeeded him, but Nasir Jung, the second son, seized his father's treasures, and, having bought over the army, proclaimed himself subhadar of the Deccan.

Nasir Jung and Mohommed Ali, Nawab of the Carnatic, were supported by the English under Lawrence, but the character of these princes was so disgusting to the English, that we abandoned their cause, and the French under Bussy defeated Mahommed Ali and Nasir Jung at Cuddalore. Nasir Jung was shot by the Nawab of Cuddalore in 1750. Muzaffir Jung the elder son of the Nizam-ul-Mulk, was then proclaimed subhadar of the Deccan, but his triumph was of short duration, for he was assassinated by the Nawab of Kurnul in 1751. His younger brother, Salabat Jung, was installed at Aurungabad as subahdar of the Deccan by Bussy, and French rule was gradually extending over the fair fields of the South. It was, indeed, only with the greatest difficulty that the English maintained their position in Madras.

The great Peishwa, Bajee Rao the first, died, leaving a son, Balajee Bajee Rao, or Nana Sahib, as he was commonly called amongst his country people, who succeeded his father, but not without considerable opposition, for the ascendancy of the Brahmin Peishwas had always been viewed with jealousy by almost all the Mahratta chiefs of different lineage. In 1749 the long reign of Sáho, the Mahratta Raja, the grandson of Sivajee, the prisoner and protegé of Aurungzebe, the patron of three generations of Brahmin Peishwas, came to an end. Having no son to succeed him, he was disposed to adopt his relative and old enemy, the Raja of Kolapore, but the same absence of heirs in the case of the Raja seemed a strong objection to his nomination. Some attempt was made to substitute a remote descendant of Wittojee, the great uncle of the hero of the Deccan, but Tara Bhye, the widow of Ram Raja Sivajee's son, declared that after the death of her son, Sivajee the Second, she had concealed a posthumous son of his, and she now demanded that this alleged grandchild should be recognised as the prospective sovereign of the Mahrattas under the title of Ram Raja II. Sáho's wife, who thus saw herself robbed of the power she had anticipated, as regent during the minority of the remoter candidate, was determined not to abandon the game without a struggle. Balajee, the new Peishwa, mistrusted both ladies; but the dislike that prevailed against the Brahmin ascendancy rendered it almost impossible that he should follow his inclination, suppress the Raja-ship altogether and proclaim himself head of the State. He managed both the rivals, however, with considerable craft, and contrived so that Sukwar Bhye on the death of the Raja felt compelled to carry out her avowed intention of suttee. A deed had been executed by the dying Raja, empowering Balajee to "manage the whole government of the Mahratta Empire, on condition of his perpetuating the Raja's name, and keeping up the dignity of the house of Sivajee, through the grandson of Tara Bhye and his descendants."* Tara Bhye watched all these arrangements with a jealous and disapproving eye, and determined to bide her time. Apparently absorbed in the cares and education of the young Raja, who lived at Satara, she never ceased to scheme for the overthrow of Balajee's power.

He now marched against Salabat, Viceroy of the Deccan, but his expedition came to a sudden end. News reached him that Tara Bhye had retired into the fort, and after in vain endeavouring to persuade her grandson to throw off the yoke of the Peishwa, had turned upon the miserable youth with fierce invective railing at him as an impostor and a changeling, whilst he ordered the old orthodox Mahratta troops by whom

* Major Grant Duff.

she was surrounded, to fire on the Raja's people. She invited Dunnajee Guikwar to join her in ridding the capital of the Brahmin clique, and turned the guns of the fort upon the town, which was occupied by the Peishwa's troops. But the Guikwar shortly afterwards fell into Balajee's hands, and Tara Bhye was left to defy the Peishwa alone. This she continued to do, and, aware of the jealousy with which he was regarded, Balajee was afraid to proceed to extremities with her. Her energy, her ability, her prestige with the people, all made her a dangerous enemy, and after a time terms were agreed upon between them. She retained possession of the fort of Satara, and of the Raja's person and establishment, whilst the Guikwar was bound to yield permanently half the revenues of Guzerat to the victorious Balajee. Balajee now turned his arms once more against Salabat who was forced to cede territory between the Taptee and the Godavery to the Peishwa, whose army twice within a short time overspread the Carnatic, and established the Mahratta supremacy in the Deccan.

From the fall of Beejanuggur in 1565 until 1761, a Hindoo dynasty had reigned in Mysore until Hyder Ali, the successful adventurer, general, and minister, deposed his master and usurped his throne. In 1766 he invaded Malabar and took Calicut. The English, the Mahrattas and the Nizam formed an alliance against him, but the Nizam went over to Hyder, and the Mahrattas took to plundering, and thus the first Mysore war ended in the discreditable peace of Madras, 1769. In 1778 Hyder Ali, the Nizam, and the Mahrattas were all united against the English. The Carnatic was desolated, and so critical had the position become in Madras, that a message was sent to Warren Hastings at Calcutta for assistance. Sir Eyre Coote presently coming to the aid of the English, Hyder Ali was defeated, and dying shortly afterwards, was succeeded by his son Tippoo. The second Mysore war was ended by the treaty of Mangalore, 1784. The third Mysore war gave us the half of Tippoo's dominions which we shared with our allies. The siege of Seringapatam and the death of Tippoo in 1799 concluded the fourth war, after which the ancient Hindoo dynasty was restored to a limited sway, and the family of Tippoo pensioned off by Government.

Balajee, after the battle of Paniput, sickened and died. He was succeeded by his second son, Madu Rao, appointed to the office of Peishwa by the reputed descendant of Sivajee, Ram Raja, of Satara. He was succeeded by his younger brother, Narayana Rao, who was almost immediately murdered by his uncle Ragoba. Ragoba in 1773 assumed the dignity of Peishwa himself. In 1776 the representative of Narayana Rao's posthumous son, Madu Rao Narayana (believed by some writers to be a supposititious child) signed with Warren Hastings the Treaty of Purhandur. The seventh and last Peishwa, Ragoba's son, the odious Bajee Rao, was born in 1774. The captive of Satara, Ram Raja, died in 1777, and was succeeded by an adopted son, known as Sáho II. The mother of Madu Rao poisoned herself, and in 1795 Madu himself committed suicide. Bajee Rao II. now filled the office of Peishwa. The whole Mahratta confederation was in a state of disruption, and in 1802, after Holkar had seized Poona, the Peishwa fled for protection to British arms, and signed the Treaty of Bassein, which gave the British the Malabar coast and the command of the Indian ocean, and by which the once redoubtable Mahratta Confederation was virtually brought to an end. This was the result of the first Mahratta war. The second Mahratta war ended in the victories of Sir Arthur Wellesley at Assaye and Argaum in the Deccan against Scindia and the Rajah of Berar; and by Lord Lake at Delhi, where he defeated Scindia's brigades trained by French officers, when he restored Shah Alam to the throne, and subsequently he crushed, at the obstinately-contested field of Laswarree, Scindia's remaining battalions. And the third Mahratta war in 1804-5, Lake drove Holkar, the only remaining unbroken Mahratta power, in headlong flight, after the loss of his guns at Deeg, into the Punjab, and established the British as the paramount power in India. Bajee Rao II., the great grandson of the first Peishwa, was the last who filled that great office, which with him, after lasting 100 years, finally terminated. He was an unworthy descendant of the great men who had been his predecessors. He was distinguished, even in the Eastern world, by dissimulation and debauchery of the lowest kind. So cowardly, that he fled before his enemies like a hunted hare; he was the tool and willing instrument of the basest of ministers, Trimbukjeet Dainglia, at whose instigation he is supposed to have caused the assassination of the able and upright Gunga Dhur Shastree, the minister of the Guikwar, then on a special mission to his court; this being only one amongst many of the crimes he committed under the influence of his profligate favourites. The only redeeming quality he appears to have had was some consideration for the fortunes of those who had adhered to him in his reverses. When he assented to deposition and resigned himself a captive to our hands, he stipulated as a condition that his faithful followers should be cared for.

He surrendered in 1818 to Sir John Malcolm, who, to the astonishment of all acquainted with Indian affairs, guaranteed him an annual pension of eight lakhs of rupees or £80,000 per annum. Having no children, Bajee Rao II. adopted a son who was to succeed to his vast wealth, but not to the pension or title of Peishwa. This young man, described at the time of Bajee Rao's death as "quiet and unostentatious, not at all addicted to any extravagant habits, and invariably showing a ready disposition to attend to the advice of the British Commissioner," was none other than the infamous Dundoo Punt, better known as Nana Sahib. Resentment against the British Government, for disallowing his claim to succeed to the Peishwa's titles and pension as well as to his private fortune, amounting to £280,000, seems to have inspired him with a revengeful bitterness that only bided its time to blaze forth in unrelenting fury, and when the annexation of Oude under Lord Dalhousie gave a plausible pretext for resentment, it is said that princes and native chiefs, who had hitherto held back, now responded to his appeals, and swore to further him in his projects of revenge.*

The history of the Indian Mutiny needs no repetition here. The Nana was proclaimed Peishwa by the rebel Gwalior contingent and others. After passing through many vicissitudes and losing every battle, the blood-stained and perjured slaughterer of innocent women and

* Sir John Kaye's "History of the Sepoy War."

† Meadows Taylor's "Manual of Indian History."

children fled to Bithoor, attended by a few horsemen, "and as he rode through Cawnpore his horse flecked with foam, he might have met the public criers proclaiming that the Feringhees had been well nigh exterminated, and offering rewards for the heads of the few who were still left upon the face of the earth. But the lie had exploded, and his one thought of that moment was escape from the pursuing Englishman. Arrived at Bithoor, he saw clearly that the game was up, his followers were fast deserting him. Many it is said reproached him for his failure. All, we may be sure, clamoured for pay. His terror-stricken imagination pictured a vast avenging army on his track; and the great instinct of self-preservation prompted him to gather up the women of his family, to embark by night in a boat, to ascend the Ganges to Futtehgurh, and to give out that he was preparing himself for self-immolation. He was to consign himself to the sacred waters of the Ganges, which had been the grave of so many of his victims. There was to be a given signal through the darkness of the early night, which was to mark the moment of the Ex-Peishwa's suicidal immersion. But he had no thought of dying. The signal light was extinguished, and a cry arose from the religious mendicants who were assembled on the Cawnpore bank of the river, and who believed that the Nana was dead. But covered by the darkness, he emerged upon the Oude side of the Ganges, and his escape was safely accomplished."* The holy men proceeded without delay to plunder the palace of their quondam benefactor.

Thus vanished from the scene, like a baneful meteor, the guilty shadow of the once renowned and imperial Peishwas.

* Kaye's "Sepoy War."

CHAPTER XI.

THE REMARKABLE WOMEN OF INDIA.

Princess of Scinde—Beautiful Sultana Rezia of Delhi—Hindoo Queen of Gurrah—A Sultana Regent—Mother of Sivajee.

Before describing the origin and progress of British rule in India, a few words on the women of that country who, by their beauty, ability, and courage, have powerfully affected its history, may not be uninteresting.

Accustomed as we have been to regard all Eastern women as both mentally and morally inferior, and accepting broadly the fact of their imperfect education, subordinate position and secluded lives, it is with a feeling of surprise akin to admiration that we recognise the startling influence exercised by women on the fate of the Eastern world,—an influence not to be attributed to mere personal charms alone, nor to the infatuation of a besotted passion, which any given sovereign may have felt for this or that favourite of the harem, but conspicuously due (in combination with beauty) to ability, energy, craft, perseverance and ambition on the part of those who have come prominently to the front in the history of India. The seclusion of high-caste Hindoo women was probably not so strict in earlier ages as at present, but that their separation from the outer world was considered both desirable and expedient there can be no doubt. The wife was enjoined to give her entire devotion and obedience to her husband; she was to lead a life of seclusion, and to keep herself from contact with the world. Men were told to honour the women of their family lest "it wholly perish;" and it is added that whereas, in families where the women are not held in honour, "all religious acts become fruitless," in those, on the other hand, "where a husband is contented with his wife, and she with her husband, "will fortune assuredly be permanent."*

It would almost seem as though the general subjection of women had been more than counterbalanced by their individual supremacy in those countries where the very title of "Sultana" sounds, in Western ears, nearly synonymous with that of a toy; a beautiful, soul-less, graceful creature, helpless and useless, meant to be, and sent to be, simply and solely, "a moment's ornament." Too childish for companionship, too ignorant for opposition, too helpless for self-dependence, the Moslem faith instils the inferiority of the female sex as an article of religion. "Women," it says, "are only superior in craft and cunning." They are not allowed to read the holy books—they are not permitted to eat with their husbands—they are debarred from inheriting paternal property. Seclusion is their portion and ignorance their fate.

The history of the remarkable women of India has yet to be written, but a brief glance at some of the more prominent female figures who have illustrated Eastern story by their charms, courage and devotion may not be without interest to the reader. It will, at any rate, go far to show that the "coming woman," the capable, enduring, heroic, high-souled woman, determined, skilful,

* Colebrooke's *Asiatic Researches.*

dominant and predominating is not so entirely a product of the West, or a dream of the future, as some of the subjugators of the sex would have us believe.

The Princess of Scinde.—Of the extraordinary resolution shown by Indian women, we have a striking example as early as 711 A.D., in the conquest of Scinde by the Arabs.

Amongst the numerous female captives of Scinde were two beautiful princesses, who were reserved for the harem of the Commander of the Faithful, Walid, the sixth caliph of the house of Ommeia. When the elder was introduced to her future lord, she burst into a flood of tears, and declared that she was now unworthy of his notice, having been already dishonoured by his nephew' Casim, before she was sent out of her country. Enraged at the insult offered to him by his inferior, and inflamed by the sight of her beauty and distress, the caliph sent orders that Casim should be sewed up in a raw hide and sent to Damascus. When he produced the body to the princess, she was so overjoyed at the sight, that she exultingly declared Casim had been innocent, but that she had now avenged her father's death and the ruin of her family! This heroic lady and her sister met with a cruel and ignominious death.*

The beautiful Sultana Rezia ascended the Imperial musnud at Delhi on the deposition of her brother in 1236. "Rezia Begum," says Ferishta, "was endowed with every princely virtue, and those who scrutinize her actions most severely, will find it to be in her no fault that she was a woman."†

* Briggs' *Ferishta;* Pottinger's "Travels." † Briggs' *Ferishta.*

Not only was she beautiful as the day, but her energy, ambition and judgment were such, that twice during the lifetime of her father Altamish, he entrusted his kingdom to her care. "The burden of power," he said to his omrahs when he appointed her as regent, during his absence on his southern campaigns, "is too heavy for my sons, even though I had twenty such, but not too heavy for Rezia, delicate though her body may be, she has in her more spirit than all of her brothers put together."

The fair sultana on ascending the throne, daily gave audience, habited as a sultan. "She discarded her female apparel and veil, wore a tunic and cap like a man, gave public audience, and rode on an elephant without any attempt at concealment."* She reformed abuses, revised the laws, and fulfilled the enthusiastic predictions of her nobles and her people. But unfortunately her great ability did not shield her from weakness, and by the elevation to power of an Abyssinian slave, she roused the jealousy and excited the indignation of her nobles.

In the rebellion that ensued, her favourite was killed, but Rezia, who saw her cause to be desperate, managed to fascinate by love or by ambition one of the rebel chiefs, who married her, and joined his forces with hers against his former associates. After two bloody battles she was made prisoner along with her husband, and both were put to death.†

"With a look," said her grand vizier, "she could revive her dying friends, or render helpless her most powerful foes." Yet her charms had no weight against the

* Sir Henry Elliot's *Historians.*

† Elphinstone's "History of India."

vindictive fury of her rebellious nobles, who slew her without remorse after a reign of three years and six months.

The story of Pudmani, the Beautiful, at the siege of Cheetore under Alla the Sanguinary (A.D. 1300) has been told in another chapter.* It affords a touching illustration of that high Rajpoot courage and devotion which inspired even the women and children of this fearless race with heroism, and enabled them to brave death rather than incur dishonour.

The "johur," or the ordeal of death, far from intimidating them, was welcomed as the means of re-uniting husbands and wives, fathers and children, and conducting to the warrior's paradise the woman who had loved her warlike lord. Many utterances of heroic Rajpoot wives and widows adorn the records of Eastern courage. "Tell me, Badul," cried the wife of Gorah, one of the defenders of Cheetore, uncle of the beautiful Pudmani, "tell me, how did my love behave?"

"O mother," replied the boy, "how further describe his deeds when he left no foes to dread or admire him?"

"My lord will chide my delay," exclaimed the high-souled woman, as waving a fond and smiling farewell to the stripling, she sprang into the devouring flames of the funeral pile awaiting her.†

During Akbar's invasion of the Deccan more than one startling proof of the heroism of its women was brought home to him. The revolted Bahadoor Kahn,

* See Chapter on Rajpootana. † Sullivan.

Sultan of Guzerat, having fallen into the hands of the Moguls (1560) his mistress, said to be one of the most beautiful women ever seen in India, became the property of a Mogul chief renowned for his fierce and cruel nature. Finding resistance to be unavailing, she appointed an hour to receive him. Her attendants adorned her with her most splendid jewels, dressed her in magnificent attire, sprinkled her couch with perfumes, and left her to receive her conqueror in state. Drawing a mantle over her face, she lay down to rest, and it was only when her attendants approached to warn her of the presence of her future lord, that they discovered the gentle slumber she had feigned was the last long sleep of death.

The Hindoo queen Durghetti, who reigned over the small territory of Gurrah, is another woman famed in the history of the Deccan for her beauty and accomplishments, her heroism and constancy. Ten sovereigns of her race had already reigned in succession over the fertile and prosperous district which was hers by inheritance. Bent upon developing the resources of her happy little state and increasing the prosperity of her people, the spirited Hindoo queen turned all her attention and energy to those ends. Aseph Jah, one of Akbar's generals, determined to overthrow her power and conquer for his master her smiling territory. Without a moment's hesitation the queen called together her peaceful and peace-loving subjects. They responded to her appeal with ready devotion, and burning with indignant enthusiasm, she placed herself at the head of her troops. A helmet on her head, a quiver at her side, a lance in her hand, she advanced to meet the invading Mogul. Perceiving that her troops, new to the art of warfare, were advancing upon the enemy in disorder, she sounded a recall, re-formed and harangued them, telling them that they were to wait for a signal from the royal elephant, on which she was herself seated, before advancing. Surprised by this unexpected resistance, the Moguls were driven back and left 600 dead upon the field. But Durghetti's nobles refused to carry out her tactics and follow up their advantage by a night attack upon the discomfited troops of Aseph Jah, and when on the following day he renewed the engagement with fresh reinforcements, they fled in confusion, leaving guns and arms in the hands of the enemy. The courageous queen, supported by four of her chieftains, bore the brunt of the battle, holding out valiantly after all hope was at an end. Her friends implored her to fly—her son fell at her side, pierced through the eye by an arrow—the princess, deserted by her troops, was in imminent danger of falling into the enemy's hands. Turning to the chief officer of her household, "Haste!" she cried, "let your dagger save me from the crime of putting an end to my own existence! We are overcome in war, but we need not be vanquished in honour!" Her faithful servant had not, however, the courage to fulfil this her last request and, seeing that her exhortation could not prevail over his affection, she snatched the dagger from his side "and satisfied the immortal longings of her soul."*

* Sullivan, Elphinstone and others.

Chand Sultana is one of the most distinguished women that have ever appeared in India. She was acting as regent for her infant nephew, Bahadur Nizam Shah, of Ahmednuggur, and she was no sooner aware of the approach of the Moguls (under Akbar about 1595) than she applied herself to conciliate the king of Beejapoor, her relation, and at the same time to reconcile the heads of other interested parties, that all might be united to resist the power whose ambition threatened equal danger to all. Her defence of Ahmednugger is famous in history. She superintended the workmen and directed the mining and trench work, exposing herself to the same dangers as the rest. Two mines had already been rendered useless by her counter-mines, but unfortunately before means could be taken to render it ineffectual, a third mine was fired, the counter-mines blown up, and a large breach made in the wall, by which such a panic was created, that the besieged were on the point of deserting their posts and leaving the breach open to the advance of the storming party. But Chand Sultana, with a naked sword in her hand, clad in complete armour, a veil over her face, sprang into the breach, and, having thus rallied her troops, she continued her exertions until every power within the place was brought against the assaulting Moguls. Matchlock balls and arrows poured on them from the works—guns were brought to bear upon the breach—rockets, gunpowder and other combustibles were thrown amongst the crowd in the ditch, and the garrison in front opposed so steady a resistance, that, after an obstinate and bloody contest, the Moguls were obliged to withdraw. The activity and energy of the regent were not slackened during the night, and the Moguls, finding next day that the breach was built up to such a height as to render it impossible to mount it without fresh mines, a truce was agreed upon on both sides. Mahommed Khan, whom Chand Sultana had appointed her Prime Minister, plotted against her; her government became more and more disturbed by internal factions, and whilst she was negotiating a peace with the Moguls, the soldiery, instigated by her opponents, broke into the female apartments and treacherously put her to death.

Chand Sultana is the favourite heroine of the Deccan, and is the subject of many fabulous stories. Even Khafi Khan mentions her having fired silver balls into the Mogul camp, and the common tradition at Ahmednugger is that when her shot was expended she loaded her guns successively with copper, with silver, and with gold coin, and that it was not until she had begun to fire her jewels away that she consented to make peace.

The history of Tara Bhye, given at page 72, is another proof of the ambition, ability and energy of Indian women, whilst that of the mother of Sivajee, the popular hero of the Deccan (born 1627) deserves mention. She was of good family and a woman of so much ability and character that during his father's absence in the Carnatic, Sivajee was left to the care of his mother and of his father's agent, a Brahmin. He appears from the first to have looked to her for counsel and sympathy in all his undertakings, his great object in life being to free himself from Mahommedan control. His tutor and guardian, Dadajee Konedeo, at first endeavoured to disuade the youth from his wild undertakings, but, failing to do so, he appears to have succumbed to the force of Sivajee's character and to have come at last to share his views.

His mother, an enthusiast in religion, believed herself to be visited by the goddess Bowhanee, whose revelations shadowed forth the future freedom of the Mahrattas from Mahommedan yoke, and the future greatness of her son. Later on, when his fame became established, no one doubted but that his mother's dreams and visions, which had become popular amongst his people, were in reality the divine revelations they pretended to be. He remained devoted to his mother, claimed her blessing on all his undertakings, however questionable, and never ceased to pay her every honour that affection and respect could dictate.

CHAPTER XII.

THE REMARKABLE WOMEN OF INDIA.—*continued.*

Noormahal,* Consort of Shah Jehangire—Arjamund Banu,† (of the Taj), Consort of Shah Jehan—The Emperor's Daughters.

Noormahal.—No more extraordinary example of the triumph of beauty and ability over precedent, tradition, and every prejudice, religious as well as social, exists, than that of Noormahal, the light of the harem, who for twenty years, as the wife of Jehangire, reigned, with a power as absolute over the mighty empire of Hindostan as that exercised by Semiramis and Cleopatra over the kingdoms of Assyria and Egypt.

Her father, Chaja Aiass, a Tartar of noble blood but poor circumstances, became later the High Treasurer of the Empire of Hindostan, but his daughter Noormahal was born in the days of his adversity amongst the wilds of Western Tartary as her parents were wandering, in search of fortune, towards India. The beautiful Noormahal frequently accompanied her mother to the harem of Akbar, and here Prince Selim, heir to the throne, saw and loved her. He demanded her hand of her father, who replied that his daughter was promised to Shere Afkun, a young Persian lord. Noormahal, who appears

* Afterwards Noorjehan. † Or Mumtazmahal.

to have been of a practical turn of mind, thought it wiser to take the magnificent Shere Afkun than to incur the danger of mating with the future Emperor. The Emperor Akbar absolutely refused to interfere or annul the engagement, and Shere Afkun was determined not to renounce his right—even for the heir to the crown—to the most beautiful woman in the world.

When Akbar died, and Selim ascended the imperial musnud, under the name of Jehanghire, Shere Afkun was soon removed to a happier sphere, and the lovely Noormahal transferred to the Zenana of the Emperor.

For some reason which does not appear, she remained six years in absolute seclusion; but the talk of her wit and beauty which reached the Emperor's ears at length determined him on visiting her. He found her in a plain muslin dress, surrounded by slaves dressed in the finest brocades and cashmeres. She had learned the charm of modesty during the period of her retirement; and, with downcast eyes, she stood before the Emperor in all the unadorned simplicity of her dazzling beauty. The first question he asked her was why her slaves were dressed so much better than their mistress? to which the cunning Noormahal shrewdly made answer, "Those born to servitude must dress as it shall please those whom they serve. These are my slaves, and I make the burden of their bondage pleasant to them by every indulgence in my power. But I am your slave, oh, Emperor of the world! and must dress according to your pleasure, and not my own." Casting a necklace round her neck of forty pearls, each worth £4,000, Jehangire ordered the clever intrigante to be proclaimed Empress of the

World. From the humblest apartments of the Zenana she at once removed to those of the Sultana. She was permitted to assume the title of Shahi, or Empress; to change her name from Noormahal, Light of the Harem, to Noor Jehan, Light of the World; whilst the besotted monarch caused to be inscribed on the gold coin of the realm: "Gold has acquired a hundred degrees of excellence in receiving the name of Noor-Jehan." He was then forty-four years of age. Like another famous Eastern Queen, "age could not wither her, nor custom stale her infinite variety," and for twenty years her magnificence dazzled Hindostan. It was she who gave away the smallest as well as the greatest official appointments. From Western Tartary came crowds of cousins to share in the brilliant fortunes of the superb Empress. Her father was Prime Vizier; her brother, Asiph Khan, was first Omrah; Shah Jehan, the Emperor's favourite son, married her niece, the daughter of Asiph Khan; whilst Prince Sheriar, Jehanghire's third son, married her own daughter by her first husband, the luckless Shere Afkun.

Led by her, Jehanghire was induced to ill-treat and mistrust Mohabit Khan, to whom he had been thrice indebted for the safety of his kingdom; and in return Mohabit, by a *coup-de-main*, seized the Emperor and carried him off to his own camp. Noormahal escaped in disguise, and, calling her brother Asiph to her aid, mounted her elephant and prepared to rescue the Emperor. Though her daughter was wounded in the fray and sank fainting at her side, this daring woman pursued her way, until at length her troops were overwhelmed and she was forced to fly to Lahore.

Mohabit accused her of having planned her husband's death, and she was conducted by him before the Emperor to make her defence. "You, who are Emperor of the Moguls," said Mohabit, exhorting the infatuated monarch to throw off her dangerous influence, "ought to follow the example of God, who is no respecter of persons." But the beautiful and specious Noormahal prevailed; and when the Emperor, affected by the sight of her tears, appealed to Mohabit to spare her, the chivalrous soldier replied, That the Emperor of the Moguls should never ask a favour of him in vain, and signed to the guards to relinquish their prisoner. Noormahal survived her husband eighteen years; but from the hour of his death she retired altogether from affairs of state, and closed her life amongst the gardens and palaces of the royal residence of Lahore.

Arjamund Banu.—Although not distinguished by the craft and ability of her predecessor, Arjamund Banu, the heroine of the Taj Mahal, has been handed down to posterity by the story of her beauty and unbounded influence over the Emperor Shah Jehan.

It was the custom in those days, as it is in our own, for ladies to hold fancy fairs, and to sell their merchandise to the highest bidders. Shah Jehan, then a prince residing at his father's court at Agra, attended a bazaar where the Emperor had commanded that the nobles should give whatever price was asked for their wares by the fair stall-keepers. Prince Jehan, pausing before the booth of Arjamund Banu, the daughter of the Vizier Asiph Jah, and wife of Jemal Kahn, was so struck by her beauty and grace that when she asked him £12,500 for a piece of sugar candy, cut in the shape of a diamond, the infatuated young man smilingly paid the fancy price demanded for her bon-bon by this enterprising saleswoman. He invited her to his palace; and when, after three days' *séjour* with him, she returned to her husband, she felt much aggrieved that her lawful lord received her less warmly than she considered becoming. She immediately complained of her tyrant's fit of the sulks to Shah Jehan, who quickly found a remedy against the recurrence of such attacks of temper. He ordered him to the elephant garden, that he might there be destroyed. Jemal Kahn, upon this unpleasant news, hastened to the prince and humbly begged that he might be allowed to explain. Permission was graciously accorded, when he judiciously declared that his reserve had not proceeded from coldness, but from a sense of his unworthiness to take to his bosom the being who had been honoured by the attention of the son of the great Mogul. A royal suit and the command of 5,000 horse was immediately bestowed upon the accommodating husband, and the lady was transported forthwith to the seraglio of the prince. She possessed, it is said by historians, the wit and beauty of her aunt, Noormahal, and the wisdom and integrity of her grandfather Aiass. She is spoken of as that virtuous woman who is proverbially a crown to her husband, whose only wife she remained during twenty years, and when she died the Taj Mahal at Agra, that exquisite dream in marble, bore witness to the devotion and attachment which even her memory was still able to inspire.

The daughters of Shah Jehan.—The daughters of Shah

Jehan were important actors in the scenes of his eventful reign. They were all three women of beauty, talents and accomplishments. Jehanara, the eldest, was remarkable alike for wit and beauty. Her devotion to her father knew no bounds; and he had so high an opinion of her judgment, that his will became in many cases subservient to that of his lovely tyrant. Nevertheless, a terrible story of the summary vengeance he wreaked upon a favoured lover shows that affection did not altogether blind him to the possible effects of his daughter's somewhat too elastic morality. He paid her an unexpected visit; and, in the hurry and confusion occasioned by the inopportune attention, Jehanara could think of no better place wherein to conceal the contraband lover than in one of the huge cauldrons made to hold water for the bath. Then, after affectionately enquiring after her health, he insisted on the restoring and curative effects of hot water, and desired that fires should at once be made under the cauldrons in order that she might without delay experience the agreeable results he described. Jehanara dared not resist; and, feigning unconsciousness of her agony, her father remained conversing cheerfully and affably with his miserable daughter until a servant brought him word that the unhappy lover was boiled to death, when, without uttering a word of reproach, he amiably took his departure. His second daughter, Ranchenara Begum, was acute, artful, intriguing and ambitious, and as devoted to Aurungzebe as Jehanara was to Prince Dara, her father's eldest son, and heir-presumptive. Later, when Dara had been defeated by Aurungzebe, and his wife and son placed with Jehanara under close restraint, it was the younger sister Ranchanara Begum, who scented out all the plots and intrigues at Court and confided them to Aurungzebe. The gentleness of Suria Banu, the third daughter, kept her aloof from political intrigue and family dissension. Jehanara tenderly nursed her father through his last illness, and survived him many years. Her brother Aurungzebe was eventually reconciled to her; and amidst the ruin and desolation of the pearl mosque at Delhi, may still be deciphered the last injunction of "the perishable pilgrim," Jehanara Begum: "Let not any person desecrate my tomb with any other thing than earth or flowers, for these are fitted for the resting place of a Holy Spirit."*

* Sullivan.

CHAPTER XIII.

THE REMARKABLE WOMEN OF INDIA—*continued.*

Ahalya Bhye the Good, Queen of Indore—Tulsee Bhye the Cruel, Regent of Indore.

Ahalya Bhye, the Queen of Indore, or, the dominions of Holkar.—Ahalya Bhye was the widow of the only son of Mulhur Rao Holkar, the founder of the Holkar dynasty, and on the death of her only son, who died in early childhood, soon after the death of his grandfather, assumed, according to the custom of the Mahrattas, the administration of the country.

The long, peaceful, and successful reign of this illustrious lady was at its commencement vehemently opposed by the intrigues and machinations of Bagonath Rao, the uncle of the then Peishwa, who endeavoured to force upon the Queen the adoption of a child whose future movements might be subject to his guidance or that of his agents.

This scheme was entirely frustrated by the wise conduct of the princess aided by the determination of the chiefs of the Mahratta States, to uphold "the legitimate rights of the widow of Mulhar Rao's son."*

* Malleson's "Native States of India."

In India during the latter half of the eighteenth century, the power of the sword was supreme, and in nothing was the wisdom of the Ranee, Ahalya Bhye more remarkable than in her choice of the commander of her troops.

Tukajee Holkar, who was appointed to this high office, was not related to, although of the same tribe as, Mulhar Rao. He was of mature age, unambitious, of excellent character, possessing sound sense, but without brilliant qualities. Ahalya Bhye soon gave Tukajee a large share in the general administration of the country, but whether he was near the capital or in the more distant provinces, he served the Ranee with the utmost fidelity and respect during her long reign of thirty years.

Her Highness had representatives at most of the Courts of India. The administration of justice was scrupulously attended to, the Queen herself being at all times accessible and attending to the most insignificant cases when reference was made for her decision. The accounts of the State receipts and disbursements were kept with the most scrupulous exactitude.

"During thirty years of rule," says Colonel Malleson, "perhaps no prince or princess ever conciliated more respect from foreign sovereigns than did this illustrious Hindu lady. She was extremely pious, much given to devotion, yet she found time to attend to the important affairs of state." She transacted business from 2 p.m. to 6 p.m., and from 9 p.m. to 11 p.m. Her dominions were but once invaded and then unsuccessfully, and the internal administration was equally fortunate, for nowhere were the people more happy or prosperous. She built forts and made roads, and Indore, the present capital, she found a village and left a wealthy city.

Fortunate, and held in the highest regard as a ruler, yet the loss of her children under peculiarly painful circumstances, left on her life an impression of sadness which no success in public affairs could alleviate.

Ahalya Bhye died in 1795 at the age of sixty, utterly exhausted by the cares of State. According to Sir John Malcolm this famous lady "was of the middle stature and very thin; her complexion, which was of a dark olive, was clear; and her countenance is described as having been to the last hour of her life agreeable. She was very cheerful, seldom in anger, possessed a cultivated mind, was quick and clear in the transaction of public business, and even flattery appears to have been lost upon her."*

Honoured and held in reverence during life for her piety, virtues and good deeds, she died universally beloved and lamented.

Tulsee Bhye, Regent of Indore.—Tulsee Bhye was beautiful, cruel and profligate, and met with a tragical end—a contrast in every respect to Ahalya Bhye.

She was the protegé of a sectarian Brahmin, and would have been considered his daughter did not the vow of celibacy of the holy man forbid such a supposition.

A Mahratta adventurer thought he might promote his own interests through the influence of her beauty on Jeswunt Rao Holkar, the Maharajah of Indore. The prince saw Tulsee Bhye, was at once captivated, and,

* Malleson's "Native States of India," and Sir John Malcolm's "Central India."

notwithstanding that she was a married woman, had her at once placed in the harem, while the husband was sent to prison. Some lingering feeling induced her to entreat her spell-bound lord to liberate the unfortunate husband, who, on receiving a dress of honour, a horse and a small sum of money, departed to seek his fortunes elsewhere. The influence of this new ornament to the harem became supreme over the prince and the State and continued until Holkar became insane, when she was appointed regent, and having no children adopted a son of the Maharajah by another woman. The people bore with her cruel and abandoned conduct until at last, having executed her Prime Minister, an old, popular, and faithful servant of the State, and having appointed a worthless paramour to his high office, her power over the army became little more than nominal, and as she was suspected of intriguing with the English with a view to their protection, some of the leading men in the State conspired against her. She was ruthlessly slain almost in the midst of her soldiers but not a hand was raised to rescue her—beauty and appeals for mercy were unavailing. Thus miserably ended the cruel and criminal career of the beautiful Tulsee Bhye.

Tulsee Bhye was beheaded on December 20, 1817. Her accomplishments and character are thus described by Sir John Malcolm:—"Tulsee Bhye," he writes, "was not thirty years old when she was murdered. She was handsome, and alike remarkable for the fascination of her manners and quickness of intellect. Few surpassed her in fluent eloquence, which persuaded those who approached her to promote her wishes. She rode with grace, and was always, when on horseback, attended by a large party of the females of the first families of the State. But there was never a more remarkable instance than in the history of this princess, how the most prodigal gifts of nature may be perverted by an indulgence of vicious habits. Though not the wife of Jeswant Rao, yet being in charge of his family, and having possession of the child, who was declared his heir, she was obeyed as his widow. As the favourite of the deceased and the guardian of their actual chief, she had among the adherents of the Holkar family the strongest impressions in her favour, but casting all away, she lived unrespected and died unpitied."*

* Malcolm's "Central India."

CHAPTER XIV.

THE REMARKABLE WOMEN OF INDIA—*continued.*

Begum Sumroo of Sirdhanah—Walter Reinhart—Chief Officers—Colonel le Vaisseau—George Thomas, a common sailor, afterwards a Rajah—Begum's Court—Adopted Son, Dyce-Sombre—Domestic Chaplain, Father Julius Cæsar.

*The Begum Sumroo,** born about 1753, was the illegitimate daughter of a Mohammedan of Arab descent. She was also reported to have been a native of Cashmere, and to have been originally a dancing girl. On the death of her father she and her mother, in order to avoid the persecution of the legitimate heir, removed in 1760 to Delhi. It is not certain when she entered the family of Sumroo, nor even that she ever became his wife. This Sumroo was a native of Treve in the duchy of Luxemburg, his real name, Walter Reinhardt, but more familiar to us by his Indian soubriquet of Sumroo or Sombre. He had come to India as a sailor in the French navy, deserted to the British service, and joined the first European battalion raised in Bengal. Deserting again, he joined the French garrison at Chandernagore, and was one of the few who followed Law when that officer refused to surrender the place to the British. After the capture of his gallant chief, Sumroo, under

* Or Zeb-ul-Nisa, the ornament of the sex, christened Johanna Nobilis.

Meer Cassim, Nawab of Moorsedubad, advanced against the English, and by the Nawab's orders, on his arrival at Patna he put all the English prisoners to death. All suspected of being friends of the English were assassinated, and Sumroo, firing volleys into the prisoners' rooms, about 200 British, including the Resident and all his followers, met with a cruel end. Sumroo, sold his sword first to one party and then to another, as interest might dictate. After his death,* which took place at Agra, 1778, his soldiery were maintained by his supposed widow, and the Mogul Minister who perceived her to be a woman of extraordinary ability, put her—instead of her step-son by another Mussalmani, who was a minor—in possession of the lands which had been held by Sumroo for the support of his troops. Her army is stated to have consisted of five battalions of Sepoys, about 300 European officers and gunners, with forty pieces of cannon and a body of Mogul horse. This efficient little army was engaged in many parts of India. A detachment of it fought under Scindia against Wellington at Assaye, and on another occasion operated against the Seikhs; and, after quelling a rising in the Cis-Sutlej States, this energetic and loyal lady suddenly appeared with her European officers in the palace of the Emperor at Delhi, and overawed by her presence Rohilla conspirators, causing them to regain their camp on the other side of the Jumna. In 1781, she embraced Christianity. She founded a Christian mission which grew by degrees into a convent, a cathedral, and a college; and there were some 1,500 native and Anglo-Indian Christians resident at Sirdhanah.

* The widow of one of Sumroo's descendants still occupies a house and park near Meerut.

Here she kept up princely state, and in 1792 married Colonel le Vaisseau, who was one of the chief European officers of her little army. Her troops, not approving of this arrangement, revolted and a revolution broke out at Sirdhanah in favour of her step-son, Zafaryab Khan, or Aloysius Reinhardt, residing at Delhi with the title of Nawab. The Begum and Le Vaisseau escaped, but were pursued. They agreed that neither was to survive the other, and when the soldiery came up a scream from the female attendants of the Begum caused Le Vaisseau to look into the litter. The white cloth on her breast was stained with blood. She had stabbed herself, but the dagger glancing aside on the breast-bone, she had not the courage to repeat her blow, or rather, as it is alleged by many, had no intention to do so. Her husband put his pistol to his temple, the ball passed through his head, and he fell dead to the ground.

The Begum was carried back to the Fort, stripped of her property, and tied under a gun. Here she remained several days, and must have died of starvation but for the kindly offices of a faithful *ayah*, who supplied her more pressing necessities.

She appealed to George Thomas, an Irishman, formerly her chief officer, who commanded her troops in the dashing charge which rescued the Emperor at Gokalgurh, but now the Rajah of Hansi.* With the generosity which is a characteristic of his nation, this man whom she had illused for years, hastened to her rescue with a body of troops, and reinstated her in her dominions, and restored to her her army, which she

* See note at the end of this chapter.

retained unmolested for the rest of her life. Her troops having already, before Thomas appeared in the field, found out the total inefficiency through insobriety of their new chief Zafaryab, and having become tired of being their own masters, plundered him to the skin, and were thankful to return to their allegiance. Unwilling to compromise her position a second time as Sumroo's heir, she never again gave way to the softer emotions of the heart. Death soon relieved her of all anxiety concerning her stepson. He died of the effects of intemperance, leaving a daughter who married Mr. Dyce, an Eurasian, and became the mother of Mr. D. O. Dyce-Sombre, who, with his sisters was adopted by the Begum, and whose melancholy story is fresh in the memory of the present generation.* The management of her territories occupied most of her time and attention, and their effective supervision absorbed her energies. In addition to the territory round Sirdhanah, the Begum possessed a moderate Principality fifty miles south of Sirdhanah, and another near Delhi. Peace and order were well kept throughout her dominion, no lawless chiefs were allowed to harbour criminals or defraud the public revenue. The soil was maintained in complete cultivation. The peasants were sometimes obliged to plough their fields at the point of the bayonet.

Thomas describes the Begum at that time as small and plump, her complexion fair, her eyes large and animated. She wore the Hindustan costume made of the most costly materials. She spoke Persian and Urdu fluently, and attended personally to business, giving audience to

* Keene's "Fall of the Moghul Empire."

her native employées behind a screen. At Durbar she appeared veiled, but in European society she took her place at table waited upon exclusively by maid servants. She was an imperious, unscrupulous woman of immense force of character.*

Bishop Heber in his delightful journal mentions the Begum Sumroo as "a little queer-looking old woman, with brilliant but wicked eyes, and the remains of beauty in her features." He says she was generally respected both by her soldiers and the people of the country, and possessed considerable talent and readiness in conversation, but that he heard terrible accounts of the ears and noses she had cut off, and of her vindictive and unrelenting tyranny. He also alludes to the story of the poor Nautch girl whom she caused to be buried alive, but does not give the reason of this ferocious act, either considering the details unfit to be recorded by the pen episcopal, or his informant having judged them to be of a nature better withheld from their reverend hearer. Whatever her defects may have been, she was a brave leader in the field and a wise and successful ruler of her fertile territory. She once, when co-operating with the imperial army, rescued the Emperor from a critical position, for which service he called her his daughter, a designation of high honour and dignity, and conferred upon her the title of Zeb-ul-Nisa, the ornament of the sex. No province in India appeared better administered than Sirdhanah.

The writer has a lively recollection of seeing the Begum in extreme old age, shortly before she died, seated in Durbar, robed in the finest Cashmere shawls, with a jewelled turban and embroidered slippers, one of her

* Ibid.

pretty little feet resting on a footstool, smoking her hookah and chatting familiarly with her European visitors seated in a semicircle on her right and on her left. The native vassals and sirdars of Her Highness were numerous and had no seats assigned them, and as they approached to pay homage, the Chamberlain, or Master of the Ceremonies, proclaimed with a loud voice their style and titles.

The Begum bore herself bravely while seated in her great chair rolled up in her Cashmeres, and her large black eyes were bright and full of humour. On one occasion, when admitted too early to the Durbar hall before the aged queen was seated, the writer was amazed to see how bowed, and shrunk and feeble she was, but as soon as she had taken her place all idea of physical infirmity vanished.

At this time Mr. Dyce Sombre, the Begum's adopted son, was all powerful at her little Court, and no one could be more courteous and kind than he was, and his two sisters were then married to officers in the service of Her Highness, one an Englishman and the other an Italian nobleman. The Begum was affable and kind in manner, hospitable and charitable, but was unable entirely to emancipate herself from the old feelings of one accustomed to despotic authority. She had a fairly equipped army of 5,000 men, cavalry, infantry, and artillery, and, like all Oriental potentates, their pay was frequently greatly in arrears. About the time alluded to there was to be a parade of troops before the palace, some of the men refused to fall in unless they received some portion of their over-due pay. The aged lady watching their proceedings from the balcony, immediately issued orders for execution of the malcontents, and was with some difficulty persuaded by her European officers not to have recourse to such summary proceedings.

She built a beautiful church, taking St. Peter's at Rome as her model. She entertained two priests as domestic chaplains, one an Irishman, Father Macdonald; the other an Italian, the well-known Father Julius Cæsar, afterwards by the Pope raised to the episcopate.

In 1836 this very remarkable and energetic lady died in extreme old age, and when the writer was in Rome not long after, he heard of the liberality of her alms and her princely donation to the Pope, and that a church with special services was set apart for masses for the repose of her soul. Her statue surmounting a group in white marble by Tadolini stands over her tomb in the church which she built at Sirdhanah. The chief portion of her great wealth is now being enjoyed in this country by the heirs of her adopted son, the late D. O. Dyce Sombre.

NOTE—George Thomas, the Sailor Rajah, was a common sailor in the British Navy, who, having deserted his ship, and having wandered about in various parts of India, entered the service of the Begum, and rose to be one of her chief officers. The young Irishman was brave, handsome, and generous, and gave every indication of capacity for command and administrative ability of no common order.

His dashing bravery was signally shown when he at the head of a detachment of the Begum's troops, rescued the Emperor Shah Alam from a critical position, and changed the fortunes of the day during the determined sortie of the garrison of Gokalgurh, in 1788.

Some years after this the Begum having married M. le Vaisseau, a Frenchman in her service, Thomas left her in disgust.

Soon after this Thomas entered into correspondence with several native chiefs, and was soon in charge of an extensive territory yielding a large revenue, and when he appeared iu public was escorted by a chosen body of horsemen.

The Begum, instigated by her husband, invaded Thomas's new district, but was recalled by a revolution at Sirdhanah, which led to her deposition, when Thomas forgot all past injustice, and came to the rescue with all the generosity and chivalry of a warm hearted Irishman.

Thomas, soon after leaving Sirdhanah, was adopted by a powerful native chief of a capricious character, and who not long after placing our adventurer in charge of certain wild and almost inaccessible districts, died insane. This and other circumstances in those lawless times fraught with change and vicissitude, enabled the enterprising seaman to achieve for a time independent sovereignty.

Hansi, the chief town of a district between Delhi, the Punjab, and Scinde, had fallen into decay, but he rebuilt the town, and restored the ruined fortifications, and such was his reputation that the people gladly returned to sow and till once more the long-neglected fields.

Here, to use the words of Rajah Thomas, "I established a mint, and coined my own rupees, which I *made current*, (!) in my army and country . . . . . cast my own artillery, commenced making muskets, matchlocks, and powder . . . . . till at lengh, having gained a capital and country bordering on the Sikh territories, I wished to put myself in a capacity, when a favourable opportunity should offer, of attempting the conquest of the Panjab, and aspired to the honour of placing the British standard on the banks of the Attock."

Thomas having extended his conquests towards the Punjab, cherished no less a design than the conquest of that country, and having achieved his purpose, was, Nearchus like, to descend the Indus, and lay his conquest at the feet of his liege lord, George III.

But the days of the sovereignty of the sailor Rajah were numbered.

General Perron was now all powerful at Delhi and in Upper India, and he too had been a humble sailor, and in the plenitude of his power he would not brook the proud independence of the British seaman, and strange to say, the two men now stood face to face as representing England and France, rivals for the supreme power in Hindoostan.

On Thomas's refusal to acknowledge the supremacy of Perron, his territory was invaded and his capital besieged, and after an heroic resistance, the brave sailor Rajah was allowed to retire to British territory on the 1st January, 1802. He died a few months afterwards on his way to Calcutta.

Begum Sumroo took charge of his family, but they have long since merged in the native population.

It would have been well had the British Government cast the shield of protection over Thomas in his manful struggles against Mahratta lawlessness, and the still encroaching and daring ambition of France, but at that time the country ruled by Thomas was regarded as distant from the British territory as Cabool is now.

This extraordinary man gave peace to a turbulent country, and put an end to the perpetration of crimes which the British Government has found it difficult to deal with successfully.

So completely had the Rajah identified himself with his people, and isolated himself from his own countrymen, that when Lord Wellesley asked him to send him some account of his dominions, he begged that he might be allowed to send it in Persian, as he had forgotten English.

He reigned for four years with great success and beneficence, and it is much to be regretted that he was not able to return to enjoy some portion of his hard won honours and wealth and to spin stupendous yarns about the famous pagoda tree in his native Tipperary.*

* I have followed in the above, Keene and the authorities he quotes.

CHAPTER XV.

THE REMARKABLE WOMEN OF INDIA—*continued.*

Lutchmee Bhye, the Rebel Queen of Jhansi—Her wrongs—Her revenge and heroic death.

Lutchmee Bhye, the fierce Ranee of Jhansi, must not be passed over in silence. The great blot on the otherwise successful and brilliant administration of Lord Dalhousie was his policy of annexing native states, which lapsed to the paramount power from the want of heirs. Perhaps of all annexations the small Mahratta State Jhansi was the worst. It was usual in Mahratta States for the widowed queen to exercise sovereign power during the minority of the heir to the throne, or to adopt an heir should there be no legitimate claimant. In this case, on the death of the Rajah, the Queen was not only denied the power of adoption, which according to the custom of her country she considered her right, but she was deposed under humiliating and aggravating circumstances, and the Principality incorporated with the British dominions.

Having deprived the Ranee of all power and authority, and sequestrated her husband's private estate, the British authorities had the incredible meanness to call upon her to pay the Prince's debts out of the slender provision they had awarded her. The Ranee petitioned and remonstrated in vain. We had no mercy, no consideration for the deeply injured woman, and we cannot be surprised that when in the hour of our tribulation we cried to her for succour, her ears were closed against us, and that she knew no mercy.

The Ranee was in the prime of life, of a goodly presence, able, acute, a perfect mistress in the art of dissimulation, and knowing how to bide her time. That time came when our rebellious Sepoys were bent on uprooting all established authority and making an end of the English rule by fire and sword.

At Jhansi there was the usual staff of civilians with detachments of native troops of all arms. The Europeans numbering about seventy in all. The little force at Jhansi was not slow to follow the example of their mutinous comrades elsewhere. The Queen had by this time embodied troops of her own under the plea of self-protection. Appeals from the English to the Ranee for aid or protection were vain. No answer was returned, the messengers being slain at the palace gates, and soon the handful of English men, women, and children were, in cold blood, ruthlessly butchered, after having been by the natives in our service most treacherously and cruelly betrayed.

The British exterminated and their power laid in the dust, the Queen issued from her palace with flaunting banners, and was proclaimed sovereign of the State.

It is matter of history how the Ranee defended her ill-gotten power; the siege and taking of Jhansi being one of the most brilliant feats of arms of Sir Hugh Rose and his gallant army; and how when the relieving army under Tantia Topee was defeated she escaped through the force surrounding her. Having succeeded in joining the forces of Tantia Topee, the amazon queen was conspicuous at the head of her horsemen at the battle of Kunch, in the vain attempt to bar the advance of the British on Calpee on the Jumna, the great arsenal of the rebels in that part of India.

Driven from Calpee with heavy slaughter, the broken forces of the enemy fled to Gwalior, where the mutinous contingent opened its ranks to receive them, and where the able, but craven Tantia Topee deputed by the so-called Peishwa, Nana Sahib, assumed the chief command.

The brave young Scindia and his able and loyal minister, Sir Dinker Rao, had to fly for their lives. At Gwalior, strongly entrenched round the great rock fortress, the rebels made their last stand. After three days of stubborn resistance they were finally crushed.

On the third day their leader Tantia Topee fled in good time as usual, but the Ranee, in male attire, accompanied by a lady of the palace, was found dead on the field of battle pierced by sword as well as bullet.

Thus died in the prime of her days, as she desired,—with her sword in her hand, the blood-stained and vindictive queen. None of the rebel host displayed such courage and conduct as the fated Ranee, and notwithstanding her many crimes we cannot withhold our admiration for her proud and undaunted bearing when adversity overwhelmed all around her.

CHAPTER XVI.

THE REMARKABLE WOMEN OF INDIA—*concluded.*

Kudsia Begum of Bhopal—Sekunder Begum, her great qualities—Begum Shah Jehan, the present Ruler.

Sekunder Begum, of Bhopal.—This distinguished lady was descended from Dost Mahomed, an Afghan nobleman, who during the anarchy that prevailed on the death of the Emperor Aurungzebe, took possession of the territory adjacent to the town of Bhopal, and called his new-made domain Bhopal, after his capital.

At a moment when the arrival of General Goddard's force of 4,000 or 5,000 men on the western coast was of vital importance, the way was barred across the peninsula by all the princes of Central India save one. That one was the Nawab of Bhopal, who not only gave free passage through his country, but liberally supplied the necessities of the army. This well-timed hospitality laid the foundation of a friendship which has never been broken and has been on several occasions of the utmost value, both to this country and Bhopal.

In 1817 Nuzzer Mahomed, the able and upright minister of Bhopal, having married the daughter of the previous Nawab, concluded a treaty with the British

8

government, which guaranteed the country to himself on certain not very onerous conditions.

On his death, his widow, the Kudsia Begum, became Regent, and a marriage was arranged between his nephew Jehangire Mahomed Khan and his only daughter, the Sekunder Begum. On this Jehangire was to be declared Nawab, but the queen regent, the Kudsia Begum, who was only seventeen when the reins of government were placed in her hands, had become enamoured of power, and postponed the celebration of the nuptials on various pretexts. At last, on the mediation of the British Government, the Kudsia Begum retired on a handsome provision, and Jehangire was duly invested as Nawab in 1837.

The Sekunder Begum was formed to rule, from her abilities, her resolution, and lofty aspirations. She quarrelled with her husband and went to live with her mother, where she remained for six years watching events.

About this time the profligate career of Jehangire was brought to a close, and after some delay, in February 1847, Sekunder Begum was appointed sole regent for her only child, a daughter.

"In six years she paid off the entire public debt of the State; she abolished the system of farming the revenue, and made her own arrangements directly with the heads of villages. She put a stop to monopolies of trades and handicrafts; she brought her Mint under her own management; re-organised the police, and made many other improvements. In fact she displayed in all departments of the State an energy, an assiduity and an administrative ability, such as would have done credit to a trained statesman."*

The Begum was not only an able and successful administrator, but a vigorous and heroic ruler.

When the storm-cloud of 1857 broke upon Central India, the Begum never faltered. She sheltered British officers. She put down with a strong hand her own mutinous contingent. She soothed the excitement of her capital, and gave peace and order to her territory.

"She did all this under great difficulties: when the contingent raised in Bhopal and commanded by British officers had mutinied, when her mother, who had become a bigot, and her uncles, who were weak-minded and priest-ridden, were urging her to declare a religious war against the infidel. But the Begum never faltered. She was true to the last."

If the Begum was wise and courageous she was also generous and liberal to aid, to reward, and was prompt in all things.

To us she gave soldiers and supplies of all kinds without stint, and her own people who stood by her and us in the hour of trial, when the hearts of men were failing them through fear of the tribulation that was upon them, were munificently rewarded. For important services to the paramount power, Sekunder Begum had additional territory awarded her with powers and privileges much coveted by native states, and in 1863 Her Highness was invested with the dignity of the highest grade of the Star of India.

* Malleson's "Native States of India."

This famous Begum of Bhopal was of small stature and fragile frame, and continued her wise rule until her death, in October, 1868.

The sentiments of the government of India regarding the character and services of Sekunder Begum are expressed in the following extract of an Order issued by the Viceroy. After stating the profound regret with which the Government had received intelligence of the demise of that illustrious lady, the document continues:—"Her Highness had conducted the administration of this principality since the year 1847, when she was first appointed regent, with ability and success, until the day of her decease. In the early years of her rule, she improved the system by which the revenue of the State is collected, abolished monopolies, regulated the Mint, re-organised the police, and gradually increased the revenue, while she effectually diminished the public debt. In later times, by her support of the cause of male and female education, by her superintendence of works intended to supply her capital with pure and wholesome water, by the construction of serais and roads, and by other improvements, she gave convincing indications of real and abiding interest in the progress of her people and in the prosperity of her country. But it was by her firm conduct during the great mutiny that she established a more direct title to the acknowledgments of the head of the administration.

"Her unswerving fidelity, her skill in the management of affairs at an important crisis, the bold front which she presented to the enemies of the British power, and the vigilance with which she watched over the preservation of Englishmen, were acknowledged by Lord Canning, in open durbar, in terms of well-deserved praise and commendation, and the gratitude of the British Government was further evinced by a grant of territory which its owner had justly forfeited in open rebellion, by a recognition of the right of succession, according to the custom of the principality and the Mahomedan law, and by the bestowal of one of those titles which the Sovereign of Great Britain, as the fountain of honour, has instituted to reward good services performed in India, either by natives of the country or by the British servants of the Crown."

The daughter, Begum Shah Jehan, at once succeeded. She, too, has one child, a daughter, Sultan Jehan, who was married on February 1, 1875, to Meer Ahmed Ali Khan Bahadur, a nobleman of Afghan descent. She has learned English. The Begum of Bhopal receives a salute of 19 guns.

CHAPTER XVII.

ORIGIN AND PROGRESS OF BRITISH RULE IN INDIA

BOMBAY PRESIDENCY.

Rivalry of Portuguese, Dutch, French and English in the East—First English ship—First factory, Surat—The transfer of the Island of Bombay from Charles II., the dowry of his Queen to the East India Company in 1668—Gradual spread of English rule over the provinces which Sivajee and the Peishwas had wrested from the Moguls and minor sovereigns of the Deccan—Mahableshwar—Poona—Oomrawuttee—Goa.

HAVING traced the history of India, from the earliest times to the overthow of the Mahratta supremacy and the extinction of the Mogul dynasty, we have now to describe the modest origin and wonderful progress of British rule in India, resulting in a dominion more solid and assured in the contentment of the people, as well as more prosperous and brilliant, than that under Akbar the Great or Aurungzebe. Before describing the origin and progress of the British in India, a very brief recapitulation will render the subject clearer and more interesting.

It has been already seen that in the cold grasp of the aged and bigotted Emperor Aurungzebe the sceptre of the Great Mogul had imprinted upon it the germ of decay.

From Cabul to Cape Comorin authority was shaken. On the North West the Afghans and Seikhs were arming, and the Mahrattas in the South, having recently defeated the Emperor in the field, hung like a cloud on the Western Ghats ready to lay waste and pillage the plains of Hindostan. So soon as the master's hand was withdrawn the fairest provinces in India were to be the prizes to be contended for by rebellious vassals, adventurers, and plunderers.

Early in the sixteenth century the Portuguese by doubling the Cape of Good Hope and establishing a paramount influence in the eastern seas, and extensive commercial relations between Europe and the East, by this route, they supplanted the Venetians and Genoese who traded with India via Syria and Egypt.

Portugal having become little more than an appanage of the Crown of Spain, its colonial dominion received a blow from which it never recovered.

The Dutch with characteristic energy and perseverance towards the end of the sixteenth century followed the example of the Portuguese, and succeeded in commanding and retaining a large share in the eastern trade as well as considerable political influence.

The magnificent results obtained from the adventures of the Portuguese and Dutch were not lost upon the rest of Europe, and even Louis XIV., the Grand Monarque, declared that it was not beneath the dignity of a gentleman to trade with India. About the year 1660 companies or associations were formed for prosecuting the trade with India, and the representatives of the two great nations, that were destined in a comparatively short period to contend for the empire of India, were merely merchants and supercargoes with bills of lading, and invoices of their wares for their credentials. The strangers in many instances by the perfidy of the native princes had to convert their stores and factories into fortifications, and their clerks into officers of the native troops they had embodied for their defence, and thus they became conquerors in self-defence—masters instead of suppliants for protection and leave to trade.

The French and English were forced continually to make common cause with one or other of the contending princes, and in this way the superiority of the West over the East became demonstrated.

The predominance of the English and the French over the natives of the country, led to a jealousy and conflict of interests inevitable between the two great rivals of the West, who, instead of being merely allies in subordination to the native Princes, Soubadars, Nawabs, and Rajahs, had gradually become principals in the arena, whether of politics or war, and a great portion of the last century was occupied by their varying and stirring fortunes in their bold attempts to seize the falling sceptre of empire.

Subsequent chapters being devoted especially to the doings of other European nations in India, it is desirable to confine our attention in this exclusively to the progress of our own countrymen in India.

Surat &c.—"The first English ship which came to Surat, was the Hector, commanded by captain William Hawkins, who brought a letter from the company, and another from the king, James I., to the great Mogul Jehangire, requesting the intercourse of trade.

"The Hector arrived at Surat in August, 1608."*

The first formation of an English factory took place at Surat, in 1612, under the protection of the Emperor Jehangire, which controlled all the factories from Cape Comorin to the Red Sea and Persian Gulf, with additional privileges accorded by the Emperor Aurungzebe in consequence of his admiration of the successful resistance of the English factory to Sivajee when he plundered the city.

The town of Surat, 150 miles north of Bombay, lies on the Taptee not far from its mouth, contains 130,000 people, and is still the seat of a considerable trade, however fallen from the high estate it once enjoyed, before Bombay sprang up to supersede it. Here in the 17th century, for about seventy years the young East India Company drove the bulk of its modest trade by permission of the Mogul emperors. Passing northward by the still populous town of Baróch (or Broach), in these days a busy cotton-mart, and by Baroda, the capital of the Gaikwar's State, we come to Ahmedábád, formerly one of the noblest cities in India in the days of the Bahmani kings of the Deccan, and still remarkable for the beauty of its chief buildings and the remains of palaces, mosques, and aqueducts which bear witness to its olden glories. Yet grander are the remains of Muhammadan architecture to be found at Beejápòre, the capital of an old and splendid Pathán dynasty overthrown by the arms of Aurungzebe. Within the

* Orme's Fragments.

mouldering walls and among the massive ruins of a vast city that once rivalled Delhi and Agra, only ten thousand people now dwell.

Bombay, the capital of Western India, and the most populous city in the empire next to London, and the most thriving in the whole Peninsula. At Bombay His Royal Highness the Prince of Wales on the 8th November, 1875, first placed his foot on Indian soil when commencing his memorable tour, and received a loyal and enthusiastic welcome. The city and its suburbs, containing altogether about 650,000 souls, spread over a group of islands, which joined together by causeways, form a kind of promontory with one long horn at the eastern or Colaba end, and a shorter one from the Malabar Hill, while Back Bay carries its deep arch between them. The breadth of this promontory never exceeds three miles, and its total length from Colaba to Sion is about fifteen. Two ranges of whinstone rocks, rising sometimes 190 feet above the sea, give Bombay a beauty of outline wholly wanting to the uniform flatness of Calcutta and Madras. A noble bay on the eastern or Mazagon side of the island, affords one of the finest harbours in the world.

Of the earlier history of Bombay, or Mumbai, as the Mahrattas call it, there is little worth mentioning before it fell into the hands of the Portuguese in 1632. At that time it seems to have been little better than a sickly salt-marsh. In 1661 it was ceded to England as part of the dowry of Catherine of Braganza. Seven years later, Charles II. handed it over to the East India Company at a quit-rent of £10 a year. For some years the English settlement had to contend with the twofold dangers of an unhealthy climate and foreign attacks. In 1686 the seat of government and of the Company's trade on that side of India, was shifted from Surat to Bombay, and in 1708 Bombay was formed into a Presidency, like Madras and Calcutta, with a Governor and Council of its own.

From that time the city grew steadily, both in political and commercial importance, through all the troubles which harassed Western India in the last century. Practically safe from foreign invaders, it became the centre of a flourishing trade, and the meeting-place of traders and refugees from countries far and near. Its prosperity culminated with the American war of 1861-64, which for a few years threw the command of the cotton trade of the world into the hands of Bombay merchants, and the cotton-growers of Western India.

With the return of peace came a sudden collapse, the more disastrous for the gambling mania which had seized upon the leading citizens of Bombay. Since then, however, the city has gradually emerged from its sudden eclipse, and still runs Calcutta a close race for commercial pre-eminence—a race in which it may yet prove the winner, were it not for the vast producing districts in the rear of the metropolis. In some respects Bombay has already outstripped its eastern rival. The native town, with its broad bazaars and many-coloured house-fronts, is one of the most picturesque in India. In public buildings of architectural beauty, in the public spirit of its native citizens, especially the Parsees, in culture, enterprise, social progress and general well-being, no other Indian city can touch the capital of the west.

In the eighth century, not long after the Arab conquest

of Persia, and the establishment of Islám in the room of the old national sun-worship, the Parsees, a small remnant of the unconverted race, were driven by steady persecution from their retreats in Khorásán, to the isle of Ormuz in the Persian Gulf. Their ill-fortune still following them, they took shelter, first at Diú, in the Gulf of Cambay, and some years later in Guzerát. Here under certain conditions they were allowed to dwell, and to build the temples which held the sacred flame kept ever burning in honour of their god—the pure and bright Ormuzd. From Guzerát they gradually made their way over Western India, until at last a new Parsee settlement sprung up in Bombay itself, where the Parsees have since taken the lead in every field of commercial enterprise, and social progress.

Of late years a new industry has gained a firm footing in Bombay. At this moment eighteen cotton mills are at work in the Island, and thirteen more are nearly completed—to say nothing of the mills which Bombay capitalists are founding in Surat, Ahmedabad, Madras, Nágpore, and the Deccan. Railways connect Bombay with nearly all the chief cities of India—*viâ* Jubbulpore and Allahabad, it is connected with Delhi and Calcutta, and another line places it in railway connection with Madras. Its water supply is now brought chiefly from a great reservoir at Vehár, some fourteen miles off. Six miles from the city, in the island of Elephanta, are the famous Caves, masterpieces of old Buddhist and Jain architecture, hewn out of the solid rock, and still wonderful to look at even in their decay. The cave-temples of Kanhari, in the neighbouring island of Salsette will also repay a visit, although they cannot vie with the more imposing beauty of those at Kárli on the road to Poona.

On the Western Gháts, some thirty miles from Bombay, is the pleasant hill-station of Matherán, about 2,500 feet above the sea, noted for its verdure, and the views it offers of the surrounding country. Further south on the same range is the larger station of Mahábleshwar at a height of 4,500 feet above the sea, the Simla as it were of Bombay, near which springs the sacred source of the Kistna.

Poona.—The city of Poona, the ere-while capital of the Maharatta Peishwas, lies 74 miles south-eastward from Bombay, on a treeless plain about 2,000 feet above the sea. It still contains about 100,000 inhabitants, and forms the military head-quarters of Western India.

Oomrawuttee.—In the fertile province of Berár peculiarly suitable for the cultivation of cotton is the large and rising town of Oomrawuttee, the great cotton-mart for Central India.

Goa.—Sailing down the coast from Bombay, we come to Goa, the ancient seat of Portuguese rule in India, and still in its decay an interesting relic of the greatness associated with the names of Vasco da Gama and Albuquerque. Its harbour ranks next to that of Bombay, and a Portuguese Viceroy still holds his little court in the modern town. But it is in Old Goa, now a mass of nearly deserted ruins, that the monuments of former greatness alloyed by religious fanaticism may be looked for in the magnificent cathedral, a few fine churches, and a convent hardly to be surpassed for size and grandeur by any in Europe. Lower down the coast stands Cochin, where Vasco da Gama died in 1525, and a little above it is Calicut, where he landed for the first time in 1498.

CHAPTER XVIII.

ORIGIN AND PROGRESS OF BRITISH RULE IN INDIA—*continued.*

MADRAS PRESIDENCY AND BRITISH BURMAH.

Wars with the French—Clive—Coote—Dupleix—Labourdonnais—Bussy—Nawab of Carnatic—Madras—Arcot, heroic defence of—Vellore, mutiny of—Gillespie and the 19th Dragoons—Ootacamund—Tinnevelley—Pooree—Juggernath—Rangoon—Moulmein.

THE beginnings of Madras date from the founding of an English settlement in 1625 at Masulipatam; but the town of Madras, the great seat of English rule in Southern India, dates its origin from 1640, when the first English factory on the site of the present city was turned into a fortified post, under the name of Fort St. George.

A hundred years later came the wars with our French rivals, signalised by the dashing deeds of Clive, Lawrence, Forde, Coote, and other heroes, and crowned at last, after several reverses, by the firm establishment of our sway along the whole of the Coromandel Coast.

In 1746 the French under Dupleix and Labourdonnais took the town of Madras, and soon after Anwar-ud-din, Nawab of the Carnatic, sent an army of 10,000 men to demand the cession of the town. This large army suffered a disgraceful defeat by Paradis at the head of 230 Europeans and 700 Sepoys.

This action of no great magnitude in itself was fraught with momentous consequences, for it demonstrated to Europeans and natives, how impotent a native force, however numerous, was to cope with the disciplined valour of Europeans, or even with that of natives if led by Europeans.

For a brief period nothing could be more brilliant than the career of the French in the Carnatic, under the auspices of Dupleix and the gallant Bussy. The vain-glorious and Bobadill-like doings of the former, his pillar of victory, and the town built to perpetuate his name are mentioned in a subsequent chapter.

In this part of India the fortunes of the English were reduced to the lowest ebb, when a new actor appeared on the scene, the "heaven born soldier" Clive, a young clerk or writer in the service of the East India Company, who having distinguished himself greatly as a volunteer, had obtained a commission in the army, and earned still further distinction.

Clive having obtained permission from the then Governor of Madras, with a handful of men to seize the important fortified town of Arcot, the capital of the Nawab of the Carnatic. The garrison seeing Clive and his men marching steadily to the attack during a storm of thunder and lightning, thought they were fire proof, and panic-striken fled before them, abandoning the fortifications.

The heroic and successful defence of this place against overwhelming odds, led the way to other victories over the French and their Allies, but Clive, whose genius and bravery had done so much to advance the prestige of the British, was now called to achieve other and more arduous exploits in Bengal, and was obliged to leave to another the glory of giving the *coup de grâce* to the French influence in that part of India.

In 1759 the gallant Colonel Eyre Coote came with a moderate reinforcement of troops, and encountered the French army under Lally and Bussy at Wandewash, when the French army was totally routed, and the heroic Bussy made a prisoner. In 1761 Pondicherry surrendered. Lally was beheaded in Paris in 1766, and three years afterwards the French East India Company was dissolved.

Thus the dream of a French Empire in India was at an end.

A little later began the hard fight for empire between the English and the House of Hyder Ali, the Jugurtha of India, which was to issue in the capture of Seringapatam in 1799, in the death of his son Tippoo, and the utter overthrow of his dynasty. In the next two years, parts of the Nizam's country and the whole of the Carnatic were added to the dominions ruled from Madras, which had become the seat of a separate Presidency in 1654.

Madras, the capital of southern India, contains a population of 500,000 and spreads over a length of nearly four miles, with an average breadth of two and a quarter. A good deal of this space is filled up with gardens and enclosures, or "compounds," as in India they are generally called. Most of the public buildings and the merchants' houses front the sea, which here thunders along the beach in lines of breakers so heavy that no ship can approach or ordinary boat can live in them, as a rule, but the Mussula boats and the Katamarans of the country pass through these breakers with impunity. In spite of its open roadstead, Madras contrives to do a fair amount of trade with foreign countries; and when Mr. Parkes's scheme for a close harbour with curved breakwaters shall have been carried out on the lines already sanctioned, the capital of Southern India may yet come much nearer the commercial greatness long since achieved by Calcutta and Bombay.

Arcot.—Arcot, the former capital of the Carnatic, lies inland on the railway from Madras to Beypore. It is a large and prosperous town, memorable for the glorious defence which Clive and a few hundred Sepoys and Englishmen made in 1751 against the repeated onsets of the Nawab, Chunda Sahib's powerful army, with his French allies.

"Military history records few events more remarkable than this memorable siege. Its conduct at once placed Clive in the foremost rank of distinguished commanders. Justly has it been said that he was 'born a soldier.'* At the time when with a handful of men, most of them unpractised in the operations of war, he defended the fort of Arcot against a force several thousand strong, his military experience was small, while of military education he was entirely destitute. His boyhood had passed in idleness, or in the reckless

* Major Lawrence, "Narrative of the War on the coast of Coromandel."

perpetration of mischief, while the few years which he had numbered of manly life had, for the most part, been occupied with the details of trade. Deprived of all the means by which, in ordinary cases, men are gradually prepared for the duties of military service or command, he showed himself a perfect master of the arts of war. Like all other eminent commanders, he communicated to those under him a spirit of devotedness and self-abandonment, which is among the most graceful, as well as the most valuable qualities of a soldier. An instance of this occurred among the native troops employed in the defence of Arcot, which is alike honourable to them and to their commander. When provisions became scarce, and there was ground for apprehending that famine would compel a surrender, the sepoys proposed that their diet should be restricted to the thin gruel in which the rice was boiled, and that the whole of the grain should be given to the Europeans, as they required more nourishment."*

Vellore.—At a short distance from the frontier of Mysore, Vellore was chosen, after the fall of Seringapatam, as the future residence of the family of Tippoo Sultan, and was garrisoned by a wing of the 69th Europeans and two regiments of Native Infantry, one of the latter being largely recruited from the soldiers of Tippoo's own army.

Changes introduced in the dress of the Sepoys of the Madras army had engendered a spirit of distrust and disaffection especially at Vellore.

* Malcolm's "Life of Clive."

"At 3 o'clock on the morning of the 10th July, 1806, the two native regiments at Vellore rose in sudden mutiny, attacked the European barracks, where some 370 men of the 69th Foot were yet sleeping, poured volley after volley into their helpless victims, and shot down thirteen officers coming out of their rooms."*

A British officer on duty outside the fort, hearing the firing inside, immediately proceeded to Arcot, nine miles distant, and in fifteen minutes after his report, the gallant Colonel Gillespie with two squadrons of the 19th Dragoons had started for Vellore, having left orders for the rest of his regiment with the galloper-guns to follow without delay. A native cavalry regiment obeyed with alacrity the trumpet-call and was speedily in the saddle. When Gillespie arrived at the gate of Vellore, the hard-pressed British soldiers drew up by means of a rope the gallan tcolonel, and began at once the work of retribution; the galloper-guns meanwhile proclaiming their arrival by blowing open the gates, when the Dragoons dashed in, followed by the black horsemen, who emulated the ardour of their European comrades in putting to the sword all implicated in this treacherous, blood-thirsty, outbreak. Of the gallant 69th, ninety-five officers and men lay dead and nearly as many wounded. But the family of Tippoo were mercifully spared the punishment of their evident participation in the movement, for they and their servants had encouraged the mutineers both by word and deed, and had hoisted the tiger-striped banner of their father with his insignia over the palace.

* Trotter's "India."

There is nothing finer in history than this prompt and heroic ride to save.

If there had been a Colonel Gillespie at Meerut in 1857, what might we not have been saved?

Utakamund.—What Simla is to Calcutta and Mahábleshwar to Bombay, the beautiful hill-station of Utakamund in the Neelgerries is to Madras. Lying more than 7,000 feet above the sea, this healthiest of Indian sanitaria has a smaller rainfall and a more even temperature than any of its Himalayan rivals. Nearer Madras are the Shevarai Hills, forming part of the Eastern Ghâts, and offering a pleasant retreat in the hot-weather to those who may shrink from the longer journey to Utakamund or to the Palnai Hills still further South.

Pooree.—On the northern frontier of the Madras Presidency, but under the Government of Bengal, lies the province of Orissa, a land of hills and wood fringed by a narrow seaboard through which the Mahánuddee flows by numerous outlets into the Bay of Bengal. The seat for many centuries of successive dynasties, Hindoo, Yavan, and Muhammadan, Orissa was finally rescued from Maharatta inroads in the beginning of the present century. Its chief town, Cuttack, has a considerable trade and a population of 40,000. Far more famous is the ancient and holy city of Pooree at its southernmost corner. Hither from all parts of India flock crowds of Pilgrims, eager to wash out their sins by worshipping at the shrine of Juggernath, or Vishnu, whose far-famed pagoda towers to a height of nearly 200 feet from the midst of 120 smaller temples, and in whose service some 20,000 men, women, and children are constantly employed.

Rangoon and Moulmein.—Crossing the Bay of Bengal, past the jungle-covered islands, the Súnderbunds, and the mouths of the Ganges and the Brahmapútra, we sight the hilly coast of Araccan, conquered from the Burmese in 1826, and now forming part of British Burmah. Its chief town, Akyáb, is a small but flourishing seaport. After rounding Cape Negrais, Bassein on the most westerly mouth of the Irrawáddy is the first place that calls for passing notice. On the Rangoon river, a broad branch of the Irrawáddy lies crowned by its great Golden Pagoda, the populous and flourishing city of Rangoon, not only the maritime capital of Pegu, which, with the rest of that province, fell into our hands during the Second Burmese War of 1853, but the Capital of British Burmah, and where the Chief Commissioner of the province resides. To the East of Rangoon, a little way up the broad and deep Salwín river, is the important town of Moulmein, the most important town of Tenasserim, another Burman province ceded to us in 1826. With its broad streets of teak-built houses, its fine markets, roomy quays, and a population already numbering 20,000, Moulmein is one of the healthiest towns and most thriving seaports in British India.

Near the Gulf of Manar, and less than one hundred miles to the south of the town of Madras, is Tinnevelly, noted chiefly for its native Christians and a pearl-fishery of no great importance. Further up the coast is Negapatam, and a few miles up the Cávaree lies Tanjóre, remarkable for its pagodas and a considerable trade in silks and muslins of home manufacture. Further inland on the same river is the town of Trinchinoply, which played an important part in the wars of the last century, and still carries on a respectable trade in gold filagree-work, cheroots, and cutlery. Higher up the coast is Pondicherry, the last important relic of French power in Southern India, a power which for some years, under Dupleix and his successors, fought hard for mastery against its English rival, but happily fought in vain. With the capture of Pondicherry from the brave but hapless Lally by the redoubtable Sir Eyre Coote in 1761, French supremacy in India virtually received its death-blow.

While the English and French were struggling with varying fortune for supremacy in the Carnatic, and the Deccan, events of the utmost importance affecting the future empire of India were about unfolding themselves in Bengal, the richest and most populous of all the provinces which owned allegiance to the Mogul.

CHAPTER XIX.

ORIGIN AND PROGRESS OF BRITISH RULE IN INDIA—*continued.*

BENGAL PRESIDENCY.

Job Charnock—Prince Azim—Emperor Ferokshere—Hamilton—Mahratta ditch—Aliverdi Khan—Suraj-ud-doula—Fort William—Black Hole——Calcutta—Howrah—Barrackpore—Serampore—Plassy, Battle of—Clive—Meer Jaffier—Moorshedabad—Patna—Benares.

While the power and influence of the British were already considerably advanced at Bombay and Madras on the opposite sides of the peninsula, nothing could be more feeble or unpromising than their efforts to establish a footing in Bengal, arising in a degree from their own violence, which led to their expulsion from Hooghly and other factories; but their privileges were restored through the intervention of Mr. Boughton, whose surgical aid had been of service to one of the daughters of Shah Jehan and subsequently to the Viceroy of Bengal.

But the real foundation of our rule in Bengal was laid by Job Charnock's successful negotiation* in 1695,

* Job Charnock, when agent or chief of the East India Company's Factory at Calcutta, happened to be present at the preliminary arrangements for a suttee, when he was so interested by the distress and beauty of the young widow, who was very reluctant to quit this sinful world, that he ordered his guards to rescue her. They lived happily together for years, and had a family, and when she died, Charnock sacrificed yearly a cock upon her tomb. The fair Hindoo instead of becoming a Christian had unfortunately made Job a pagan.

when the villages of Chatanatti, Calcutta, and Gorindpur, were bought from Prince Azim, then Viceroy of Bengal and the grandson of Aurungzebe. Soon after this time the Emperor Ferokshere was unable in consequence of indisposition to receive his bride, a fair princess of Rajpootana, and was so overjoyed at this cure by Mr. Hamilton the surgeon of the British embassy, that he asked him to name his reward, on which Hamilton patriotically asked for additional privileges and protection for his countrymen to trade. Five years later the works of Fort William on the Hoogly, outside Calcutta, were rising from the ground, as a bulwark against Mahrátta and other foes. The Mahratta Ditch, dug in 1742, marked the modest boundaries of the new Presidency, which, covering only a few square miles of ground, was content to flourish under the protection of Aliverdi Khan, the Soubadár or Viceroy of Bengal. His grandson, Suráj-ud-doula, picked a quarrel with his English neighbours, which issued in the capture of Fort William, and the dreadful incidents of the Black Hole, where, in one hot night of June, 1756, one hundred and twenty-three men and women out of one hundred and forty-six in all, died miserably of heat, thirst, and overcrowding in a guard-room only twenty feet square, lighted by two small windows strongly barred. For a moment the English power in Bengal seemed utterly and for ever dead.

But a new life awaited it at the hands of Clive and Admiral Watson. In the following January Calcutta was retaken, and on the 23rd June, 1757, the hosts of Suráj-ud-doula were finally routed by Clive's little army near the village of Plassy, on the road to Moorshedabad.

Calcutta.—Of the many cities of India famous either in the past or the present, politically or commercially, Calcutta, as the capital of our Indian Empire, and the great outlet for the trade of Bengal and Upper India, claims in an especial manner our attention. Lying about one hundred miles up the Hoogly it has grown, from a group of small villages into a city stretching about four miles and a half along the noble river just named, with a breadth of less than two miles, and a population now reckoned at more than 400,000. Calcutta, or Kálikatta, derives its name from the Hindoo goddess Káli, whose worship is still common in Bengal, and among whose votaries were the Thugs or Stranglers—a class of professed thieves and murderers, whom Sleeman, and other officers of the Company, were engaged some forty years ago in hunting down. So thoroughly was that work done, that the Thug no longer dares to pursue his horrible calling within reach of a British magistrate. The white town of Calcutta, which sweeps back from the river and Government House, round the broad Maidan or plain behind Fort William to the Cathedral founded by Bishop Wilson, has some right to be called "the City of Palaces," from the imposing look of the large, lofty, white two-storied houses, with deep pillared verandahs, which reminded Bishop Heber of St. Petersburgh. Government House itself is a noble building in the Italian style, which London might well envy. Some other of the public buildings, notably the Courts of Justice, the Currency Office, the Post and

Telegraph Offices, a church or two, one or two hotels, and the merchants' offices are handsome structures; but the Cathedral is unworthy of being the Metropolitan Temple of the Church in India, and the black town is a mass of mean-looking houses huddled along narrow and dirty streets.

Between the Maidan (a grassy plain) and the river lies Fort William, half hidden behind its deep moat, and capable of holding 15,000 men. Fifty or sixty years ago it was one of the strongest of modern fortresses, and its strength even now, if it were properly armed, would no doubt suffice to protect the city from any approach by water. The river itself in front, is generally alive with shipping from all parts of the world, and with all kinds of native craft, from the crank, high-sterned dinghy, with its naked rowers, to the great corn-boats slowly bearing their freight up stream; steamers from Europe, models of engineering ingenuity, contrasting strangely with the primitive craft of the country.

In the Mall, or Course along the river, and in the bazaars, you may see people of many different races, clothed in every kind of garb, from the sleek black Bengálee, in robes of pure white, to the tall, fair, but dirty-looking merchant from Cabul, in his high turban and loose sheepskin tunic. "Strings of rude bamboo carts, drawn by slow oxen, impede the progress of well-appointed broughams, bearing rich merchants to their counting-houses; and the splendidly-equipped scarlet orderlies of the viceroy's body-guard, are seen side by side with the tawdry and ill-mounted ruffians who hang on the skirts of some petty native despot. Everywhere the completeness, polish, and brilliancy of Europe, are seen contrasted with the rudeness, squalor, and tawdry finery of Asia.*

Across the Hoogly and now connected with Calcutta by a floating bridge, is the important suburb of Howrah with its docks, the terminus of the East Indian Railway, which runs up to Delhi, and also links Allahabad to Jubbulpoor. Another and more pleasant suburb is Garden Reach, on the Calcutta side of the river. Here still lives the Ex-king of Oude, whose dethronement in 1856, however well deserved, may have helped to bring about the general rising of that province in the following year. During the Mutiny, the Calcutta Volunteers, mostly English merchants and traders, kept order and restored tranquillity to the metropolis, which was greatly disturbed, notwithstanding the noble bearing of the Governor-General and Lady Canning, the latter showing her fair face in the fashionable drive as usual. In these latter days, the Maidan has twice witnessed the gathering of high English officers and richly-decked native princes, to take part in the splendid pageant of a Chapter of the Star of India, held on each occasion by a Prince of our own Royal House. A little up the river is Barrackpore, the head-quarter of the Presidency division of the army, with a country house and park for the Governor-General, and on the opposite bank is Serampore, the old seat of missionary enterprise in Bengal, and for many years a Danish settlement before its transfer to the Company in 1845. A few miles

* *Times of India* "Handbook of Hindustan."

higher up is the French settlement of Chandernagóre, which was taken by the English, but finally restored to France in 1816.

Plassy.—Ninety-six miles north of Calcutta, on the route to Moorsehabad. Ever to be had in remembrance as the scene of Clive's wondrous victory!

But the turning point of our fortunes which converted at a blow traders into heroes and statesmen deserves more than a passing allusion.

No wonder if the heart of the "heaven born General" faltered for a moment on the eve of such a crisis—it was either—victory or ruin! "Clive was unable to sleep; he heard through the whole night the sound of drums and cymbals from the vast camp of the Nabob. It is not strange that even his stout heart should now and then have sunk, when he reflected against what odds, and for what a prize, he was in a few hours to contend.

"Nor was the rest of Surajah Dowlah more peaceful. His mind at once weak and stormy, was distracted by wild and horrible apprehensions. Appalled by the greatness and nearness of the crisis, distrusting his Captains, dreading every one who approached him, dreading to be left alone, he sat gloomily in his tent, haunted, a Greek poet would have said, by the furies of those who had cursed him with their last breath in the Black Hole.

"The day broke; the day which was to decide the fate of India. At sunrise the army of the Nabob, pouring through many openings from the camp began to move towards the grove where the English lay. Forty thousand infantry, armed with firelocks, pikes, swords, bows and arrows, covered the plain. They were accompanied by fifty pieces of ordnance of the largest size, each tugged by a long team of white oxen, and each pushed on from behind by an elephant. Some smaller guns under the direction of a few French auxiliaries, were perhaps more formidable. The cavalry were fifteen thousand, drawn not from the effeminate population of Bengal, but from the bolder race which inhabits the northern provinces; and the practised eye of Clive could perceive that both the men and the horses were more powerful than those of the Carnatic. The force which he had to oppose to this great multitude consisted of only three thousand men. But of these nearly a thousand were English, and all were led by English officers, and trained in the English discipline, conspicuous in the ranks of the little army were the men of the Thirty-Ninth Regiment, which still bears on its colours amidst many honourable additions won under Wellington in Spain and Gascony, the name of Plassey, and the proud Motto "Primus in Indis." The battle commenced with a cannonade in which the artillery of the Nabob did scarcely any execution, while the few field-pieces of the English produced great effect. Several of the most distinguished officers in Surajah Dowlah's service fell, disorder began to spread through his ranks, his own terror increased every moment; one of the conspirators urged on him the expediency of retreating. The insidious advice agreeing as it did with what his own terrors suggested, was readily received. He ordered his army to fall back, and this order decided his fate, Clive snatched the moment, and ordered his troops to advance. The confused and dispirited multitude gave way before the onset of disciplined valour. No mob attacked by regular soldiers was ever more completely routed. The little band of Frenchmen who alone ventured to confront the English were swept down by the stream of fugitives. In an hour the forces of Surajah Dowlah were dispersed never to reassemble; only five hundred of the vanquished were slain. But their camp, their guns, their baggage, innumerable waggons, innumerable cattle remained in the power of the conquerors. With the loss of twenty-two soldiers killed and fifty wounded, Clive had scattered an army of near sixty thousand men, and subdued an empire larger and more populous than Great Britain."*

Under a new Nawáb of Bengal, set up by the conquerors, large districts around Calcutta were added to the Company's rule. In 1765 all Bengal, Bahár, and Orissa were made over to the Company by Shah Alam, the Mogul Emperor, as a kind of fief, to be held on payment of a fixed tribute. In the time of Warren Hastings, the first and greatest Governor-General of India, these rich and populous provinces dropped by force of circumstances into the entire possession of their English masters, who also gained a footing in Benares and Allahabad.

Moorshedabad—On the Bhauguruttee has long since dwindled from its former splendour, as the capital of successive Nawábs of Bengal, is the place where the victor of Plassy, flushed from his overthrow of one king, set up another in his stead. This city was formerly the head

* Life of Clive by Malcolm.—Macaulay's Critical and Historical Essays.

quarters of the silk trade, and is still celebrated for its exquisite carving in ivory.

Patna.—Turning thence up the Ganges, we come to the rich and populous city of Patna, 380 miles from Calcutta, peopled chiefly by Mahommedans, and famous as the scene of several English victories, of a massacre of English prisoners by the ruffianly Walter Reinhardt, otherwise Sumroo, in 1763, and in later days of many a Mussulman plot against our rule. Patna is alike famous for its opium and rice.

Benares.—Forty miles further from Calcutta, on the left bank of the Ganges, towers Benares, the holy city of the Hindoos, in a stately semicircle above the broad river, presenting to the first view a rich confusion of temples, palaces and ghâts, or bathing-stairs, interspersed with clumps of trees, and crowned by two lofty minarets, which recal the palmiest days of Mogul rule. The city itself is a dense maze of narrow crooked streets, often lined by lofty and noble stone houses, and generally thronged by Brahmins, pilgrims, Fakeers, traders, and Brahminee bulls. At all hours the numberless shrines are visited by eager worshippers bearing gifts, while the Gháts are daily trodden by thousands of people met for bathing, praying, preaching, bargaining, gossiping, or sleeping. So sacred is deemed the Ganges at Benares that the police have occasionally to restrain the over-zealous pilgrims from seeking eternal bliss by immolating themselves in its turbid waters. At once the Oxford and the Mecca of India, Benares also ranks amongst the very wealthiest of Indian cities, and drives a lucrative trade in kincobs, brocades, and other rich fabrics.

Here, too, it was that Warren Hastings, amidst a whole populace in arms against their Rạjah's seeming oppressor, quietly finished the draft of his treaty with Scindia, while faithful messengers stole out of the city with demands for succour from the nearest military post. And here it was that Neill's timely daring and Tucker's heroic firmness, prevented a mutinous outbreak in 1857 from blazing into a general revolt.

CHAPTER XX.

ORIGIN AND PROGRESS OF BRITISH RULE IN INDIA—*continued.*

PRESIDENCY OF BENGAL AND NORTH WEST PROVINCES.

Mahrattas—Tragical occurrences—Alamgire II.—Vazir Gazi-ud-deen—Shah Alam II.—Battles of Buxar, Patna and Guya—Carnac and Munro—M. Law—Allahabad—Cawnpore—Lucknow—Oude—Agra.

For the latter part of the eighteenth century, the Mahrattas were the dominant power in the Deccan and Hindostan, but their disunion and rivalry, not only gave opportunity for the intrigues of other adventurers at the Imperial Court at Delhi, but rendered the permanency of their own widely extended dominions impossible.

The Mahrattas frequently without any apparent design but to prove their own ubiquity and daring, insulted the Emperor, flaunting their banners and defying his authority under the very walls of his palace, and even when entrusted with the highest offices leaving their liege lord to the mercy of the unscrupulous and blood-thirsty miscreants, who, in times of violent vicissitude and revolution, had too frequently a footing within the palace, and who stopped at no outrage or crime to gain their ends, or of those who employed them.

A short time before the fatal field where the Abdallee Shah of Afghanistan, the most renowned soldier in Asia, had humbled the pride and broken the power of the Mahrattas, the infamous Vazir Gazi-ud-deen had the unfortunate Emperor, Alamgire the II., assassinated. The heir apparent, Ali Ghohur, afterwards Shah Alam the II., previous to this having bravely cut his way through his enemies, entered into an arrangement with the then Governor of Allahabad for the recovery of Bengal, Behar, and Orissa, the prince being the legally appointed Soubadar of these provinces.

As the movements of the prince greatly influenced our progress in Hindostan, while it led to the consolidation and permanency of our rule in the lower provinces, a few words as to his personal appearance and character may not be out of place on his advent—to him a new arena of politics and war.

The prince at this time was about 40 years of age, handsome, tall, and of a dignified presence, brave, and almost too merciful to his enemies, without enterprize or force of will, fond of pleasure, and too compliant to those about him; the character of his ancestor Aurungzebe was like that of Louis the XI., while that of Shah Alam resembled that of Charles the II., abandoning great designs for sensual gratifications.

Such was the royal adventurer who driven by adverse fate, sought a precarious footing in the wide dominions which by right were all his own.

The news of his father's death, and the appointment of his own son Prince Jewan Buckt to act in Delhi as Regent in his absence, at last reached the exiled prince, when he was at once proclaimed and acknowledged as Shah Alam the II., or Conqueror of the World.

Shah Alam established his Court at Allahabad, at the confluence of the Ganges and Jumna, and made various excursions with such troops as he could collect into Behar, with a view of extending the limited territory subject to his sway. He encountered the British forces under Major Carnac and Major Munro (afterwards the famous Sir Hector Munro) at Buxar, at Patna, and finally at Guya.—In all these actions the Emperor was defeated, although supported by the powerful Viceroy of Oude, Meer Cossim, with the miscreant Sumroo and his trained battalions, and the distinguished French adventurer, M. Law, who, when deserted by all, refused to surrender his sword, but was received by the British with honor and hospitality.

It was after peace was restored, and a small addition had been made to the territory subject to the Emperor for his pressing necessities, that the powers and privileges of the British over Bengal, Behar, and Orissa were extended, and they were made perpetual collectors of revenue. And in return his vassals and servants were pleased to confirm Shah Alam in the possession of the scanty remains of sovereignty at Allahabad.

Allahabad.—Allahabad, the present capital of the North-West Provinces, is commanded by a strong fort which marks the meeting of the blue waters of the Jumna with the turbid flood of the Ganges. The city, which is about five hundred miles from Calcutta, was an important place in the Mogul days, when its old Hindoo name of Prág was exchanged for the one it now bears, Allahabad or the city of Allah. It still boasts a population of 100,000, and retains its old sanctity in Hindoo eyes. During the Mutiny, the sepoys quartered there suddenly rose upon their officers, some of whom were cruelly murdered, and the city with the surrounding country was given over to anarchy and plunder, until Neill's timely arrival with his Madras Fusiliers encouraged the resistance already made by Brasyer's Sikhs, secured the Fort itself from further danger, and finally drove the rebels away from that neighbourhood.

Cawnpore.—On the right bank of the Ganges is Cawnpore, an old city with 110,000 inhabitants and a large trade, especially in saddlery and other articles of leather manufacture. On the plain outside once stood perhaps the largest cantonment in India, before the British outposts were advanced to Umballa and Ferozepore. From two of the barracks poor Sir Hugh Wheeler and his undaunted but ill-fated garrison maintained for three weeks of June 1857, a hopeless defence against swarms of rebels, led by the infamous Nána of Bithoúr. From the banks of the neighbouring river, his ruffians began their cowardly and cruel slaughter of men without arms, and women and children who had been promised a safe conduct to Allahabad. Of the hapless survivors, four only lived to greet their advancing countrymen; the rest were either slain on the spot, or reserved for that final massacre, whose still fresh traces told their tale of horror to Havelock's heroes on the memorable 16th July. The well into which the still warm bodies of the victims had been thrown has since been covered with a memorial figure, and surrounded with a handsome parapet, while a beautiful garden seems to relieve, in some degree, the sad memories of the place. The Prince of Wales during his recent tour paid with his usual good feeling a reverent visit to the last resting place of the slaughtered innocents of his country.

Lucknow.—From Cawnpore let us cross the Ganges, and follow the road taken by Outram, Havelock, Neill, and afterwards by Lord Clyde to Lucknow, once the capital of the Náwabs of Oude and subsequent kings. This large, picturesque, and populous city—which at one time contained some 300,000 souls, a number now greatly reduced—stretches for four miles along the right bank of the Goomtie, here spanned by two bridges. Its noble-looking mosques and semi-Italian palaces, surrounded sometimes by green and wooded parks, awaken in the mind a sense of grandeur and beauty, which a nearer view of the streets and buildings does not tend to deepen. Some of the buildings, however, and one or two of the streets are well worth seeing. The ruined Residency still attests the fierceness of the struggle waged for months in 1857, by a small but noble garrison of men and women against the whole armed strength of Oude. Of the cool courage and heroic endurance shown by all who shared in that defence it is impossible to speak too highly. Of those who fought and fell there, the first alike in rank and worth was the noble Sir Henry Lawrence, the greatest soldier-statesman of his day. Neill's death just outside the Residency, in the very moment of victory, cast a shadow on the glorious deeds that marked the first relief of Lucknow—soon to be rendered still more deep by the loss of Havelock, the hero of that brief but brilliant campaign. How bravely Outram, the Bayard of the Indian army, held the post of danger, into which he and Havelock had forced their way through fearful odds, until Sir Colin Campbell came up to the final rescue, need not be told again. The latest memories of Lucknow, are connected with the visit of the Prince of Wales, with his splendid welcome by the once rebellious, but now loyal Talukdars of Oude, and with the kindly and gracious words addressed by him to some of the sepoy veterans, who stood so loyally by our countrymen throughout the trials of the siege.

Eighty miles east from Lucknow, on the banks of the Gogra, stands the ancient and populous city of Oude, dear to Hindoos as the former seat of one of the oldest and most powerful Hindoo dynasties centuries before the Christian era.

On the north-western border of Oude, lies the fruitful and well-watered province of Rohilchund, forming part of the North-Western Provinces. Its chief towns, Bareilly, Shahjahánpur, and Morádábád, are the centres of populous districts, which in 1857 were given over for a time to all the horrors of mutiny and rebellion.

Agra.—Placed on the Jumna, is the once imperial city of Agra, known to the Moguls as Akbarábad, or the city of Akbar, greatest and wisest of the old Emperors of Hindustan. The city, which he may be said to have founded, still boasts a population of 145,000, and was captured by Lake in 1803.

Sometime before the Mutiny, it became the seat of our rule in the North-West Provinces. Within the city are one or two fine streets of stone-built houses and at least one noble mosque, the Jumma Masjid. But its greatest ornaments are the picturesque fort of red sandstone, built by Akbar, and further up the river, that exquisite "dream in marble," the Táj-Mahal, which Akbar's grandson Shahjehán reared with the aid of Italian architects, to the memory of his lovely and well-beloved Queen, Mumtaz-i-Mahal, the Flower of the Palace. This gem of Eastern art, for such it is, with its tapering minarets, upswelling marble dome, delicate trellis work, and gracefully flowing mosaics, is unsurpassed, as Elphinstone rightly observes, by any other building in Europe or Asia, "for the richness of the material, the chasteness of the design and the effect at once brilliant and solemn." Even in Florence its mosaics in *pietra dura* are unequalled. Its stately grace and perfect symmetry of form, must strike the beholder from almost any point of view; but it is seen to best advantage, either from across the river, or else by moonlight, glistening in white softness through the long dark avenue of cypresses which, from a majestic gateway, lead up to its broad marble basement.

The Fort itself, in which our beleaguered countrymen found safe shelter during the worst days of 1857, contains many beautiful buildings of stone, marble and inlaid work, dating from the times of Akbar and Shahjahán. Among these the exquisite Moti Musjid, or Pearl Mosque, with its graceful arches and clustering domes, fills the foremost place. Here, too, are the marble-floored rooms once inhabited by ladies of the Imperial Harem, and the palace where Shah-Jahán passed his latter days, a state-prisoner, by sufferance of his son Aurungzebe. The civil and military lines spread for some distance over the plains outside the city. Akbar himself lies buried in a noble mausoleum at Secundra, a few miles distant from Agra, so vast that Lord Lake was said to have quartered a regiment of Horse in its Arches. Mahommedans to this day visit this tomb with as much awe and reverence as if the great Emperor was almost divine. Twenty miles south-east from Agra, at Futtepore Sickri towers the great mosque, whose lofty gateways and vast quadrangle, still attest the architectural glories of Akbar's reign.

On the Jumna, thirty-five miles north-west of Agra, is *Muttra*, an old Hindoo city famed for its shrines and sacred monkeys. Many years ago two young English officers in sport wounded one of these sacred animals, which created such a commotion by the screams of his countless relatives, that the people rose in a frenzy of religious enthusiasm, and the Englishmen, to save themselves, forced their elephant to cross the river, but as the animal rolls in the water, only the mahout or driver reached the opposite bank. Muttra was also the favourite head-quarters of Madojee Scindia, the Pateil,* when he was supreme director and protector of the Emperor.

* Or beadle, or headman of a village as he loved to call himself in the plenitude of his power. This office in his native village was hereditary in his family.

CHAPTER XXI.

PROGRESS OF BRITISH RULE IN INDIA—*continued.*

NORTH-WEST PROVINCES.

Shah Alam II.—Viceroy of Oude—Meer Cossim—Sumroo—Mahrattas—Golam Kadir—Scindia—Lord Lake—Bahadour Shah—Delhi and its vicissitudes—The Koh-i-noor and the Peacock Throne—Mahdajee Scindia—Daulat Rao Scindia—Holkar—Ochterlony—Alarm in the Palace—Mutineers—The King, the Captain of the Guard, and the Physician—Willoughby fires the Arsenal—Siege—Capture—Englishmen dine in Palace of Mogul—Hodson at Hoomayoon's tomb—Surrender of King and Princes—Grand reception to Prince of Wales—Proclamation of Empress.

After the battles of Patna, Buxar and Guya, the Emperor Shah Alam II. resumed his residence at Allahabad, and the Viceroy of Oude had favourable terms granted him and nearly all his teritory restored. Meer Cossim fled despoiled and deserted by the viceroy and his former tool, Sumroo, for protection to the Rohillas, where he died; and Sumroo with the remnant of his force entered the service of the Rajah of Jeypore.

Soon after this the Emperor got tired of his modest retirement and mimic court, and was easily persuaded by the Mahrattas, who had reasons of their own for wishing to have the charge of the person of the sovereign, to return to the palace of his ancestors at Delhi, and in 1771 contrary to the advice and urgent remonstrances of his English friends and protectors, Shah Alam accompanied Scindia to the imperial city, where he was received with great manifestations of loyalty and rejoicing, and was enthroned with every circumstance that could give splendour to so august a ceremonial.

The Maharattas were from 1771 to 1803 the masters of Hindostan, under Scindia, the Pateil, and his successor, but for a space the attention of this renowned warrior and crafty politician was absorbed in his attempts to achieve supremacy in the court of the Peishwah, as he had already succeeded in doing in that of the Emperor.

In this season of neglect, a wretch, Golam Kadir, an Afghan, aided by the discontent of the Mogul nobles, under the Maharatta rule, forced himself with his immediate followers into the palace and compelled the helpless emperor to appoint him his Vizier, the highest office in the state.

This atrocious ruffian having, it has been said, received at the hands of the emperor an irreparable wrong in his early youth, thirsted for revenge on the imperial house. No sooner was he installed in office than he filled the palace with those devoted to his interests. After grossly insulting the emperor and his family, he with his own hands blinded the aged monarch, tortured the princes, and outraged the sanctity of the haram in frantic attempts to obtain possession of fancied hidden treasure. After heaping every insult and degradation on the inmates of the palace, and having collected a vast amount of valuables, having robbed the ladies even of their personal ornaments—scared by the rumour of the too tardy approach of Scindia, Golam Kadir collected his booty, and after burning a portion of the palace, sought safety in flight, during the darkness of the night. This ferocious assassin came to a dreadful end. In a vain attempt to escape with the most valuable jewels, he fell from his horse and was secured by the country people and sent to Scindia, who had now resumed his functions as Lieutenant-General of the kingdom. After having been degraded and tortured in the most dreadful manner, his head was cut off and placed at the feet of the now blind, aged, prostrate emperor whom he had so remorselessly insulted and outraged so recently. Shah Alam remained poor and neglected by Scindia, until rescued by Lord Lake, in 1803. One of the grandsons who had been tortured in the presence of the emperor, was Bahadour Shah, who witnessed in his palace at Delhi in 1857, the massacre in cold blood of Englishmen, women and children.

Delhi.—Nearly a thousand miles by road from Calcutta. For miles before the eye rests on the tall red sandstone walls and bastions of the city founded, or rather rebuilt by Shah-Jehán, the ground is covered with the ruins of former Delhis, or of the yet older Hindoo city of Indraprastha. Successive dynasties, Hindoo, Pathán, and Mogul, have left the traces of their olden splendour in or about the city, whose name to Englishmen will always recal at once the darkest and the brightest page in the history of our Indian Empire. From the day when Pritwí Rajah, the last Hindoo King of Delhi, fled before the onset of Muhammad Ghori's Afghan horsemen in 1193 A.D., to the hour when Nicholson's stormers planted the British flag once more on the walls of the great rebel stronghold, in September, 1857, Delhi has lived on through a long train of chequered experiences such as perhaps no other of the world's chief cities can match. Every foot of ground within or around its walls is indeed historical. To tell of all that has happened there would be tantamount to writing the history of Hindustan. No other city, not even Rome herself, has witnessed such swift and frequent alternations of success and suffering, peace and bloodshed, greatness and humiliation, good government and fearful tyranny. In the fourteenth century it was well-nigh unpeopled, in order that Muhammad Toghlak might indulge his whim for transferring the seat of empire to the Deccan. Of course the attempt failed, and Delhi throve again under his humane successor, Feroze Shah. But the last days of that century beheld its streets piled with dead, and its houses gutted of their wealth, by order of the merciless conqueror Tímoor the lame.

For many years after 1450 the citizens had a long rest from suffering under the wise rule of Balól Lodi. Then came a time of further trouble, which ended in the conquest of Delhi by Báber, the brave, chivalrous and jovial founder of the Mogul dynasty, in 1526. During the long reign of his grandson Akbar, contemporary with our own Elizabeth, Delhi flourished as it had never done before. For about two centuries it continued to reflect the greatness and the splendid tastes of its Mogul rulers, from Akbar to Aurungzebe. Its outward glories culminated under Shah-Jehán, to whose princely tastes are due the noblest streets in the modern city, and the magnificent fortified palace, with its lofty red stone walls, its stately balls of marble and mosaic, and its wide arcaded courts, surpassing in magnificence, according to Heber, the Kremlin at Moscow. He, too, it was who built the great Jamma Musjid, one of the noblest mosques in the world, and who surrounded the city with walls and noble gateways, covering a circuit of seven miles.

Early in the eighteenth century the Imperial City was rudely awakened from its long rest, to go through a new course of trials and disasters, now due to civil commotions, now to new invaders from without. Hardly had it escaped the attack of Bájee Ráo's Mahrattas in 1737, when it fell a prey to the greed of the Persian savage, Nádir Shah, who, after renewing the massacres of Tímoor, carried away from the plundered city many millions' worth of treasure and jewels, including the Koh-i-noor, the chief ornament of the famous Peacock Throne of Shah-Jehán. Some years later, the Great Mogul of that day was blinded and slain by his own Vizier, and for months contending factions filled the city with their murderous havoc. Three years afterwards, in 1756, Delhi was plundered by a new invader, Ahmed Shah, the Duránee King of Afghánistán. The work of ruin was carried on by the Mahrattas, who, in 1759, despoiled and disfigured the still lovely palace of Shah Jehán. There, too, it was that the infamous Gholám Kádir, in 1788, "with his own hands shared in the torture of the Royal Family, and the blinding of the helpless old Emperor, Shah Alam." By that time the Mahrattas, recovering from their crushing defeat at Paneeput in 1761, came again swarming over Hindustan, and the poor blind descendant of Akbar was presently replaced on his shadowy throne by Mahdajee Scindia, who for some years ruled the country in his name. Under his successor, Daulat Rao Scindia, the helpless puppet and virtual prisoner of his new protectors, held his mockery of an Imperial court, until the capture of Delhi by Lord Lake in 1803, when the poor old man was found "seated under a small tattered canopy, the remnant of his royal state, with every external appearance of the misery of his condition."

From that moment all Delhi, outside the palace where Shah Alam still reigned over his own household, passed under the rule of that Company to whom Shah Alam, in 1765, had granted the government of Bengal. Thenceforth, save for Holkar's sudden dash on Delhi in October, 1804, baffled by Ochterlony's gallant defence, nothing ruffled the peace of the famous city until in the early morning of the 11th of May, 1857, the mutinous troopers of the Third Bengal cavalry, which had been unaccountably allowed to escape from Meerut, clamoured loudly under the palace windows of the king for help and leave to enter the city—they had overthrown the English and had come to fight for the King and the Faith. The troopers cried to the king with a loud cry, for a great fear was upon them, for they thought in their terror that they saw the gleam of the avenging sabres of the British dragoons in headlong pursuit of the scared and frantic troopers—but alas of the magnificent European brigade at Meerut, not a man moved in pursuit of these traitors and murderers.

If swift retribution had followed their blood-stained steps, what prolonged anguish might we not have been spared! what horrors might *not* have been averted! Hearing their cry, the king summoned to his presence Captain Douglas, the Commandant of the Palace Guards. In the Hall of Audience, supporting his tottering limbs with a staff, the aged monarch met the English captain. Douglas said that he would descend and speak to the troopers; but the king implored him not to go, lest his life should be sacrificed, and laying hold of one of his hands, whilst Ahsonoollah, the king's physician, took the other, imperatively forbade him to go down to the gate.*

In vain the Captain of the Palace Guards delayed the troopers for a moment, and only for a moment, for there were traitors within, as well as without, the great stronghold of the Moguls, the clatter of horses' feet in the streets and the fierce shouts of the troopers, followed by a great multitude—proclaimed that the first act of the great drama was consummated by our mutinous soldiery —a dome-like cloud rose above the arsenal fired by the heroic Willoughby—Delhi had fallen—the Mogul was restored!

The grandson of Shah Alam looked on without a protest at the butchery of English men, women and children within the palace where he himself, in 1788, had been tortured by order of the ruffian who had put out his grandfather's eyes. It was not long, however, before Muhammad Bahádur Shah and his family reaped the reward

* Sir J. W. Kaye.

of their weakness or their crimes. An avenging force of Englishmen, Seikhs and Goorkas sat down before the blood-stained city, and after several months of hard fighting and stern endurance, the storming columns won their way through the breaches made by their guns, into a stronghold guarded by many times their own number. When we took possession of the fortified palace, on the 20th September, "it is related that a sentry was found at each gate, with his musket on his shoulder, grim and immoveable, prepared for his doom." "The British standard was hoisted, and the Englishman celebrated his victory by ordering dinner in the Dewan-Khas, with its lustrous marble walls and lovely arabesques,"* and realised as he looked at the golden letters inlaid in the white marble under the cornice the truth of the famous inscription quoted by Moore —"If there is a Paradise on earth it is this—it is this." But where was the great Mogul? The king with his family and thousands of armed retainers had removed to Hoomayoon's tomb, an enormous structure, a short distance beyond the walls of Delhi. Hodson, the fierce and renowned partisan leader, had sought and obtained leave to receive the sword of Bahadour Shah. "So Hodson went forth from his resting-place, and stood out before all, in the open space near the beautiful gateway of the tombs, a solitary white man among so many, awaiting the surrender of the king and the total extinction of a dynasty the most magnificent that the world has ever seen."* The king was not

* Sir J. W. Kaye.

allowed to return to the palace, but was placed in honourable confinement in a private dwelling. Next day Hodson with a hundred of his troopers received the surrender of three of the princes with thousands of their followers, but unfortunately when near Delhi, fearing an attempt to rescue the princes, he deliberately shot the Shazadas with his own hand, thus dimming the lustre of his recent conduct, which had been noble and heroic. Two of these unhappy princes had in the words of Sir Archdale Wilson "been most virulent against us," and several other princes of the family were afterwards caught and hanged for the part they had borne in the massacres of May. The sentence of death passed some months later on the king himself, was commuted into one of transportation for life, and the white-haired convict disappeared from the scene of his ancestral glories to end his days in a distant corner of Pegu.

The grand reception given to the Prince of Wales at the old imperial city will long be held in remembrance, as it concentrated as it were in one view the past, the present, and the future. The old Mogul nobility, the magnificent palaces and mosques of their once imperial house were in the assured possession of the stranger, when artillery, infantry and cavalry in splendid array ushered in the Prince their future Emperor, from whose gracious bearing they might gather happy omens for the future. The Prince, before quitting Delhi, held a grand review of all arms on that ever-memorable ridge, some of the troops and officers occupying the points they held so bravely during the siege; and as he rode along the line of British soldiers, the haughtiest and most energetic of native princes was proud to ride on the right hand of the English prince and avow himself the faithful servant of our Queen.

At Delhi, on the 1st of January, 1877, Queen Victoria was proclaimed Empress of India by Lord Lytton, her viceroy, in the presence of her vassal kings and long descended princes, with their armed retainers and clansmen around them; some arrayed in complete armour like the Paladins of old, some in gorgeous raiment, stiff with barbaric pearl and gold; all this mighty host stood forth with drooping banners in homage to their empress.

Old imperial Delhi has witnessed many a grand and stirring spectacle, but not in the palmiest days of Shah Jehan or Arungzebe was there such an array of princely splendour, or loyalty to the imperial throne so significant.

NOTE.—Delhi, besides being for ages the seat of empire, has ever from its geographical position commanded a mighty trade—its bankers and merchants being famed for their riches and extensive commercial relations —its jewellery and embroidery being preferred to all others. Within the walls of Delhi there are the termini of three lines of railway—the East Indian, from Calcutta, the Rajputana State line from Bombay, and the terminus of the Scinde, Punjab and Delhi railway from Kurrachee.

CHAPTER XXII.

PROGRESS OF BRITISH RULE IN INDIA—*continued.*

NORTH-WEST PROVINCES, PUNJAB AND SCINDE.

Pâneeput—Meerut—Simla—Umritsur—Lahore—Peshawur—Mooltan—Sukkur, Bukker, and Roree—Shikarpore—Jacobabad—Dadur—Hyderabad—Kurrachee.

Páneeput.—On the not far distant plains (from Delhi) of Paneeput the drama of Empire was enacted over and over again. On those plains, Báber and his Moguls overthrew, in 1526, the hosts of Ibrahim Lodi, the last of the old Pathán kings of Delhi, and so founded the dynasty which, with one brief interval, held its sway for the next two hundred and fifty years. Thirty years later, on the same field, the youthful Akbar crushed out the last hopes of the rival Afghan dynasty of Shír Shah. In 1761, the field of Páneeput witnessed the shock of two great armies fighting over the death-stricken body of the Mogul Empire. The victory won by Ahmed Shah's Afghan and Mogul warriors on that day of terrible slaughter, proved equally fatal to the House of Báber, and to the growth of that Mahratta empire which Sívajee and his successors had striven to rear on the ruins of that of the Mogul. This celebrated battle, which permanently affected the fate of the Moguls and Mahrattas, removed many obstructions from the path of the continually advancing and victorious British, and well merits a passing notice.

The Mahrattas having invaded the Punjab roused the resentment of the Abdallee king of Afghanistan, who once more crossed the Indus at the head of his fierce and veteran horsemen.

Ahmed Shah, who had been a man of war from his youth, was at the time the most renowned general in Asia, far-seeing, patient, skilful, indefatigable, prompt, and resolute. Sedasheo Rao Bhow,* his Mahratta opponent, without experience in war, was imperious, contemptuous, and headstrong, but brave in action.

The forces were about equal, leaving out of calculation the clouds of irregular horsemen which hovered about both armies. Nothing could be more simple than the dress, arms and camp equipage of the northmen, while the men of the south, with their officers decked out in cloth of gold (degenerate sons of the great Sivajee!) they emulated in all their appointments the splendour of the Mogul glories of bygone days with their vast pavilions, the gilded tops of which were never again to reflect the slanting rays of the evening sun to welcome the return of the doomed warriors, who now humbled by famine, were sadly and sternly prepared for the worst; and what a contrast did they present to the proud and glittering array which entered that encampment only a few short weeks before!

* Bhow—a Hindoo title.

The Mahrattas were in a camp strongly entrenched, and began to suffer from the want of supplies, when the Bhow sent a letter to his friend, the Nawab of Oude, who was negotiating for terms with the Afghan king. "The cup is now full to the brim, and cannot hold another drop. If anything can be done, do it, or else answer me plainly at once; hereafter there will be no time for writing or speaking."

When the Mahrattas were reduced to their last meal they issued forth from camp determined as they swore to conquer or die. To quote the words of Grant Duff, "The ends of their turbans were let loose, their hands and faces were anointed with a preparation of turmeric, signifying that they were come forth to die; and everything seemed to bespeak the despondency of sacrifice prepared, instead of victory determined;" but their ancient valour and *élan* did not desert them in this extremity. They came on like a whirlwind, and for a moment the fierce onset of the Mahratta horse appeared to shake the tried veterans of the Abdallee and in some portions of the field to force them to give ground, but the tenacity and strength of the north, aided by a skilful general, prevailed against the misdirected, fiery, and impetuous valour of the south. The victory was complete. The general-in-chief of the Mahrattas and the Peishwa's son, with Scindia and many men of note, fell on this fatal field. The renowned Holkar fled. Maharastra was filled with mourning, and the spirit of the people appeared crushed.

Thenceforth India lay at the mercy of any power strong enough to take advantage of the weakness and confusion caused by the rout of Páneeput, and the conqueror's subsequent retreat to his own country. Four years later, the victor of Plassy, Clive, became the virtual master of Bengal, while his countrymen in Southern India, fresh from the death-blow they had inflicted on their French rivals, were already marching forward on the path of assured dominion.

Meerut.—Forty miles to the north of Delhi lies Meerut, famed for its cheerful hospitality and rich verdure. Here the mutiny first showed itself red-handed with fire and slaughter of the helpless, and here too with the most magnificent brigade of Europeans—horse, foot and artillery, the frantic sepoys were allowed to escape, to put the garrison and Budmashes of Delhi into a blaze of rebellion, which was the signal for a conflagration all over the country. As remarked in a preceding chapter, if that handful of native cavalry which led the revolt had been either crushed in their lines or pursued even to within the gates of Delhi, what blood and treasure, what unspeakable anguish to English hearts and homes might have been spared!

Simla, &c.—Proceeding northwards, past Kurnául and Umbálla, we cross the low Sewálik Range that forms an outwork to the Himalayas, and winding up by the hill-station of Dugshai, arrive at last on the wooded slopes of Simla, towering from eight to nine thousand feet above the level of the sea, in full sight of the great central range, its icy pinnacles glistening in the silent air as far as the eye could reach. Amidst the deodars and rhododendrons of this Indian Capua, the rulers of India, and as many as possible of their countrymen, spend the hot and rainy months of each year, recruiting mind and body with the breezy air, healthful exercise, much cheerful society, and all the silent influences of grand mountain scenery. Ever since the days of Lord Dalhousie, Simla has been the usual head-quarters of the Indian Government for more than half the year. Dárjeeling, on the borders of Sikhim, is the summer retreat of the Government of Bengal, Ninee Tall, in Kamaon, for that of the North-West Provinces, and Murree, on a lower range of the Himalayas, beyond Ráwalpindee, of the Government of the Punjáb. At the last-named hill-station, as well as Kisaulee, Dugshai, Subáthoo, and Landour, English troops and invalids are generally quartered.

Umritsur.—The road from Simla eastward, brings us across the Sutlej at Rúpur, where Lord Auckland had a courtly meeting with Runjeet-Singh, to Jullunder, chief town of the district occupied by us after the first Seikh war. On the line of the Scinde, Punjab and Delhi Railway thence to Láhore lies Umritsur, the sacerdotal and commercial capital of the Punjab, the Holy City of the Seikhs, famous for its temples, its sacred tank, "Amrita-Saras," or Fountain of Nectar, and its commercial wealth and enterprise; its merchants having extensive business relations with Central Asia, on one hand and on the other with Calcutta and Kurrachee, its industries include the manufacture of calicoes, silks, and shawls.

Láhore.—Láhore, the political capital of the Punjáb, lies on the Rávee, and embraces within its walls a circuit of seven miles. Like other cities that lay in the path of invaders from beyond the Indus, Láhore had for many centuries been held by the lieutenants of successive dynasties, from the days of Mahmúd of Ghuzní until it became the capital of the consolidated and powerful kingdom of Runjeet Singh, whose ashes lie nobly enshrined close to the citadel where he dwelt. Ruins of former cities may be seen for miles round the present capital which still contains about 100,000 inhabitants, and possesses mosques, temples and palaces of interest and magnitude. The Emperor Jehángire lies buried across the Rávee, in a stately tomb surmounted by four tall minarets. North of the city are the Shalimar Gardens, where Shah Jehán and his ladies were wont to enjoy the cool shade of marble-floored summer-houses, made cooler by the playing of numberless fountains. Entered by Lord Gough's troops in 1846, Láhore was finally placed under our rule in 1849, when the whole Punjáb became ours by right of conquest, and the boy-successor to the throne of Runjeet Síng became in England a happy and honoured country gentleman. During the eventful year of 1857 the Punjáb was ruled by a noble band of Englishmen, Lawrence, Montgomery, Macleod, George Barnes, Edward Thornton, Douglas Forsyth, Macpherson, Corbet, Sydney, Cotton, John Nicholson and Herbert Edwardes. In the absence of their chief the dire calamity broke out in various stations, when a few of these men took counsel together and decided on the complete disarmament of the large force of native soldiers at Lahore; and this was done so well that no blood was shed and no murmur was heard.

The armourers and cutlers of Lahore have been long celebrated for their swords and other implements of war.

The reception of the Prince of Wales was very striking, from the noble stature and bearing of the chiefs and their retainers, many of them being sheathed in armour.

Pesháwur.—From Láhore the main road takes us north-westward across the Land of the Five Rivers, by Gujerát, the last great battle field of the Seikhs and English; Jhelum, where Alexander and Porus fought and Sir Walter Gilbert led his flying column in chase of the routed Seikhs; Ráwal Pindi, where the last of the Seikh veterans gave up their arms; across the Indus at Attok, where Gilbert's guns and cavalry nearly caught up the retreating Afghans—to Pesháwur, which overlooks the mouth of the formidable Khyber Pass, forced so brilliantly in 1842 by the Sepoy and English soldiers of Sir George Pollock. This city, built by Akbar, and afterwards the seat of an Afghan dynasty, from whose hands it was wrested by Runjeet Singh, is still important as the great frontier outpost, or watch tower, of British India. Here, as at Láhore, a great danger was timely averted in 1857, by the tact and courage of British officers entrusted with the task of disarming a whole brigade of Sepoys before they could rise against our countrymen.

Mooltán.—Mooltán, on the lower Chenáb, contains some 80,000 inhabitants, and carries on a thriving trade in silks, shawls, brocades, and cotton cloths of its own making. Its history may be traced back to the time of Alexander, if the Malli whom he conquered lived in Mooltán. In the eighth century of our era it was taken by the Arabs, by Mahmud of Guzni in the eleventh, by Tímur in the fourteenth, and by Runjeet Singh in 1818. The murder of two English officers here in 1848 by order of the Seikh governor Mulráj, brought on the second Seikh war, in which Herbert Edwardes won his first laurels by driving Mulráj back into his stronghold, and keeping him there until a British force came up to complete the work he had begun. During the Mutiny of 1857, two Sepoy regiments were here disarmed by a mere handful of English gunners. The railway links Mooltan with Láhore, and a like connection with Kurráchee will be completed when the "missing link" is constructed between Mooltan and Kotree, the upper terminus of the Scinde line, opposite Hydrabad, on the Indus.

Shikarpore.—A populous town about twenty miles from Sukkur,* on the route from Scinde to Khorasan and Afghanistan by Dadur, the Bolan Pass and Quetta. It is renowned for the extent of its banking relations over the East.

The subjoined account, though long, is not only so picturesque, but so illustrative of the personal characteristics of the tribes and nations on the N.W. frontier, that I transfer it without abridgement.

The Great Bazar or main street, almost bisects the city. "We have specimens of at least a dozen nations, not including ourselves. The little Bráhui, with his flat face, broad limbs and stalwart shoulders clothed in a robe of camel's hair, stands gazing like an Epicurean at the tempting store of the halwai or confectioner. Knots of Afghans are chaffering noisily about the value of their horses, ponies and dromedaries. You may see

* Sukkur is on the right bank of the Indus and Roree on the left, with Bukkur a rocky island between them. This is the point at which it is proposed to bridge the river for the Indus Valley Railway.

what these men are by their tall, large forms, eager utterance, fiery eyes and energetic gestures. Though not allowed to carry arms, their hands are deep in their waistbands, as if feeling for the wonted Charay, the long, single-edged dagger which they use with such effect. It is about the size of the old Roman sword, and it speaks volumes for the stout-heartedness of the wielders. The wild, sun-blackened Beloch, whose grizzled locks and scarred cheek tell mutely eloquent tales of the free-booter's exciting life, measures the scene with a gaze that means 'what a waste of loot!' or turns, with the action of a cat-o'-mountain, upon the running footman preceding that pulpy Sindi rider in the brocaded cap and dress of padded chintz: the 'flunkey' has taken the liberty of pushing the knight of the road out of the way. The huge and brawny Mullá from Swat, an Eastern friar of Copmanhurst, all turban and kammerband (waist-shawl) the clerical calotte and cassock of El-Islam, looks down with infinite depreciation upon the puny Sindis amongst whom he has come to live and thrive. Fierce, bullying Pathans, the Afghan 'half-castes' of the plains, dispute with smooth-tongued Persian traders : Kandahar meets Multán, intent only upon capping cheating by cheating; the tall turban of Jaysalmir nods to the skull cap of Peshín, and the white calico sleeve of Kackh and Gujerát is grasped by the hairy claw of Kelát. Now, a grimy Moslem cook pours a ladleful of thick oil upon a fizzing mass of kabábs, whose greasy steams, floating down the Bázár, attract a crowd of half-famished ryot navvies and ditchers, to enjoy, in imagination, the 'pleasures of the table.' Then a smooth-faced Loháná asks you 40 rupees for a goat-tog chogheh, or cloak, whose worn condition reduces its value to 12 or less.

"Here, a Bhátiya vendor of dried fruits, sugar, spices, opium and hemp—the *tout ensemble* fragrant as a druggist's shop in the dog days—dispenses his wares to a knot of Jat matrons and maidens, with a pair of scales and a set of weights which would make justice look her sternest. And there grim Indine Chalybes—blacksmiths, tinmen, braziers and others—are plying their ringing, clanging, clattering, clashing trade in a factitious temperature of 150° Fah., and in close proximity of a fire that would roast a lamb.

"Yet heard through all this din is the higher din of the human voice undivine. Every man deems it his duty on 'Change to roar, rather than to speak—none may be silent—even the eaters of pistachios and the smokers of tobacco must periodically open their throats to swell the clamour floating around them. Except when the crafty Hindús transact business with fingers hidden under a sheet, not a copper pice changes hands without a dozen offers and refusals, an amount of bad language and a display of chapmanship highly curious to the Western observer."

"The typical man (of the Shikarpúri Hindús proper), is a small, lean, miserable-looking wretch, upon whose wrinkled brow and drawn features, piercing black eyes, hook nose, thin lips, stubbly chin and half-shaven cheeks of crumpled parchment, avarice has so impressed her signet, that everyone who sees may read. His dress is a tight little turban, once, but not lately, white, and a waistcloth in a similar predicament; his left shoulder bears the thread of the twice-born, and a coat of white paint, the caste-mark, decorates his forehead. Behind his ear sticks a long reed pen, and his hand swings a huge rosary—token of piety, forsooth! That man is every inch a Hindu trader. He may own, for aught we know, lakhs of rupees; you see that he never loses an opportunity of adding a farthing to them. He could, perhaps, buy a hill principality with a nation of serfs; yet he cringes to every Highlander who approaches his cloth-shelves, or his little heaps of silver and copper, as though he expected a blow from the freeman's hand. Scarcely a Moslem passes without a muttered execration upon his half-shaven pate, adown whose sides depend long love-locks, and upon the drooping and ragged mustachios covering the orifice which he uses as a mouth. There is a villanous expression in Shylock's eyes, as the fierce fanatics void their loathing upon him; but nothing in the world would make him resent or return slight for slight—nothing but an attempt to steal one of his coppers, or to carry off a pennyworth of cloth.

"This Shikárpúri, having few or no home manufactures, began long ago to devote his energies to banking, and in less than half a century he overspread the greater part of inner Asia. From Turkey to China, from Astrachan to Cape Comorin, there was hardly a considerable commercial town that had not its Shikárpúri or the Shikárpúri's agent."

"The fair sex at Shikárpúr, both Moslem and Hindu, has earned for itself an unenviable reputation; perhaps we can hardly be surprised by the fact. The women are far famed for beauty, the result of mixing with higher blood—for freedom of manners amounting to absolute "fastness"—and for the grace with which they toss the kheno or ball. These attractions have often proved irresistible to the wild Highlanders that flock to the low country bringing for sale their horses, woollens and dried fruits. You will see more than one half-naked, half-crazy beggar, who, formerly a thriving trader, has lost his all for the love of some Shikárpúri syren. By these exploits the fair dames have more than once involved their lords in difficult and dangerous scrapes. Moreover, when the young husband that was, returns home old and gray, to find a ready-made family thronging the house, scandals *will* ensue—there are complaints and scoldings; perhaps there is a beating or two before matrimonial peace and quiet are restored. The Hindus of the other Indine cities have often proposed to place their northern brethren under a ban till they teach their better halves better morals." *

Jacobabad and Dadur, the former the head-quarters of the renowned Scinde horse, called after the celebrated General John Jacob, who reclaimed the land from the desert, planted it with trees, and adorned it with flowers and shrubs; but it has become unhealthy and its existence imperilled by rivers in the vicinity changing their beds; a more stable site for the cantonment appears desirable. Dadur is a small town near the mouth of the Bolan Pass and about 65 miles from Jacobabad, and the proper terminus of the long-needed railway from Sukkur.

Hydrábád.—Hydrábád, the old capital of Scinde, lies

* "Scinde Revisited," by Captain Richard Burton, 1877.

on the left bank of the Indus, not far from the ancient Tatta at the top of the delta, where the sailors of Nearchus were so alarmed by the noise of the rushing tide in the narrow creeks, which they mistook for the roar of monsters of the deep, coming to swallow them up. Hyderabad is in communication with Mooltan and other places by means of steamers and native craft on the Indus, and is opposite Kotree, the upper terminus of the Scinde Railway, being a little more than 100 miles from Kurrachee, through which it has access to the sea. Its artisans are noted among other things for their skill in making swords, matchlocks, and various other kinds of arms. It was near this city that Napier's small force routed the numerous and brave Beloochee troops, the famed "barbarian swordsmen" of the Scinde Ameers, in February, 1843, and so brought the whole province under British rule, and enabled him to say—*peccavi!*

Kurráchee.—But the most important city in that part of India is Kurráchee, on the Arabian Sea, near the low range of hills which divides Scinde from Beloochistan. During the last thirty years its growth in size and commercial importance, as the main outlet for the trade of Scinde and the Punjáb and adjacent territory has been largely aided by the vast improvements made in its harbour, under the direction of Mr. W. Parkes, consulting engineer for the harbour to the Secretary of State for India. The Scinde Railway connects Kurrachee with Kotree on the Indus, and when the line is extended to Mooltan, Kurrachee, from its geographical position as the European port of India, and its unrivalled accessibility during the prevalence of the south-western monsoons, will command much of the trade which now finds its way from the Punjáb and N.W. Provinces to Calcutta on the one hand and Bombay on the other. Already ships of very large tonnage can enter and lie in its harbour at any part of the year, and more than a thousand vessels, including coasters, now yearly enter the port of Kurráchee.

Having given an outline of the progress of British rule in India, and some description of the chief actors in the crowded arena of politics and war, as well as a glance at the places where great battles had been fought, or revolutions accomplished, it might be well, before turning to the summary of the acts of the several Governors-General, or to the subsequent chapter on the Native States, to remind the reader of the provinces immediately subject to the British crown.

The division of British India into three Presidencies, Bengal, Madras, and Bombay, has been modified by the division into provinces, each ruled by a Lieutenant-Governor or Chief Commissioner. Madras and Bombay retain on the whole their former limits, but the overgrown Presidency of Bengal has been broken up into Bengal Proper, Assam, and British Burmah, the North-West Provinces, and the Punjab; to which may be added the Central Provinces, formed out of the old Sagur and Nerbudda districts, the lapsed Mahratta State of Nagpore, and part of Bundlechund. Each of these provinces represents a certain phase in the conquering career of the grand old East India Company.

CHAPTER XXIII.

SUMMARY—GOVERNORS-GENERAL.

FROM PLASSY, 1757, TO PROCLAMATION OF QUEEN VICTORIA AS EMPRESS OF INDIA, 1877.

Clive—Governor of Bengal—Warren Hastings, 1st Governor-General—Lord Cornwallis—Lord Teignmouth—Lord Wellesley—Lord Minto—Lord Hastings—Lord Amherst—Lord William Bentinck—Lord Auckland—Lord Ellenborough—Lord Hardinge—Lord Dalhousie—Lord Canning, 1st Viceroy—Lord Elgin—Lord Lawrence—Lord Mayo—Lord Northbrook—Lord Lytton.

UNTIL the battle of Plassy in 1757 the progress of the British in India was little better than a series of obscure, if heroic struggles, for leave to trade, and to defend their limited possessions against the exactions and capricious tyranny of the native rulers of the country, or the jealousy of foreign rivals in eastern enterprize.

The battle of Plassy was the turning point of our fortunes, the commencement of our dominion. Clive, the Warwick of the time, deposed one king of Bengal and set up another.

In 1759 the Dutch squadron was captured in the Hooghly; while in the following two years the French were defeated at Wandewash by Sir Eyre Coote, they were driven out of the Carnatic, and by the fall of Pondicherry their power was annihilated.

12

In subsequent years the British, with ever-advancing standards, take Moorshedabad, Monghyr, and Patna, and after defeating the Emperor Shah Alam II. and the Viceroy of Oude, aided by the ex-Nawab of Bengal, Meer Cossim, had the power hitherto exercised by right of conquest legally confirmed by an imperial edict constituting them the imperial Dewans or collectors of revenue for the provinces of Bengal, Behar, and Orissa, on payment of a moderate tribute.

In 1767 Clive leaves India, and Hyder Ali, the Sultan of Mysore, appears in the field, and two years afterwards he suddenly approaches Madras when a peace is arranged. He said, "I do not fear the English from what I see, but from what I do not see!"

Warren Hastings, 1772—85, the first Governor-General, discontinues payment of tribute to the Emperor of Delhi. During his reign the Rohillas were defeated; Salsette fell to our arms. Colonel Maclean, the agent of Hastings in England, tendered his resignation in consequence of dissatisfaction of Home Authorities, which is accepted, but Hastings repudiates the act of his agent and retains his high office. About the same time Lord Pigot, Governor of Madras, is unlawfully arrested by his own council and dies. Renewal of war with France; Pondicherry capitulates to General Munro. In 1780 Captain Popham carries Gwalior by escalade; Bassein surrenders to Goddard. Scindia is defeated by Carnac and granted favourable terms. Colonel Baillie's force is cut to pieces by Hyder Ali. Sir Eyre Coote takes command of Madras army and defeats Hyder Ali in repeated engagements. In the same year, 1781, the Dutch settlements in India and Ceylon were taken by the English. Cheyt Singh, Rajah of Benares, deposed by Hastings with extraordinary coolness and resolution, under most perilous circumstances.

Braithwaite's force annihilated by Tippoo Sultan. Naval engagement with French without result. Death of Hyder Ali. Hastings concludes a treaty favourable to England with Oude, and aids in spoliation of the Begums.

In 1783 the brave and distinguished veteran Sir Eyre Coote, sinks under infirmity and the toils of war. There is peace with the French, but war with Tippoo Sultan, which was concluded in the following year.

Various accusations were brought against Hastings, and the chief accuser was a Brahman, Rajah Nuncomar, who was himself soon after found guilty of forgery and hanged.

Besides the conquest of Rohilchund, Hastings was involved in many and great wars with the Mahrattas and Hyder Ali of Mysore, and sent at a critical moment, as already mentioned, with that prescience for which he was remarkable, a small force under Colonel Goddard from Calcutta to Surat, which in the face of many difficulties it effected, having defeated the armies of Scindia and Holkar and taken Bassein by assault.

It was to meet the expenditure incurred by these wars that he was led to demand the large sums of money from the Rajah of Benares and the Begums of Oude.

However we may deplore the means used for raising funds necessary for carrying on to a successful issue the great designs of the Governor-General, he acted with a single eye to promote the prosperity and glory of his country by consolidating and extending its dominion, over whose destiny he watched with a vigilance that never slumbered, a resolution that never faltered, or enquired too nicely into the means to attain the end.

In 1785 Hastings returns to England, and in 1787 is formally impeached by the Commons before the House of Peers, when Burke and Sheridan deliver most eloquent orations, and in 1795 he is acquitted but financially almost ruined by the expense of the trial, and was allowed to live and die utterly neglected by the government. In extreme old age when he appeared to give evidence at the bar of the House of Commons every head was uncovered by a simultaneous impulse to do reverence to the great patriot and statesman.

Lord Cornwallis, 1787—93.—After an interval of two years Lord Cornwallis was appointed Governor General, and in 1791 takes command of the army in the field, defeats Tippoo Sultan under the walls of his capital, Seringapatam, and many strong places surrender to his arms. In the following year he appears again before Seringapatam, when Tippoo gives two of his sons as hostages, cedes territory, and pays a large sum of money.

But however successful as a soldier, Lord Cornwallis is better remembered in connection with the permanent settlement of the land tax in Bengal.

Lord Cornwallis was for his eminent services raised to a Marquisate.

Sir John Shore, Lord Teignmouth, 1795—98, who carried out the non-intervention policy of the Court of

Directors, the period of his rule was not distinguished by very important events; however, he was neither deficient in promptitude nor courage when he felt he was called upon to interfere in the deposition of the illegitimate and worthless Nawab Nasir Ali of Oude in the face of a dangerous opposition. Sir John Shore was elevated to the peerage as Lord Teignmouth, and sailed from India in March, 1798.

Lord Mornington, Marquis Wellesley, 1798—1805, commenced his magnificent rule in 1798 which was adorned by the victories of Lord Lake, Sir Arthur Wellesley, and other great commanders.

In the beginning of this century the sway of the British extended over Rohilchund and part of Oude. Lord Wellesley's wars with the Mahrattas issued in the conquest of the fertile plains between the Jumna and the Ganges, from Cawnpore up to Delhi and Meerut, in 1803.

Lord Wellesley's far-reaching imperial policy which embraced within its scope Europe as well as Asia, not only added kingdom after kingdom to the extent of our dominion, but elevated at critical periods of our history the power and glory of the British name.

By the destruction of Tippoo Saib, the ruthless tyrant of Seringapatam, and his dynasty; by the reduction of the pretensions of the Soubadar of the Deccan, the Nizam of Hydrabad; by the protection and restoration of the Peishwah; by the overthrow of the great Mahratta leaders, Scindia, the Rajah of Berar, and Holkar; by the rescue and protection of the blind, aged, and helpless Emperor of Hindostan, no rival, whether

European or native, was left in the field to contest our supremacy.

Lord Wellesley after having for seven years performed magnificent service to his country, and having in an eminent degree displayed all the kingly virtues, was elevated to a marquisate, but so mole eyed were the Court of Directors in Leadenhall Street, or so intent on profits and bills of lading that thirty years elapsed before they understood the magnitude of the services of their Governor General; at all events that period, the life of a generation, elapsed before they made him any acknowledgment.

Lord Cornwallis in 1805 resumed his high office, but only to die. He was succeeded provisionally by Sir George Barlow, whose timid policy of non-intervention and in making peace on too favourable terms with those with whom the great Lord Wellesley had been at war, left the brave Rajpoots, the allies of England, to the tender mercies of the Mahrattas, their old enemies and persecutors.

During this illomened reign the Vellore mutiny occurred.

Lord Minto, 1807—13.—During this period the war between the French and English raged with great fury, and the troops of the latter took from the French and their allies all their possessions in the east, including Bourbon and Mauritius. At this time also the rich island of Java was wrested from the Dutch.

Piracy in the Persian Gulf was suppressed. Sir John Malcolm was sent on a mission to Persia, and Mr. Mountstuart Elphinstone to Afghanistan.

The Seikhs at this time had risen to be a formidable power in the Punjab under the Lion of Lahore, Runjeet Singh, and it was apprehended that France and Russia might stir up the Shah of Persia, the Ameers of Afghanistan and Scinde, and our formidable neighbour Runjeet Singh, to form a confederacy against us.

Lord Minto, notwithstanding these sinister auguries, formed friendly treaties with all these potentates.

Lord Moira, Marquis of Hastings, 1814—23.—After the great wars of Lord Wellesley the land had still to be subdued. New quarrels with native rulers involved new conquests. The hill tracts of Kumaon were wrested in 1815 from the insolent and aggressive Nepaulese. Three years later, Ajmere, the Sagur and Nerbudda districts passed under our rule.

Lord Moira was a distinguished soldier of noble character, whose prolonged reign of nine years was distinguished by many brilliant services, by the deposition of the Peishwa, by the crushing defeat of Scindia and Holkar, by the destruction of the Pindaries (a powerful confederacy of savage freebooters), the elevation of the Nawab Vizier of Oude to the kingly dignity.

While Lord Hastings was occupied with the Mahrattas and Pindaries, the King of Burmah sent an insolent message demanding the cession of territory. The Governor-General treated the letter as a forgery, saying he fully relied upon the good disposition of the king. The ruse succeeded, and before the king made a second demand, the Mahrattas and Pindaries were disposed of, and his golden-footed majesty was speedily deprived of three of his best provinces.

The prestige of the British name was not only greatly advanced by victories in the field against apparently overwhelming numbers, but many of the strongest fortresses in India submitted to our arms. The Governor-General, who had also acted as the Commander-in-Chief, was created Marquis of Hastings, and left India amid the hearty good wishes and applause of all.

Lord Amherst, 1823—28.—First Burmese war, in which the king cedes Assam, Arracan and Tenasserim; enlarging the boundaries of the great Bengal Presidency; with a heavy pecuniary indemnity. The storming of Bhurtpore by Lord Combermere in 1825.

In 1827 Lord Amherst solemnly assured the great Mogul in his palace at Delhi that the British were now the paramount power in India.

Lord William Bentinck, 1828—35.—His administration was distinguished by peace within and without our border, and for social and economical reforms. The great act by which his name will be handed down to posterity, was the abolition of suttee, or self immolation of the wife on the death of the husband. He did much towards the extirpation of Thuggee, a tribe of professional murderers, by strangulation. At this time appeared Ramohun Roy, who desired to reform his countrymen, especially in their religious views. He came to England as agent for the king of Delhi and died at Bristol in 1833.

Lord William Bentinck was very unpopular with the army, from having, in obedience to the Court of Directors, reduced the batta or field allowance.

Lord Auckland, 1836—42.—In 1836 the British outposts overlooked the Sutlej at Ferozepore and Loodiana. Disasters occurred to our arms from interfering in the internal affairs of Afghanistan, with the view of counteracting the designs of Russia by deposing one king and setting up another, under the mistaken impression that Shah Sujah, the sovereign of our choice, was more popular than Dost Mahommed, the vigorous Ameer in chief. The retreat, sufferings and destruction of our little army cast a gloom not only over India but England, and taught our native soldiers and subjects a lesson fraught with future calamity, that we were *not invincible.*

Lord Auckland's management of the finances was successful, and his administration otherwise showed ability of no common order, but the ill-fated Afghan campaign cast a cloud over an otherwise statesmanlike career.

Lord Ellenborough, 1842—44.—Notwithstanding that the lustre of the British arms was dimmed by the retreat, the honour of England was gloriously upheld in Afghanistan by Nott in Candahar and by Sale and the "illustrious garrison" at Jellalabad, that that honour was finally vindicated and the prestige in a great measure restored, was much more owing to the conduct of the above-named commanders and the skill and determination of the relieving general, Sir George Pollock, than to the resolute councils of the new Governor-General. Having reduced the strongholds of the country, defeated the Afghans in every action, and released the prisoners, Generals Pollock, Nott and Sale returned in triumph to India and were received on the frontier by the Governor-

General with every circumstance of honour. Soon after this (1843) Sir Charles Napier was sent to Scinde. He defeated the Ameers in two pitched battles. The country was annexed without just cause, as it would appear, albeit it has prospered under our rule.

During the wars in Afghanistan and Scinde, the Mahrattas of Gwalior had been turbulent in consequence of the childhood of the Maharajah Scindia. They were defeated in two pitched battles on the same day. Maharajpore, where Sir Hugh Gough commanded, the other Punniar where General Grey was the chief.

Lord Ellenborough held opinions at variance with those of the Court of Directors of the East India Company. He treated them with disrespect, and, after an unusually short tenure of office, was suddenly recalled by the Court, in virtue of the power vested in them.

Lord Hardinge, 1844—47.—A distinguished soldier, who had seen much service in the Peninsula and at Waterloo, with the most peaceful intentions was compelled to go to war with the Seikhs, our old allies and neighbours, but jealous rivals for supremacy in India.

Since the death of the old Lion of the Punjab in 1839 the country of the five rivers had been the scene of anarchy and revolution, resulting in the assassination of several members of the royal family, and of the chief men of the State.

At length, having exterminated all the members of the family of Runjeet Singh of mature age, the Sirdars placed on the throne his last descendant, Dhuleep Singh, a child of tender years.

The Seikh army was at this time numerous, and disciplined, with a magnificent artillery, while the physique and courage of the men were of the first order; they had conquered in every field, and longed to cross swords with the British, and were not to be denied. The master's hand was gone, and the existing leaders were intriguing for the supreme power, which no one appeared strong enough to wield.

The Seikhs crossed the Sutlej (1846) and invaded British territory, when Sir Hugh Gough, Lord Hardinge and Sir Harry Smith hastened, with very inferior forces to drive them back over the boundary river, the Sutlej, which they succeeded in doing after fighting four pitched battles—Moodkee, Feroshah, Aliwal, and Sobraon.

The British army crossed the Sutlej, took possession of the citadel of Lahore, the young Maharajah, Dhuleep Singh, made his submission, peace was granted on moderate terms, Jullundur was annexed, and Cashmere was erected into a tributary State, on Golab Singh of Jummu paying £1,000,000 sterling towards the expenses of the war.

The latter portion of Lord Hardinge's tenure of his high office was adorned by his humane and successful efforts to suppress many cruel practices then prevalent amongst the aboriginal inhabitants in the remote fastnesses of India.

Sir Henry Hardinge after earning golden opinions of all returned to England in 1847, having been elevated to the peerage as Viscount Hardinge.

Lord Dalhousie, 1848—56.—Lord Dalhousie went to India with the most pacific views to promote its social and material prosperity; especially the cultivation and exportation of cotton, but soon the renewed turbulence and treachery of the Seikhs demanded the energetic action of the Governor-General in the field of politics and war.

Mulraj the Seikh Governor of Mooltan, had been privy to the murder of two British officers, the Punjab was in feverish state, the old soldiers were mustering in secret; the heavy guns and other arms which had been buried were being dug up, and once more it was evident that the Khalsa, the old Seikh army, was determined to try again the fortune of war.

Mooltan was taken by storm under General Whish; and Lord Gough, after fighting the bloody and indecisive battle of Chilleanwallah; obtained chiefly through the splendid way in which his artillery was served, a brilliant and complete victory in the battle of Gujerat.

Sir Walter Gilbert, with his flying column, in hot pursuit, compelling the fugitives to surrender, and their Afghan cavalry allies being well mounted barely escaping to their own country by the Khyber Pass.

The annexation of the Punjab was now (1849) determined. Once more the boy king sat upon his throne in the great hall of his palace, surrounded by his Court and his Sirdars, and signed in full Durbar a treaty, resigning to the English the sovereignty of his country, receiving in return a pension small in comparison of the greatness of the sacrifice, and to that which was given to deposed potentates less entitled to consideration.

The Seikhs have been amongst the most loyal subjects of the British crown, and their country has been prosperous and happy. The ever-widening circle of our rule continued to extend.

The annexation of Pegu (1852) followed from injuries received at the hands of the king of Burmah; of Nagpore, from the rajah having no heir; of Oude (1856) from the continued misery of the people by the misgovernment of the king; not to mention minor gains in Bundelchund and Sikkim.

With the retirement, in 1856, of Lord Dalhousie, the march of conquest may be said to have stopped. Very little at least has since been added to the empire, whose bounds he was but too ambitious of extending. Of all these conquests, there are very few which an impartial reader of British Indian History can condemn.

While the boundaries of the empire were greatly enlarged, every effort was made to advance the social and material prosperity of the people, the administration of justice was improved, colleges and schools were established, railways and telegraphs, roads and canals were extensively introduced.

Lord Dalhousie may have erred in annexing territory, which sowed the seeds of future woe, but on the whole his reign was vigorous and brilliant, and he may fairly be considered the greatest of all the Proconsuls after Lord Wellesley.

Lord Dalhousie was rewarded by a Marquisate, but he did not live long to enjoy it. He had indeed given his life for his country.

Lord Canning, 1856—62.—The great event of Lord Canning's reign, indeed, in the whole history of India, was the revolt of the native army of Bengal.

The alleged causes were the forcible conversion of

Mahomedans and Hindoos by the new cartridges, which were falsely said to be greased with the fat of pigs and cows, so as at once to defile Mahomedans and Hindoos alike; and that all the native states were to be annexed, like Oude.

There may have been something in these rumours, but there were other causes at work. From their fine physique and soldierly qualities we had pampered the Bengal Sepoy unduly, at the same time by our centralizing system we had taken away the power of reward and punishment from commanding officers of regiments, and as an Asiatic likes to look upon the face of the man who has power over him, thus were old bonds between officer and soldier loosened. At the same time, we left much of our artillery and arsenals in their custody—notably Delhi. We had been massacred by the Afghans and they, the Sepoys, had enabled us in our hard struggle with the Seikhs to get the victory. Why should they not fight as well without us as with us, and with our own arms and training? Pandy had become a monstrously conceited fellow, and coveted the dignity and power of command, and would have it any price.

The main incidents of the mutiny are briefly told in the preceding chapters, but all who desire a full narrative are referred to the eloquent pages of Sir John W. Kaye.

If Lord Canning was slow and reluctant to realize the gravity of the storm that was about to shake the empire to its basis, he met the tempest with calmness and resolution, and never for a moment lost his dignity and self-possession; and, when the danger was past, no one was more clement or generous.

At this period the grand old East India Company

became a thing of the past, and the Governor-General became the Viceroy of our Queen.

Among the last acts of Lord Canning was the granting of *sunnuds* or patents to the princes of India who had done good service, constituting them feudal nobles of the empire, and guaranteeing their rights and privileges, with power of adoption on failure of issue.

On the 1st of November, 1858, Lord Canning issued in the Queen's name the famous Proclamation which transferred the immediate sovereignty from the Company to the Crown, by which " Queen Victoria took the millions of India under her gracious protection, and promised to govern them according to those beneficent maxims which have always distinguished British rule. The Proclamation was translated into all the vernacular languages of India, and was read in every station and in every native court on the 1st November, 1858. Her Majesty's kind words, full of grace and dignity, doubtless did much to reassure the minds of the people, and to convince them that the intentions of their English rulers were as just and benevolent as their military strength had recently proved to be irresistible."*

Nothing can be finer than the closing words of the future Empress of India:—"When by the blessing of Providence the internal tranquillity shall be restored, it is Our earnest desire to stimulate the peaceful industry of India, to promote works of public utility and improvement, and to administer the government for the benefit of all Our subjects resident therein. In their prosperity

* Lethbridge's "Introduction to History of India."

will be Our strength, in their contentment Our security, and in their gratitude Our best reward. And may the God of all power grant to Us, and to those in authority under Us, strength to carry out these Our wishes for the good of Our people."

Shortly before leaving India Lord Canning had to deplore the loss of Lady Canning, one of the most gracious and gifted ladies that ever visited India, and whose fair face and engaging demeanour spoke of hope and better times in the darkest hour of the mutiny. Lord Canning scarcely lived long enough to receive the cordial greeting of his countrymen on his return from his arduous labours; but his lamented and premature death cannot be laid to the charge of India.

Under the most trying ordeal no one could have represented England with more manliness and dignity than the first Viceroy.

Lord Canning for his calm, dignified and resolute government of India was rewarded by a step in the Peerage.

Lord Elgin, 1862—63, gave much promise of a useful and brilliant career, when his valuable life was suddenly terminated by a disease to which he was liable, and had nothing to do with the climate.

Lord Lawrence, 1864—68.—Sir John Lawrence was rewarded by this high office for the eminent services he rendered his country when Lieut.-Governor of the Punjab. His reign was honourably distinguished by the "masterly inactivity" with which he abstained from meddling with the tangled yarn of Central Asian politics beyond our frontier. Sir John Lawrence on his return to England was elevated to the peerage as Lord Lawrence.

Lord Mayo, 1869—72, succeeded Lord Lawrence, and excited hopes of a bright future, but was to the regret of India and England assassinated by a wretched fanatic.

His noble stature and distinguished manners made an extraordinary impression on the natives of India.

Lord Northbrook, 1872—75, will long be remembered for his courage in abolishing the most unpopular, and most abhorrent to Orientals, of all taxes, the income tax; he promoted many useful measures; and his efforts were successful in mitigating the horrors of the famine in Bengal in 1874.

Lord Northbrook had the honour of receiving the Prince of Wales as his guest during his visit to India, and on resigning the viceroyalty was created an earl.

Lord Lytton, 1876.—This accomplished nobleman had the high distinction of proclaiming her Majesty Queen Victoria as Empress of India at Delhi, on the first of January, 1877. It is earnestly to be hoped that circumstances may permit Lord Lytton to pursue the wise policy of his predecessors in his high office, of abstaining as much as possible from intermeddling with Central Asian politics beyond our border. While these lines are being written, the Viceroy, the Duke of Buckingham, Governor of Madras, and Sir Richard Temple, Governor of Bombay are working together in the most harmonious and zealous manner to mitigate the distress of our fellow-subjects in India, resulting from famine and its consequences.

The magnificent donation of half a million sterling

from the people of England to ameliorate the distress of their fellow subjects in India, with the noble devotion of all the Queen's officers in India, from the Viceroy downwards, must have broken through the icy barrier of caste of the Hindoo and the pride of place of the Englishman, and established a stronger feeling of mutual sympathy and regard, and made the rigid justice and inflexible rule of the heavy handed Englishman more acceptable to the mass of the people.

How the educated natives appreciate our rule will be seen by the following extract from a recent speech of a Hindoo gentleman at a public meeting at Bombay in September, 1877.

"I am sure that every sensible and well-informed man in this country is loyal. This country for many past centuries had no government deserving the name. There was neither internal peace nor security from foreign invasion. There was no power in India which could put a stop to the evil practices of sati, infanticide, religious suicide, and human sacrifices. The whole nation presented a scene of stagnation and ignorance; but the case is now different. Under the auspices of a beneficent, civilized, and strong Government, we have become progressive. Light and knowledge are pouring in upon the country. Old prejudices and errors are vanishing. We therefore count it a great privilege to be loyal subjects of the Empress of India. There is now security of life and property, as perfect as human institutions can make it. Those who are old enough are aware of the plundering excursions of Pindaris, who, descending from the ghauts, spread terror in the Concan.

These professional robbers have been extirpated by the British Government. We enjoy liberty of speech, petition and press. We enjoy the blessings of education, useful public works, internal peace, and freedom from foreign invasions."

The events that have occurred since the abolition of the Government of the East India Company, with the exception of the great mutiny of 1857, did not, from their comparatively recent date, appear to demand more than a passing notice.

A fair review of what happened from Plassy and Arcot, to the political death of the East India Company in 1858, when, as already stated, the onward march of the conqueror was stayed, is a record of achievements of which every Englishman may well be proud. While the Court of Directors were preaching peace and commercial diligence, their servants in India were continually driven by circumstances, often unforeseen and seldom hoped for, to play the part of statesmen and soldiers, to turn their factories into fortified towns, to gather revenue as well as trade profits, exhibiting all the nobler qualities of mighty conquerors, winning province after province from weak or hostile rulers, and finally to place all India with princes as its vassals at the feet of a Company which always shrank from taking the next step on the road to a consummation so wonderful, and, for the Company itself, so short-lived. The history of those hundred years, during which our countrymen and their sepoy comrades bore the Company's flag from one end of India to the other, against the heaviest odds, over barriers the most appalling, is full of stirring appeals to the heart of every Englishman who takes an interest in his country's fortunes, and feels his blood warmed by a succession of great deeds in war and in council, deeds tarnished on the whole by few crimes and fewer reverses.

CHAPTER XXIV.

FEUDATORY NATIVE STATES.—RAJPOOTANA.

Oodeypore—Jeypore—Joudhpore—Desert States.

The Native States of India, if in that term we include every small chiefship or barony lying within our borders, and subject more or less closely to British rule, number more than four hundred and sixty, and cover an area of about 600,000 square miles, peopled on a rough reckoning by nearly fifty million souls. We may divide them locally into twelve groups, arranged in the following order :—1. The Indo-Chinese group, as typified in Manipore and other small states bordering Assam and Lower Bengal. 2. The aboriginal chiefships in Chota Nágpore, Orissa, Jeypore (in Madras), and the Central Provinces. 3. The Native States, mostly Hindoo, which girdle the western Himálayas from Cashmere to Gurhwal and Rámpore. 4. The Afghan tribes beyond the Indus. 5. The Seikh States of Sihrind, such as Puttiála, Jhend, Nabha, Náhan, and Kotgarh. 6. The Mahomedan States of Bháwulpore, and Khyrpore, in or close to Scinde. 7. The States and Chiefships of Málwa and Bundelchund, including the Mahratta States of Indóre and Gwalior. 8. The Rájpoot kingdoms of Rájpootána. 9. The cluster of little states in Káttiawár and the northern half of Bombay. 10. The Mahratta and other states in the Concan and the western Gháts, such as Kolápore and Sáwant-Wári. 11. The great Mahomedan kingdom of Hyderabád; and 12. The old Malayan States of Travancore and Cochin in Southern India, to which may be added the Hindoo State of Mysore.

These groups might re-arrange themselves into Rájpoot, Mahratta, Mahomedan, Indo-Chinese, and Aboriginal, but for the fact that in some states the mass of the people differ from their rulers in race and creed, while in others it is hard to say which race or creed preponderates. A Hindoo Rajah reigns in Travancore, for instance; a Mahomedan Bégum governs Bhopául; a Seikh dynasty holds Cashmere: the bulk of Scindia's subjects are not Mahrattas, nor do the Mussulmans outnumber the Hindoo and Dravidian races in Hyderabad. With regard to the rulers of these states, there is one easy mode of distinguishing a Mahomedan from a Hindoo dynasty. Rájah or Mahárájah, Rána, and Ráo, with the feminine Ránee, are all Hindoo titles of sovereignty, while Thákúre and Sirdár answer to our Barons. A Mahomedan Prince, on the other hand, is a Sultán, a Nawáb, or a Meer, while Khán expresses a somewhat lower rank.

Rájpootána.—Of all these States the oldest and historically the most renowned are those of Rájpootána, the land of Rájpoots or Princes, which extends from Scinde almost to the Jumna, and from Bháwulpore to the borders of Málwa and the presidency of Bombay. It is a land of rocky hills, and wide, dry, often sandy plains, covering an area of about 114,000 square miles, equal to the British Islands, peopled by ten or eleven million souls.

No small part of it is mere desert, haunted only by wild beasts of various sorts, from the nilgau to the lion. The fertile tracts afford pasture for sheep, horses, and camels, or yield crops of corn, cotton, sugar, opium, and tobacco. The inhabitants are nearly all Hindoos of various castes and tribes, from the high bred Rájpoot and the keen-witted Brahmin, to the hard-working Játs and the humble dealers in grain. The Rájpoots pride themselves on the purity of their descent from the Kshatriya, or Warrior Caste of Maru's day, and some of their princes would even trace their lineage back to Ráma, the mythical king of Oude.

Oodeypore.—Of these princes, the highest in rank by common consent is the Rána of Mewár or Oodeypore, whose kingdom has an area of 11,614 square miles, and a population reckoned to exceed a million. Centuries before Mahmud of Ghuzni invaded India, his forefathers held the country of which Oodeypore is now the capital. By some it is alleged that the blood of the Sassanian kings of Persia and that of the Cæsars of Rome meet in the veins of this feudatory prince. In the fourteenth century the renowned Hamír beat back the Pathán masters of Delhi, and recovered his capital, Cheetóre, from the successor of Alla-ud-deen. Another of his line, the yet more famous Rána Sanga, defeated the Muhammedans in battle after battle, and baffled for a brief space the might of Báber himself. His grandson, Paertáub Rána, fought hard and long against Akbar's son Jehángire, and, Cheetóre having been destroyed, founded a new capital, Oodeypore, in honour of his father Oodee Singh. The story of the first siege of Cheetore is one of the most romantic on the many-coloured page of Indian history. Rumours of the extraordinary beauty of the Protector's * wife having reached the ears of the Sultan of Delhi, Alla-u-deen, better known as Alla the Sanguinary, he made the surrender of the princess the condition of peace. He succeeded by a stratagem in capturing her husband, and by this means matters appeared to be greatly simplified. The beautiful Pudmani assembled her kinsfolk, and taking counsel of them it was agreed that if Alla would raise the siege, her hand should be his reward. She stipulated that every respect should be shown her, and all the proprieties of harem life observed. She obtained leave to enter the conqueror's camp, attended by the ladies of her household. Half an hour was to be allowed for a final farewell between the unhappy husband and wife. On the appointed day 700 litters accompanied her to the royal camp, each litter carried by six armed soldiers disguised as porters, and containing, instead of a lady in waiting, a fierce warrior of Cheetore armed to the teeth. The parting over between husband and wife, the former entered the litter waiting to convey him back to his city, whilst the supposed damsels were to remain with their devoted queen and accompany her in the conqueror's train to Delhi. But the scheme being discovered, the Rajpoot warriors sprang from their palanquins, when a bloody fray ensued. The husband and wife escaped into their capital, but the flower of the chivalry of Cheetore was the price paid for their safety. Cheetore was again

* Or chief of the confederate princes of Rajpootana.

besieged, and, on its final fate becoming apparent, Pudmani, and thousands of the wives and daughters of the inhabitants performed the johur, or immolated themselves, rather than fall into the hands of the conquerors.

Three times Cheetore was besieged and sacked, the first time, as just related, was in A.D. 1295.

Before alluding to the second siege under Bahadour, Sultan of Guzerat, in 1533, a brief mention may be made of one of the many customs of this land of romance and war, many of them akin to the usages of the feudal times in our own country, and bespeaking a common origin, or at all events apparently springing from like conditions.

From remote times there appear to have been great feudal lords in Rajpootana dwelling in large castles with lesser barons under them, with minstrels and bards in the hall to extol the gallant deeds of the cavaliers. The long-descended dames were famed alike for their beauty, their pride and their virtue, and renowned as their fathers and brothers for their devotion to the honour of their country.

The glowing pen of Colonel Tod, the Froissart of Rajpootana, thus describes a romantic and knightly usage:—"The festival of the bracelet (Rakhi) is in spring, and whatever its origin, it is one of the few when an intercourse of gallantry of the most delicate nature is established between the fair sex and the cavaliers of Rajast'han."

"Though the bracelet may be sent by a maiden, it is only on occasions of urgent necessity or danger. The Rajpoot dame bestows with the Rakhi the title of adopted brother; and while its acceptance secures to her all the protection of a 'cavaliere servente,' scandal itself never suggests any other tie to his devotion. He may hazard his life in her cause, and yet never receive a smile in reward, for he cannot even see the fair object who, as brother of her adoption, has constituted him her defender. But there is a charm in the mystery of such connexion, never endangered by close observation, and the loyal to the fair may well attach a value to the public recognition of being the Rakhi-bund Bhau, "the bracelet-bound brother" of a princess. The intrinsic value of such pledge is never looked to, nor is it requisite it should be costly, though it varies with the means and rank of the donor, and may be of flock silk and spangles, or gold chains and gems. The acceptance of the pledge and its return is by the Katchli, or corset, of simple silk or satin, or gold brocade and pearls. In shape or application there is nothing similar in Europe, and as defending the most delicate part of the structure of the fair, it is peculiarly appropriate as an emblem of devotion. A whole province has often accompanied the Katchli, and the monarch of India was so pleased with this courteous delicacy in the customs of Rajast'han, on receiving the bracelet of the Princess Kurnavati, which invested him with the title of her brother, and uncle and protector to her infant, Cody Sing, that he pledged himself to her service, "even if the demand were the castle of Rinthumbor." Humayoon proved himself a true knight, and even abandoned his conquests in Bengal, when called on to redeem his pledge and succour Cheetore and the widows and minor sons of Ganga Rana.

Humayoon had the highest proofs of the worth of those courting his protection; he was with his father in all his wars in India, and at the battle of Biana his prowess was conspicuous and is recorded by Baber's own pen. He amply fulfilled his pledge, expelled the foe from Cheetore, took Mandoo by assault, and, as some revenge for her king's aiding the king of Guzerat, he sent for the Rana Bikramayat, whom, following their own notions of investiture, he girt with a sword in the captured citadel of his foe. The Mahòmedan historians, strangers to their customs, or the secret motives which caused the Emperor to abandon Bengal, ascribe it to the Rana's solicitations; but we may credit the annals, which are in unison with the chivalrous notions of the Rajpoots, into which succeeding monarchs, the great Akbar, his son Jehangir and Shah Jehan entered with delight; and even Aurungzebe, two of whose original letters to the queen-mother of Oodipoor are now in the author's possession, and are remarkable for their elegance and purity of diction, and couched in terms perfectly accordant with Rajpoot delicacy."

On the first occasion, we have seen that thousands of the women followed the example of their queen and performed the johur; on the second 13,000 women immolated themselves; on the third, when Akbar besieged Cheetore and utterly destroyed it, 8,000 Rajpoots, with all their wives and families, performed the dreadful rite. The heroism of the women of Cheetore stands unrivalled even amongst the Rajpoots. Rinthumbor next surrendered, and the Rajpoots became, notwithstanding their daring and warlike spirit, subject to the Moguls, until the Mahrattas arose and oppressed them yet more cruelly.

It is the special boast of the Mewár princes, that none of their house ever intermarried with the Mogul Emperors of Hindustan.

Rana Raj Singh the writer of the remarkable letter quoted below could wield the sword or spear as well as the pen, and was ready, like a true knight, to do his devoir at the behest of his lady-love.

To wed with the Moslem was most distasteful to the haughty beauties of Rajpootana, and when a fair princess of Marwar was solicited in marriage by the Emperor Aurungzebe, she appealed to the chivalry of the Rana Raj Singh in these words:—"Is the swan to be the mate of the stork? Is a Rajpootnee, pure in blood, to be the wife of the monkey-faced barbarian?" The Rana hastened to the rescue, defeated the imperial escort of cavalry and bore off in triumph the lady as his bride.

Aurungzebe's bigotry* drove the Rájpoots into fresh

* "This letter (says Colonel Tod), first made known to Europe by Orme, has by him been erroneously attributed to Jesswunt Sing of Marwar, who was dead before the promulgation of the edict, as the mention of Ramsing sufficiently indicates, whose father Jye Sing, was cotemporary with Jesswunt, and ruled nearly a year after his death. My Moonshee obtained a copy of the original letter at Oudipore, where it is properly assigned to the Rana. It were superfluous to give a translation after the elegant production of Sir. W. B. Rouse.

Letter from Rana Raj Sing to Aurungzebe.

'"All due praise be rendered to the glory of the Almighty, and the munificence of your majesty, which is conspicuous as the sun and moon. Although I, your well-wisher, have separated myself from your sublime presence, I am nevertheless zealous in the performance of every bounden nor wholly unsuccessful revolts. But in an evil moment, they turned for help to the ambitious and rapacious Mahrattas, and for many years Mewár and all Rajpootána suffered grievously from Mahratta exactions

act of obedience and loyalty. My ardent wishes and strenuous services are employed to promote the prosperity of the Kings, Nobles, Mirzas, Rajahs, and Roys, of the provinces of Hindoostan, and the chiefs of Æraun, Turaun, Room, and Shawn, the inhabitants of the seven climates, and all persons travelling by land and water. This my inclination is notorious, nor can your royal wisdom entertain a doubt thereof. Reflecting therefore on my former services, and your majesty condescension, I presume to solicit the royal attention to some circumstances, in which the public as well as private welfare is greatly interested.

'"I have been informed, that enormous sums have been dissipated in the prosecution of the designs formed against me, your well-wisher; and that you have ordered a tribute to be levied to satisfy the exigencies of your exhausted treasury.

'"May it please your majesty, your royal ancestor Mahomed Jehaul ul Deen Akbar, whose throne is now in heaven, conducted the affairs of this empire in equity and firm security for the space of fifty-two years, preserving every tribe of men in ease and happiness, whether they were followers of Jesus, or of Moses, of David, or Mahomed; were they Brahmins, were they of the sect of Dharians, which denies the eternity of matter, or of that which ascribes the existence of the world to chance; they all equally enjoyed his countenance and favour; insomuch that his people, in gratitude for the indiscriminate protection he afforded them, distinguished him by the appellation of Juggat Gooroo (Guardian of Mankind).

'"His Majesty Mahomed Noor ul Deen Jehangheer, likewise, whose dwelling is now in paradise, extended, for a period of twenty-two years, the shadow of his protection over the heads of the people; successful by a constant fidelity to his allies, and a vigorous exertion of his arm in business.

'"Nor less did the illustrious Shah Jehan, by a propitious reign of thirty-two years, acquire to himself immortal reputation, the glorious reward of clemency and virtue.

'"Such were the benevolent inclinations of your ancestors. Whilst they pursued these great and generous principles, wheresoever they directed their steps, conquest and prosperity went before them; and then they reduced many countries and fortresses to their obedience. During your majesty's reign, many have been alienated from the empire, and

and Pindáree raids. At length, in 1818, when the Mahratta power had been finally broken by Lord Hastings, the victorious English held out a protecting hand to the princes of Rajpootána. A treaty made with the Rána of Mewár secured to him all his sovereign rights, limited only by the mild demands of his future protectors. British supremacy was enforced by the payment of a yearly tribute, and the surrender of the

farther loss of territory must necessarily follow, since devastation and rapine now universally prevail without restraint. Your subjects are trampled under foot, and every province of your empire is impoverished; depopulation spreads, and difficulties accumulate. When indigence has reached the habitation of the sovereign and his princes, what can be the condition of the nobles? As to the soldiery, they are in murmurs; the merchants complaining, the Mahomedans discontented, the Hindoos destitute, and multitudes of people, wretched even for the want of their nightly meal, are beating their heads throughout the day in rage and desperation.

'" How can the dignity of the sovereign be preserved, who employs his power in exacting heavy tributes from a people thus miserably reduced? At this juncture, it is told from east to west, that the Emperor of Hindostan, jealous of the poor Hindoo devotee, will exact a tribute from Brahmins, Sanorahs, Joghies, Berawghies, Sàuyasees; that, regardless of the illustrious honour of his Timurean race, he condescends to exercise his power over the solitary, inoffensive anchoret. If your Majesty places any faith in those books, by distinction called divine, you will there be instructed, that God is the God of all mankind, not the God of Mahomedans alone. The Pagan and the Mussulman are equal in his presence. Distinctions of colour are of his ordination. It is he who gives existence. In your temples, to his name the voice is raised in prayer; in a house of images, where the bell is shaken, still he is the object of adoration. To vilify the religion or customs of other men, is to set at nought the pleasure of the Almighty. When we deface a picture, we naturally incur the resentment of the painter; and justly has the poet said, presume not to arraign or scrutinize the various works of power divine.

"'In fine, the tribute you demand from the Hindoos is repugnant to justice: it is equally foreign from good policy, as it must impoverish the country; moreover, it is an innovation and an infringement of the laws of Hindostan. But, if zeal for your own religion hath induced you to

Ráná's right to make treaties with foreign powers. The revenue is £250,000. Oodeypore, the capital, is adorned with magnificent structures, and has a lake with a marble palace rising as it were out of the water. The Rana was loyal in 1857. The present prince is only eighteen years of age. He is entitled to a personal salute of 21 guns.*

Jeypore.—Next in dignity is the kingdom of Jeypore, founded in A.D. 957 by another descendant of Ráma. This State has an area of 15,000 square miles, and a population little short of two millions. Some of its rulers fought with success against the Patháin kings of Delhi, but later Rajahs succumbed to the prowess or the arts of the Mogul emperors, and gave their daughters in marriage to the house of Akbar. Among the foremost princes of this line was Jey Singh, whose reign began towards the end of Aurungzebe's, in the last days of the

determine upon this measure, the demand ought, by the rules of equity, to have been made first upon Ramsing, who is esteemed the principal amongst the Hindoos. Then let your well-wisher be called upon, with whom you will have less difficulty to encounter: but to torment ants and flies is unworthy of a heroic or generous mind. It is wonderful that the ministers of your government should have neglected to instruct your Majesty in the rules of rectitude and honour.—Tod's "Rajast'han, vol. i., p. 380, note."

* "The Guptas, on the overthrow of the Sahs, founded a second dynasty at Vallabi, in Kattiawar, and when the last of the Vallabis were driven out of Guzerat by Naushirvan, the great Sassanian king of Persia A.D. 521-579—the Vallabi Prince Goha was married to the daughter of Naushirvan. She was grand-daughter of Maurice, Emperor of Constantinople, and from her is descended the present Rana of Udaipur, or Maiwar, who thus represents at once the legendary heroes of the "Ramayana" and "Mahabharata," the Sassanians of Persia, and the Cæsars of Rome. Maiwar is the only Hindu dynasty which has outlived the thousand years of Mohammedan domination in India, and the Rana still possesses nearly the same territory which his ancestors held with

seventeenth century. His deeds of arms against the Mogul were outshone by his attainments in the arts and sciences. A renowned astronomer, he built observatories at Delhi, Jeypore, and Benáres, furnished with instruments of his own invention. The best works of the greatest mathematicians were by his orders translated into Sanscrit. The handsome modern city of Jeypore was built under his directions, remarkable for its lofty stone houses faced with a *chunam*, or stucco, almost as hard and polished as marble, and set off with frescoes, sculptures, and stone balconies enclosed in lattice-work of stone. A vast palace, and many Hindoo temples of large size, enhance the beauty of this noble Rajpoot capital.

Public inns, or *sarais*, for travellers, were freely scattered about his kingdom. Under his long and enlightened rule, Jeypore flourished as it had never done before. Then came a long period of intestine feuds, under weak and dissolute rulers, and of much suffering from Mahratta and Pindaree aggressions. Jeypore at length turned for aid to the rising British power; but the treaty of 1803, which placed her under British protection, was set aside by Lord Cornwallis, and it was

almost unvarying success against Casim and Mahmoud of Gazni, and the Afghan kings and Mogul emperors of Delhi.

"In 1809 Rajputana was thrown into disorder by the contest of the princes for the hand of Krishna Kumari, the beautiful daughter of the Rana of Udaipur. To stay the fratricidal strife and bring back peace to the land, the peerless maiden took the bowl of poison offered to her by her distracted father, and exclaiming, "This is the bridegroom foredoomed for me," drank it off and sickened, trembled, fell, and died as she spoke the words. It was a page from the Mahabharata quickened into life once more."—*Times*. Vide Appendix D.

not till 1818 that Jeypore was finally added to the list of states which paid tribute to their new overlord, the East India Company.

The present Maharajah is conspicuous as one of the ablest and most enlightened of Indian princes. Under the successful guidance of the late Colonel W. Eden, the able Political Resident at his Court he did good service in 1857. The Maharajah had a seat in the legislative council of the Viceroy, is a G.C.S.I., and is entitled to a personal salute of 21 guns. The state yields a revenue of £475,000.

Joudhpore.—Joudhpore, or Márwár, the largest but not the most populous of the Rájpoot kingdoms, with an area of more than 35,000 square miles, peopled by 2 million souls, was ruled in the middle of the thirteenth century by the Rahtóres, a Rájpoot clan who had wandered thither after the conquest of Canouj by Muhammad Ghori, in 1193. Two centuries later, one of their Rajahs, Joudh Singh, founded the city which now gives its name to the whole State. After the defeat of the great Rána Sanga, the head of the Rájpoot league against the Moguls, Joudhpore also had to bend under the yoke of the House of Báber, and to purchase peace from the victorious Akbar by giving him a Jóudhpore princess to wife. Successive Rajahs fought and ruled with distinction under their new lords; but Jeswant Singh, who had done loyal service to Shah Jehán, paid only a fitful allegiance to his crafty successor Aurungzebe, whom he fought not unsuccessfully with his own weapons of intrigue and treachery. After his death the annals of Márwár become stained with crime and confused with intestine broils. One prince murders another, only to reap in his turn the just reward of parricide at the hands of a kinswoman whose nephew he had wronged. Rival princes fight for the throne. At length the Mahrattas appear upon the scene of anarchy and bloodshed, and the brave Bijee Singh, after one successful fight, fails at last to hurl back the trained battalions of Scindia's general, De Boigne. In the days of his successors, the land is harried by swarms of Pindáree robbers, under their most ferocious leader, Ameer Khán.

At length in 1818, Márwár also passed under our protecting rule. But the troubles of the State were not yet over. Misrule, and consequent anarchy, grew so rampant, that in 1839 a British force under Colonel Sutherland marched to Joudhpore, and held that city for five months, while order was re-established under new conditions, which bound the Rajah, Máun Singh, to respect the rights of his nobles, so far as they accorded with ancient usage.

Joudhpore has a revenue of only £250,000 a year. The two preceding Maharajahs were bad rulers and incorrigible vassals. Joudhpore did good service during the Mutiny, and its present ruler bears a good character with his own subjects and with the paramount power. He is entitled to a personal salute of 19 guns and is a G.C.S.I.

The Desert States.—Bikáneer to the north and Jaisalmere on the west of Joudhpore have each a larger area than Oodeypore, but lying as they do amidst the sand-hills of the Great Indian Desert, they are very thinly peopled; the former by half-a-million, the latter by only 70,000 souls. Bikáneer was founded by a son of the Rajah who gave his name to Joudhpore. Its people are mainly Játs, a Hindoo race apparently akin to the Getæ of Latin history and to the Jutes who peopled part of Denmark and England. One of its Rajahs, Rai Singh, followed Akbar's standard in all his wars, and gave his daughter in marriage to Akbar's son, Jahángire. More fortunate than its neighbours, Bikáneer escaped the ravages of Maharatta and Pindaree greed in the 18th century. Like the other Rájpoot States it afterwards owned allegiance to the British power.

Jaisalmere was founded in the middle of the 12th century by a Bháti prince whose forefathers had once ruled in Ghuzní and Lahóre. In the latter part of the 13th century Jaisalmere was closely besieged by the troops of Alla-ud-deen Khiljí, the Sultan of Delhi. Hopeless of relief, the defenders, according to Rájpoot usage in such cases, resolved at any rate to die with honour.

Rajpoot honour demanded the "johur," or self-immolation of its women. When their destiny became inevitable, the Queen, stepping forth from amongst her attendants, replied, in answer to the summons sent by the men, "To-night we shall prepare. To-morrow's light will find us inhabitants of paradise." By daybreak next morning four thousand women of all ages gave up their lives without a murmur, and apparently without fear, the willing sacrifices of honour. The women were all put to death by fire or the sword, and then the men, headed by their sovereign, rushed forth to meet the foe, and died fighting to the last man. In the following centuries little is heard of Jaisalmere beyond its wars with Rájpoot or Afghán foes. In 1818 the Ráwa, or ruler of Jaisalmere followed the example of his brother princes, and placed his country under our protection. The capital of the State is one of the healthiest and most beautiful towns in India, built entirely of stone adorned with abundant and tasteful carvings. The ruler of Bikaneer has a salute of 17 guns, while he of Jaisalmere has a salute of 15 guns.

CHAPTER XXV.

FEUDATORY NATIVE STATES.—*continued.*

JAT AND OTHER MINOR STATES.

Alwar—Kishengarh—Dholpore—Bhurtpore—Tonk—Kotah—Keraulee—Political Relations.

The Ját States.—The other 13 States in this group are comparatively small, from Alwar with an area of 3,024 down to Kishengárh which covers only 724 square miles. Two of them, Dholpore and Bhurtpore, on the left bank of the Chumbul, are Ját States, ruled, that is, by Ját princes. Both are of recent origin. Dholpore was made over early in this century to the Rána of Góhad in exchange for his own district claimed by Scindia, and Bhurtpore was one of the little states which rose in the last century out of the ruins of the Mogul Empire. Runjeet Singh, a descendant of its founder, gave Holkar shelter within the walls of his almost inaccessible capital in 1805, an act which led to the fruitless siege of that stronghold by Lord Lake. After beating back our troops four times with heavy slaughter, the Rajah came to terms and agreed to acknowledge the East India Company as his suzerain. Twenty years later Lord Combermere led another British army against the one stronghold which had successfully braved our arms.

This time Bhurtpore was taken and its rightful Rajah restored to power in the room of the usurping Dúrjan Sál. His son, the present Rajah, enjoys a salute of 17 guns, while 15 are allotted to the Rána of Dholpore, who received a Grand Commandership of the Star of India for his loyal conduct throughout the Mutiny.

Tonk.—Another relic of the Mogul Disruption is the Muhammadan principality of Tonk, founded at the close of the last century by the terrible freebooter Ameer Khán, a Pathán adventurer from Rohilkund, whose marauding bands followed the standard of Jeswant Rao Holkar. The dominions which this soldier of fortune carved out for himself with Holkar's leave were secured to him in 1817 by the Indian Government, on condition of his renouncing all further connection with the Pindárees and reducing the number of his troops. From that time the famous freebooter eschewed his evil ways, became respectable, even devout, and governed his little State of 2,730 square miles as successfully as he had formerly ravaged its Rájpoot neighbours. His son behaved well during the Great Mutiny, but the next Nawáb, who succeeded him in 1864, was deposed in 1868 by Lord Lawrence, the Viceroy, for the part he took in murdering the uncle of one of his Thákures, or Barons. The late Nawáb was conveyed as a prisoner at large to Benáres, and his eldest son was placed upon the *Guddee*, the cushion which in India does duty for a throne. He has a personal salute of 17 guns.

Búndee.—Búndee, with an area of 2,291 square miles, dates from the middle of the 14th century. The first Rao of Búndee was a Chohan Rajpoot, who fled from

Moslem tyranny into Mewár, and afterwards founded the State which his descendants still rule. The Ráos of Búndee alternately served and fought against the Moguls. One of them in 1804 gave timely help to Colonel Monson's shattered and exhausted troops during their retreat before Holkar. His grandson in 1817 zealously aided his English allies in cutting off the retreat of the Pindárees, a service rewarded by the recovery of possessions which Holkar and Scindia had taken from his family. In 1818 Búndee also was formally placed under our protection, and its Máháraos receive a salute of 17 guns.

Kotah.—Kotah, with more than twice the area of Búndee, was an offshoot of the latter, dating only from 1625, when it was bestowed by the Emperor Jahángire on a prince of Búndee, in return for faithful services in the field. In later times Kotah paid tribute to the Mahráttas, until their overthrow paved the way for its acceptance of British suzerainty. In 1857 the Ráo of Kotah made no apparent effort to repress the mutiny of his Contingent, or to save the Political Agent from murder; for which reason four guns were taken from the number of his salute. The full number of seventeen was however restored to his successor some years ago.

Siróhee.—The Ráos of Siróhee, a small State on the borders of Mewár, and Joudhpore, claim the proud distinction of never having owned the suzerainty of any power, until in 1823 one of them agreed to pay tribute to the Indian Government in return for his admission to the benefits of British rule. In 1845 another Ráo ceded Mount Aboo as a sanitarium to the English on condition that no cows or pigeons were ever killed there. His services during the Mutiny were rewarded by a large reduction of his tribute. Fifteen guns is the number of the Ráo's salute.

Karaulee.—The little State of Karaulee was the first to claim the protection offered in 1817 by the Marquis of Hastings to the princes and people of Rájpootána. In 1852, on the death of its Rajah without a direct heir, Karaulee would have been absorbed into British India by Lord Dalhousie as a lapsed fief. But opinion in this country proved hostile to that great ruler's bold policy, and the right of a feudatory to adopt an heir in certain cases was admitted by the placing of Madan Pál on the vacant Guddee. In return for his services during the Mutiny, the new Rajah obtained a remission of his debt to the Supreme Government, and an increase of his salute from 15 to 17 guns.

Political Relations.—The relations of all these States with the Supreme Government are managed by the Governor-General's Agent from Mount Aboo, where he resides in the hot season, visiting the different States in the cold weather. For this purpose the whole of Rájpootána is divided into seven Agencies, the Mewár, the Jeypore, the Márwár, the Haráotee, and so forth. Each is under an English "Political," who transacts business with the native ministers, and combines in himself the various parts of diplomatist, head magistrate, and minister of State, with large if undefined powers of interference in the internal affairs of his Agency. The Márwár Agent holds a special Court for deciding all disputes between the different States of

Rájpootána. Besides Mount Aboo, there are two districts ruled directly by British officers. Ajmere, with an area of 2,000 square miles, was ceded by Scindia in 1818, and annexed to the Government of the North-Western Provinces. Not long afterwards the hilly tracts of Mairwára, peopled by aboriginal Mairs, passed under British keeping, and its rude inhabitants repaid the efforts of their new masters to reclaim them from their savage ways by rallying freely to our side in the troubled days of the Mutiny.

CHAPTER XXVI.

FEUDATORY NATIVE STATES—*continued.*

STATES ON THE INDUS AND ITS TRIBUTARIES.

Khyrpore—Bhawulpore—Cashmere—Punjab Hill States.

Khyrpore and Bháwulpore.—Along the left bank of the Sutlej and the Indus stretch the Muhammedan States of Bháwulpore and Khyrpore. The former, a long strip of land between the river and the desert which girdles the north-west boundaries of Rájputána, covers an area of 15,000 square miles, of which only a third is cultivated. It was founded in 1737 by Dáüd Khán, a Dáudputra, or "son of David," whose clan boasted their descent from Abbas, the Prophet's uncle. The people he found there were mostly Játs. His great-nephew Bháwul Khán, built the city which has given its name to the State. Another Bháwul Khán, nephew of the former, had to beseech English aid against the encroachments of the Seikh ruler Runjeet Singh, who had already stripped him of his possessions on the right bank of the Sutlej. English influence did its work, and subsequent treaties with Bháwulpore in the interests of our trade improved the alliance thus begun. In 1838 the Nawáb, who had long since disowned his vassalage to Candahár, formally transferred his allegiance to the Indian Government. Ten years later his Dáudpútras marched forth to aid Captain Herbert Edwardes in his brilliant achievement when he drove the rebel Mulráj back within the walls of Mooltán. In 1866, on the death of the last Nawáb, the government of the State was entrusted to the Political Agent during the minority of the rightful heir. Under Colonel Minchin's fostering care the country is fast recovering from the misrule and neglect of former days; and the young Nawáb, who is being carefully trained by an English tutor, will begin his reign in 1879 with every advantage that an upright and able ruler could desire. His salute is 17 guns.

Khyrpore on the Indus has an area of 6,000 square miles. Its ruler, Meer Ali Murád, was the youngest brother of Meer Rústum, one of the Tálpoor Ameers of Scinde, when that country was conquered by Sir Charles Napier in 1843. In the general overthrow of the Tálpoor dynasty, Ali Murád contrived to retain his share of the family estates; but his attempt to get more than his share by means of forgery was found out some years later, and duly punished by Lord Dalhousie with degradation from the higher rank of Rais, and forfeiture of part of his dominions. His salute is 15 guns.

Cashmere.—Among the Native States of Northern India, Cashmere claims the first place, with its area of 79,784 square miles and a population of above a million and a half. The present kingdom includes not only the famous valley of Cashmere, but the hill districts of Jummu, Baltistán, and Ladákh. The beautiful valley of Cashmere, 70 miles long by 40 broad, is surrounded on all sides by lofty and rugged highlands, a wilderness of mountain ridges thrown out from the great Himálayan chain, through which the Indus and the Jhelum cleave their way down into the Punjáb. The people of Cashmere are mainly Hindoo by race, with a certain admixture of the Tartar and Thibetan elements in the more mountainous parts. Successive dynasties of different races ruled the country, before it passed under the sway of the Emperor Akbar in the latter part of the 16th century. The rule of the Moguls was supplanted in the last century by that of the Persian conqueror, Nádir Shah. Eighty years afterwards the country fell into the hands of Runjeet Singh, and in 1846, after our first Seikh War, it passed by right of conquest into British keeping. But Goláb Singh, the Dogra Chief of Jummu, who had remained neutral during the war, was allowed to purchase for £1,000,000 sterling the whole province from its new masters, on conditions of fealty enforced by the payment of a yearly tribute, in the shape of one horse, twelve shawl goats, and three pairs of shawls. His loyalty stood the test of the second Seikh War in 1848-49; and his successor, Runbeer Singh, sent his troops in 1857 to bear their part in the memorable siege and storming of Delhi. An able and enlightened ruler, as things go, Runbeer Singh has done much to foster the trade, industry and moral welfare of his subjects. The revenue is £835,234. This Chief is a general in the British army, is G.C.S.I., and entitled to a personal salute of 21 guns.*

* For this and other States, see J. Talboys Wheeler's "Imperial Assemblage at Delhi."

Punjab Hill States—On the southern borders of Cashmere is the Hill-State of Chamba, an old Rájpoot principality, covering more than 3,000 square miles, and rich in forests of Deodar, which have been rented to the Indian Government. To the south and east of the Kangra District are the small States of Mundi, Sukét, and Bassáhir, which last has also rented its deodar forests to the Paramount Power. Of the 26 small Hill-States to the South of the Sutlej the largest is Náhan or Sarmúr, whose Chief rules over 90,000 subjects, and receives a salute of seven guns. The hill-station of Kasaulee (or Kussowlie) was built on land obtained from the Rajah of Baghat. These hill-chiefs are all of good Rájpoot lineage, and enjoy like their more conspicuous peers the right of adoption in default of direct heirs. Beyond the Sutlej also lies the Seikh State of Kapúrthulla one of whose Rajahs, Rundhír Singh, fought so loyally for his English friends in 1857-58, that his domains were enlarged by fresh estates in the Punjab and two Jágeers or fiefs in Oude; he is entitled to a salute of 11 guns.

CHAPTER XXVII.

FEUDATORY NATIVE STATES.—*continued.*

CIS-SUTLEJ STATES.

Putiala—Jhend—Nabha—Faredkhot—Maler Kotla—Rampore.

Putiala.—Of the Cis-Sutlej States in Sirhind, the great plain between the Sutlej and the Jumna, where the fate of India has so often been decided by the shock of arms, Putiála, with an area of 5,412 square miles, peopled by 1,650,000 souls, ranks first, both in extent and for the noble services its Chief and people rendered to our cause during the worst days of the Mutiny. Founded by a Seikh Ját in the 17th century, Putiála and several other States on the British side of the Sutlej passed under our protection in 1809. For the help he gave us some years later in the war with Nepaul, the Rajah of Putiála was rewarded with new estates. A like return was made for the loyal conduct of another Rajah during the first Seikh War. It was the same Narindar Singh who, at the outbreak of the Mutiny in 1857, at once cast in his lot with ours, placed himself and his troops at our disposal, kept the road open from Lahóre to Delhi, lent his money freely to the Indian Government, sent out his soldiers wherever they were needed for the maintenance of order or the suppression of revolt, and spared no effort which a faithful vassal might make on behalf of his liege lord. For these splendid services the Maharajah was duly rewarded by the gift of forfeited estates yielding two lakhs of rupees a year, by the right of adoption in default of heirs, and by the power of inflicting capital punishment within his own realm. His successor, Mahindar Singh, who died lately in the sixteenth year of his rule, was a well-taught, able, and enlightened prince, who spoke English, and administered justice on English principles. He was entitled to a salute of 17 guns.

Jhend.—Not less faithful in the hour of our great need were the Rajahs of Jhend and Nabha, both descended from the same clan as Patiála. Jhend, a small State of 1,236 square miles, helped Lord Lake against Holkar in 1805, and a few years later secured its independence of Runjeet Singh by acknowledging the Indian Government as its Overlord. In the two Seikh Wars Rajah Sarúp Singh stood loyally by his English masters, and in 1857 he vied with Putiála in the zeal and promptitude of his movements on their behalf. In a very few days after the rising at Delhi, the road from Kurnaul to that city was guarded by his troops. At Budlee Serai, on the memorable 8th of June, they assisted to chase the rebels into the stronghold which they afterwards helped to storm. Their Rajah himself took part in the famous siege. For these and subsequent services he was rewarded with an increase of territory, the right of adoption, the full power of life and death, and a salute of eleven guns. In person and character Sarúp Singh, was among the noblest specimens of the Seikh race. On his death in 1864 he was succeeded by his son, Rugbheer Singh, who had proved himself the worthy heir of his high-minded father.

Nabha, &c.—The Rajah of Nabha, a yet smaller State than Jhend, made ample atonement during the Mutiny for his father's shortcomings during the Seikh War of 1845. Some of his troops were sent to occupy Loodiánah, while another body did good service at the siege of Delhi. He would have placed himself at their head, but this offer was declined on the plea of his youth. The rewards conferred upon him were similar to those conferred on his kinsmen of Jhend and Putiála. Dying of fever towards the end of 1863, he was succeeded by his younger brother, who has a personal salute of 13 guns.

Of the other States between the Sutlej and the Jumna, Faridkót is the largest with an area of 643 square miles. It was founded by a Burár Ját in the time of Akbar, and its Rajah rendered us good service during the troubles of 1857. Malér Kotla is ruled by a Pathán Nawáb whose ancestors came from Cabul. These two chiefs have a salute of 11 and 9 guns respectively.

Rámpore.—The Nawáb of Rámpore rules a State within the British province of Rohilkund, having an area of 945 square miles and a population of nearly half a million. It was a forefather of the present Nawáb who fled before Colonel Champion's Sepoys in the time of Warren Hastings. In the general overthrow of the Afghan Rohillas he was allowed to retain his lordship of Rámpore as a fief of the Nawáb of Oude. For his services during the Mutiny the present Nawáb received a further grant of land. He is a good Arabic and Persian scholar, and is entitled to a salute of 13 guns. His revenue is £146,000.

CHAPTER XXVIII.

FEUDATORY NATIVE STATES—CENTRAL INDIA.

Bhopal—Bundelkhund—Gwalior—Mahrattas—Indore—Dar and Dewas.

Bhopál.—The chief Muhammadan State in Central India is that of Bhopál, lying between the Vindhya Hills and the Nerbudda, with an area of 8,200 square miles, peopled by 769,200 souls. It was founded by an Afghan follower of Aurungzebe, whose successors gallantly held their own against many an attack from their Mahratta neighbours. In 1818 Bhopál was placed under British protection. During the Mutiny the brave and able Sekundar Begum stood so loyally by the British power, that her dominions were enlarged by new grants and her dynasty assured by the right of adoption. On her death in 1863 she was succeeded by her like-minded daughter, the Shah Jehán Begum.* Her Highness is a G.C.S.I. and is entitled to a salute of 19 guns.

Bundelkhund.—Bundelkhund or the land of the Bundelas, and Bhagalkhand, peopled by the Bhagelas, both Hindoo tribes, contain a cluster of Native States, stretching from the Betwa eastward to Mirzápore. Chief of these is Rewah, a highland State with an area of nearly 13,000 square miles, the Rajah, under the vigorous lead of Captain Willoughby Osborne, showed a bold front

* *Vide* chapter XVI..

to the mutineers and rebels in 1857. His loyalty was rewarded with the hill district of Amarkantak and the right of adoption. His salute amounts to 17 guns. Next in importance comes Urcha or Tehri on the Betwa, whose Rajah became our vassal in 1812. Datia, an offshoot of Tehri passed under our protection in 1804, and Samptar, which had once formed part of Datia, in 1817. The little State of Pauna, south of Tehri, was once famous for its diamond mines. Besides these, Bundelkhund contains some 32 minor chiefships covering an area of 6,300 square miles, only one of which is ruled by a Muhammadan.

Gwálior.—Passing over the smaller States controlled by the Central India Agency, through its various branches from Western Málwa to Bhagalkhund, we come to the larger kingdoms of Gwálior and Indóre, still ruled by Mahratta princes of the Scindia and Holkar lines. The Mahrattas, so called from Maharastra, a hilly region, which they have inhabited from time immemorial. This tract, which lies along the eastern slope of the western ghats in the Deccan, abounding in mountain fastnesses and small hill forts, appeared to be a fitting nursery for the future robbers and plunderers of India. Although this race may have taken their name from that region of mountain fastnesses, where they may have in early times sought a refuge, it would appear that they must have largely inhabited the Deccan generally, for in no other way can we account for the swarms which burst forth from time to time, like a flight of locusts devouring the land, "making a solitude and calling it peace." Under Sivajee they became soldiers and conquerors, and extended their sway in all directions. Sivajee's successors became little more than State prisoners in the hands of the Peishwa or chief minister,* who ruled with a varying sway the formidable Mahratta confederacy, which was gradually formed under his auspices, some member of which, such as Scindia and Holkar carried their swarms of horsemen with or without the leave of the Peishwa up to the gates of Delhi, and became at once the masters and protectors of the Imperial throne; the advent of the English alone staying their victorious career towards the complete conquest of Hindostan.

The history of India in the last century is filled with the wars and plottings of the great Mahratta chieftains, who in the name of their nominal head, the Peishwa of Poona, strove to build up a new Hindoo Empire on the wrecks of the Mogul power.

Junkají Scindia, grandson of Ránojee, (the Pateil, or head man of his village) the founder of his line, was captured and slain after the terrible defeat of Páneeput in 1761. But his uncle Mádhojee, escaping with a wound that lamed him for life,† lived to carry his arms over great part of Upper India, to escort a Mogul emperor back to Delhi, and to rule the provinces around

* But a descendant of the renowned freebooter still reigns at Kolapore a small state on the Western Ghauts. *Vide* page 233.

† He fled from the disastrous field, but was pursued to a great distance by an Afghan, who, on reaching him, gave him so severe a cut on the knee with a battle-axe, that he was deprived for life of the use of his right leg. His enemy, content with inflicting this wound, and stripping him of some ornaments and his mare, left him to his fate. He was first discovered by a water-carrier, of the name of Ranak Khan,* who was among the

* His service was gratefully rewarded. Ranak Khan, the water-carrier, was afterwards styled the Bhaee, or brother, of Madhajee Sindia, raised to the first command in his army, and afterwards loaded with favours.

the Imperial Capital in that emperor's name. Events meanwhile brought him into collision with the English, and his defeat by Colonel Camac in 1782 issued in a treaty which bound him to remain neutral in the war which Warren Hastings was waging against other foes in the Deccan. At his death in 1794 the Mahratta power had reached its height. Nearly all Upper India paid tribute to the successor of Madhojee, and the poor old Emperor Shah Alam was a mere helpless pensioner on Scindia's bounty.

In the days of his successor, Daulat Ráo Scindia, a change for the worse set in. Already weakened by his quarrel with Jeswant Ráo Holkar, Scindia had ere long to pay the penalty of trying conclusions with the conquerors of Seringapatam. At Alygurh, Assaye, Argaum, and Láswári, his best troops, trained by French leaders, fought in vain against Englishmen and Sepoys led by Wellesley and Lake. In the last days of that eventful 1803 he had to sign the treaty which stripped him of all his conquests between the Jumna and the Ganges, as well as those in Western India; and reduced him from

fugitives: this man, placing him upon his bullock, carried him towards the Deckan. Madhajee used frequently to recount the particulars of this pursuit. His fine Deckany mare carried him a great way ahead of this strong ambling animal upon which the soldier who had marked him for his prey, was mounted; but, whenever he rested for an interval, however short, his enemy appeared keeping the same pace; at last, his fatigued mare fell into a ditch. He was taken, wounded, spit upon, and left. He used to say to the British Resident at his Court, the late General Palmer, that the circumstance had made so strong an impression upon his imagination, that he could not for a long time sleep without the Affghan and his clumsy charger pacing after him and his fine Deckany mare! ["Central India," by Sir John Malcolm.]

his virtual headship of the Mahratta League to a mere equality with the chiefs of rival States. In 1818, after the Peishwa's final overthrow, Daulat Ráo made new concessions to the power which thenceforth took the place alike of Mahratta and Mogul. Shortly after the death of his successor Junkají in 1843, the Gwálior nobles provoked a quarrel with the English, which issued in the victories of Mahárájpore and Punniár, the reduction of the Gwálior army, and the raising of a Contingent commanded by British officers.

In 1857 the brave young Jaiají Scindia, (the present ruler) under the guidance of his able minister Dinkar Ráo, strove hard to keep his own subjects faithful to his liege lords. But the Gwálior Contingent mutinied at last, and in June of that year Scindia was flying for his life from the troops of the rebel leader, Tantia Topee. Happily Sir Hugh Rose came promptly to his succour; and in less than three weeks Scindia rode in triumph through his capital which British daring had won back for its rightful master. It need hardly be said that his loyalty reaped its due reward. The country now ruled by him covers 33,000 square miles, stretching unevenly, in a disjointed way, from the Chumbul up to the Nerbudda, and reckoned to contain about 2,500,000 souls, all Hindoos of various races, with Brahmins and Mahrattas for the ruling class. The revenue is £1,200,000. There is a British Resident at the Court of Gwalior, and a British garrison in the great rock fortress. The Maharajah is a general in the British army, is a G.C.S.I., and is entitled to a personal salute of 21 guns.

Indóre.—Indóre, the State ruled by a descendant of Mulhar Ráo Holkar, a Mahratta of the Shepherd caste lies mainly in the old province of Málwa, and covers an area of 8,075 square miles, with a population of more than half a million. After the rout of Páneeput, Mulhar Ráo retired to the country he had conquered and held as a fief from the Peishwa. His successors brought fresh provinces under their sway, and engaged in frequent wars with their great rival, the house of Scindia. In the first years of this century Jeswant Ráo Holkar turned his arms against the English, but the defeats inflicted on him by Lake's warriors sent him flying to the Punjáb. The treaty of December 1805, brought him a peace cheaply purchased by the loss of part of his dominions. In 1818, soon after the defeat of the Indóre troops at Mahidpore by Sir T. Hislop, the young Mulhar Ráo Holkar, then a boy of sixteen, signed a treaty which cut off a large slice from his realm, and placed the remainder under the British guarantee. His latest successor, Túkajee Ráo Holkar, failed during the Mutiny to keep his troops from turning their guns against the English Residency and rioting in the murder of helpless English fugitives. But Holkar's share in that dismal business seems to have been purely passive, and the Indian Government never called him to account for the misdeeds of his mutinous soldiery. Unlike Scindia, whose tastes are chiefly military, Holkar takes a keen interest in revenue affairs and in the manufacture of cotton fabrics; a little too keen indeed if the stories told of him are not pure inventions. Among the crops raised in his country opium takes a foremost place. The revenue is

£500,000. There is a British Resident at Indóre and a British garrison is cantoned at Mhow, thirteen miles from Holkar's capital, which betokens his dependence on the Paramount Power. He too is a G.C.S.I., and is entitled to a personal salute of 21 guns.

Dhár and Dewás.—The little State of Dhár on the Nerbudda was also founded by a Mahratta. Its people rebelled against us in 1857, and the country was confiscated. But when it came out that the Rájah had suffered for the sins of others, he was reinstated in his former domains, except that portion which had been transferred to Bhopál. His salute amounts to 15 guns. The same number is granted to the two Chiefs of Dewás, a little State of 256 square miles.

CHAPTER XXIX.

FEUDATORY NATIVE STATES.—WESTERN INDIA.

Baroda—Kolapore—Sawant-Wari—Jinjiri—Cutch—Katiawur—Pahlanpore—Mahi Kanta—Rewa Kanta.

Baroda.—The Native States in Western India outside Scinde are very numerous and of all sizes, from a petty chiefship of a few square miles to Baroda with an area of 4,399 and a population of about two millions. This latter State includes part of Kándéish and Kátiawár with the bulk of Gujerát. Its founder, Dámajee Gaikwár (Herdsman), a successful Mahratta officer, who died in 1720, was succeeded by his nephew Pílaee who perished at the hands of assassins employed by the Rájah of Joudhpore. His son Dámajee fought at Páneeput, but lived to strengthen his hold on Gujerát. In 1780 his successor entered into close alliance with the English, who helped to make him independent of the Peishwa. Subsequent treaties brought Baroda within the circle of States dependent on the British power. In the fight for empire between the English and the Mahrattas, the Gaikwár dynasty remained true to its treaty engagements; and in 1857 Khandí Ráo Gaikwár did loyal service to his friends in need, who rewarded him with the right of adoption and the remission of certain claims on his revenue. His brother, who succeeded him in 1870, was the Mulhar Ráo whose continued misrule, followed up by an accusation of attempting to poison the British Resident, compelled the Viceroy in 1875 to depose him from the Guddee, and send him a State prisoner to Madras. A child belonging to another branch of the same family was installed as Gaikwár in his stead, and the conduct of affairs has meanwhile been entrusted to Sir Mádhava Ráo, a statesman who had already proved his worth in the government of Travancore and afterwards of Indóre. The revenue is £1,150,000. The Gaikwár's salute is 21 guns.

Kolápore.—While Sattára, the old seat of Mahratta power, has long been absorbed into British India, Kolápore on the eastern slopes of the Western Gháts, between Ratnagíru and Belgaum, is still ruled by a descendant of the famous Sívajee. In the last century Kolápore was given to acts of piracy which provoked the interference of the Bombay Government. By the treaty of 1811 the Rájah agreed to keep the peace with his neighbours, and yield up his forts in return for the British guarantee. Fresh breaches of the peace provoked sterner measures on our side, and at last in 1844 a general rising in the South-Mahratta country had to be put down by a British force. From that time the government of the State was retained in British hands until 1862, when Rájáh Sívajee, who had stood our friend during the Mutiny, was allowed to govern for himself. His successor, a promising youth, came over to England in 1871 and died at Florence on his way home in the following year. During the minority of the present Rájah, the country is administered by the Political Agent. Area 3,184 square miles; population, 802,691; revenue, £304,724; salute, 19 guns.

Sáwant-Wári.—The chief of Sáwant-Wári, a State of 800 square miles in the southern part of the Concan, is a Mahratta of the Bhosla family which once gave rulers to Nágpore. In 1730 one of his ancestors formed an alliance with the English against the pirate lords of Kolába. During the last century Sáwant-Wári and Kolápore were engaged in fighting each other whenever their taste for piracy found no sufficient food elsewhere. More than once the Indian Government had to interfere with a high hand, and in 1819 the ruler of Sáwant Wári yielded up a part of his dominions in exchange for the protection assured him by the agents of Lord Hastings. Fresh disturbances called for fresh displays of our authority in 1839 and 1844, and for many years the State was ruled by British officers. In 1867 a new Rajah was allowed to rule in fact as well as name; but after his death the country passed again under British management, the present Rajah being still a mere boy. Of the minor chiefships in the Southern Mahratta country Sánglee is the largest and most important. The Chief of Nurgúnd, whose ancestor had fought stoutly against Tippoo, was hanged in 1857 for the murder of the Political Agent, and his Jágeer was confiscated to the Paramount Power.

Jinjíra.—On the Western coast, a little to the south of Bombay, lies the small Muhammadan State of Jinjíra, ruled by a Habshee, or Abyssinian Sídee, whose forefathers held their fief as admirals of the Sultán of Beejápore, and engaged in frequent wars with the countrymen of Sivajee.

In 1733, the Sídee of that time entered into a close alliance with the English, which has never since been broken.

Cutch.—The Ráo of Cutch, that singular tongue of land which stretches from the delta of the Indus to Gujerát, with the Raun of Cutch on its northern, and the Gulf on its southern side, rules over an area of 6,500 square miles, peopled by half a million souls. The Raun itself, a desert of salt and sand at one season, becomes a vast though shallow lake at another. Low volcanic hills run across the land of Cutch, the greater part of which is little better than a desert, fringed by grassy plains and fields of rice, cotton, sugar-cane, or millet. The inhabitants are mostly Hindoos with a sprinkling of Muhammadans, and the Jháréjas, a Rájpoot tribe from Scinde, form the ruling class. The present dynasty was founded in the fifteenth century, but the title of Ráo is younger by a hundred years. In the first years of this century, rival rulers, Hindoo and Muhammadan, shared the country between them. Their quarrels and piracies brought English influence, armed or peaceful, into frequent play, in the early years of this century. In 1819, the Ráo was dethroned, and his State administered for his child-heir, until 1834, when the reins of government were handed over to that heir. In 1860 the latter was succeeded by Ráo Prágmul, an able ruler, who did his best to put down infanticide and the slave-trade, which his subjects carried on with Zanzibar. On his death in the early part of 1875, the State once more passed under British management. Under the Ráo of Cutch there are some two hundred chiefs or barons, each of whom wields almost sovereign power within his own domains. The present Rao has a revenue of £210,000, is eighteen years of age, and has two sons and a daughter, is a G.C.S.I. and has a salute of 17 guns.

Kátiawár.—To the south of the Gulf of Cutch, lies the peninsula of Kátiawár, with Ahmedabad and the Gulf of Cambay for its eastern boundary. Within its area of 21,000 square miles, a crowd of chiefs rule over some two million subjects in all, mostly Hindoos of various tribes, with a sprinkling of Patháns in the towns and of aboriginal Bheels and Kátees in the central highlands. Of these chiefs, who are said to number 216, the Nawáb of Júnagurh, descended from a soldier of fortune who rose to power in the last century, may be held to rank first. He pays tribute both to the Gaikwar and the Indian Government. The Jám of Nawánagar, a Jharéja Rájpoot whose line dates from the sixteenth century, holds a part of his domains under Júnágurh and Baroda. The Thákure of Bhaunagar, whose Rajpoot forefather settled in Kátiawár in the thirteenth century, has the largest revenue—£80,000—of any chief in the peninsula. Two other chiefships, Púrbandar and Drángdra, make up the list of those whose rulers have the power of life and death over all but British subjects. For the trial of capital offences in the remaining states, and of crimes committed by petty chiefs, there is a special criminal court, over which presides the Political Agent.

Páhlanpore.—The Páhlanpore Agency controls a group of eleven States, four Muhammadan and seven Hindoo, lying between Rájpootána and Baroda, and covering an area of 6,041 square miles. Of these, the largest is Páhlanpore, whose Dewán claims descent from a Loháni Afghan, on whom the title was bestowed by the Emperor Akbar. The present Dewán proved himself our true friend during the mutiny. Rádhanpore was founded in the seventeenth century by a Persian adventurer from Isphahán. These two chiefs alone have the power of trying for capital offences.

Máhi Kánta.—In the Máhi Kanta Agency there are three score and odd petty chiefs, whose estates, with those of the Rájah of Idar, cover an area of 4,000 square miles, peopled by 311,000 souls. The only chief worth mentioning is the Rájah of Idar, a State founded in the eighteenth century by two younger brothers of the Rájah of Joudhpore. The engagements of the remainder with the Indian Government may, in the words of Colonel Malleson, be generally described as "engagements on their part not to rob or steal."

Rewa Kánta—The Rewa Kánta States, on the east of Baroda, cover an area of about 4,900 square miles, peopled mainly by Hindoos and Bheels. Among the sixty chiefs who have feudal relations with us, the Rájah of Rájpípla stands first. The tribute which his ancestors paid to Akbar, was afterwards transferred to the Gaikwár, but a portion of it is now paid to his British protectors. Chota Oodeypore and Deogurh Baria, both founded by Chohan Rájpoots, passed under our protection in 1803. These two States yield a revenue, the one of 100,000 the other of 75,000 rupees a year. The revenues of the remaining chiefships are still smaller, though some of them have an area of several hundred square miles. Another group of small chiefships lies about the borders of Khandeish and Násik.

CHAPTER XXX.

NATIVE STATES—SOUTHERN INDIA.

Hyderabad—Mysore—Cochin—Travancore—Padukatta—Petty Hill Chiefs.

Hýderábad.—The largest Native State in India is that of Hyderábád, with an area of 98,000 square miles, larger than that of Great Britain, and a population of nearly nine millions. The first Nizám, or Subahdár of the Deccan, as he once was called, was Chín Kilick Khán, a Turkish noble whose father had held high office under Aurungzebe. Under a show of allegiance to the Delhi Emperors, Chin Kilick, otherwise Asaf Jah, extended his sway from the Nerbudda to Trichinopoli, and from Musulipatám to Beejápore. After his death in 1748, the quarrels and intrigues of his sons brought the Mahráttas, the French, and finally the English into conflict or alliance with the rival claimants to the kingly power. Our first treaty with the reigning Nizám was made in 1759, when Salábat Jang ceded one of his districts, and promised to dismiss his French allies. A few years later a fresh alliance was sealed by the cession of more territory, in exchange for a British subsidy. In the war with Tippoo Sultán in 1790, Nizam Ali found his advantage in siding with his English friends, and his prudence was rewarded with a slice of Tippoo's kingdom. After the fall of Seringapatam, the Nizám's share of Tippoo's forfeited dominions was made over to the East India Company, as a provision for the payment of those auxiliary troops which he had bound himself to maintain under British officers, for the special purposes of British rule.

His successor, Sikandar Jah, was an indolent, pleasure-loving prince, who bore little love for his English protectors. But the services rendered by his troops during Lord Hastings's war with the Pindárees and Mahrattas in 1817-19, won for their sovereign a further increase of territory, and a final release from all feudal dues to his Mahratta neighbours. From that time, however, the internal affairs of Hyderabad, in spite of English interference, fell into worse and worse disorder. The country was misgoverned, its revenues were plundered by greedy adventurers, a large body of unpaid or badly-paid soldiers preyed upon the people, the great landholders waged war with each other, the Indian Government pressed in vain for the arrears of interest due on its loans to the Nizam. At last, in 1853, British forbearance could wait no longer. Under pressure from Lord Dalhousie, the Nizám of that day ceded in trust to his English creditors the fertile province of Berár, on condition that its surplus revenues, after defraying the cost of the Nizám's Contingent, should be handed over to the Nizám's Treasury.

The capital is a large and populous fortified city, tenanted chiefly by Mussulmans of various races and sects, and adorned with numerous mosques, a fine palace, and the imposing group of buildings which form the Residency. A sea of verdure divides the city from the neighbouring cantonment of Sikunderábád. Not many miles off is the famous battle-field of Assaye, where "the Sepoy General," Sir Arthur Wellesley, with his 4,500 English and native troops routed some 50,000 Mahrattas in September, 1803.

The ruined city of Golconda is a few miles west of Hyderabad.

During the troubles of 1857, our hold on Southern India was greatly strengthened by the goodwill or, at least, the timely quiesence of Hyderabad. Happily for us, a wise and powerful minister, the Nawáb Salár Jung, guided the counsels of the new Nizám. Any incipient rising was promptly quelled, and a part of the Nizam's Contingent fought bravely under English leading, side by side with the sepoys of Bombay and Madras. In return for these services, half a million of the Nizám's public debt was cancelled, and a part of the ceded districts given back to him. His able minister became Sir Salár Jung, G.C.S.I., the new Order specially created to do honour to those Indian princes and nobles who had stood most loyally in their allegiance to the British Empire, and of those who otherwise deserved well of England for good service done for India. Under that minister's guidance, Hyderábád has ever since made steady progress in the paths of peace, order, and general well-doing. On the death of the last Nizám, in 1869, a Council of Regency, headed by Sir Salár Jung, took the government into their hands during the minority of

Afzal-ud-daula's heir, then a delicate child of only four years. Watered by the Godávari, the Kistna, the Warda, and their respective feeders, Hyderabad is rich in natural resources, which have yet to be fairly developed. Renowned in former days for the diamonds of Golconda, it has lately opened up new stores of wealth in the coal-fields which spread far along the Warda Valley. There is an English Resident at the Nizám's Court, and a strong British garrison hard by, in the suburb of Secundrábád. The present Nizam is now eleven years of age, receives a salute of 21 guns and has a revenue of £3,000,000.

Mysore.—South of the Nizám's country, lies the woody and rugged table-land of Mysore, covering a surface of 29,000 square miles, peopled by more than five million souls. Mysore, best known historically as the seat of a Mahomedan power which gave us no little cause for anxiety, from the days of Warren Hastings to those of Lord Wellesley. Two able, bold and ambitious rulers, Hyder Ali, a Pathán officer from Lahóre, and his son Tippoo, succeeded for more than thirty years in holding the spoils first won by the former, against the onsets, single or combined, of Mahratta, Mogul, and English arms.

In 1799 Tippoo Sultan relying upon aid from France, was rash enough to defy for the third time the British power, when Seringapatam was taken by storm under General Harris and Sir David Baird. After the place had fallen the body of the Sultan was found in a gateway under a heap of slain, preferring as he had said a soldier's death to an ignominious surrender.

16

For centuries before Hyder rose in the service of the Mysore Rajah, a long succession of Hindoo princes had ruled the country which Hyder was at length to win. After the fall of Seringapatam in 1799, a part of Tippoo's dominions passed within the British pale, the remainder being handed back to a prince of the dynasty which Hyder had dethroned. During his minority, Mysore was fairly governed by an able Brahmin minister; but in 1832, the misrule of its new Rajah provoked Lord W. Bentinck to relieve him of a burden he was quite unfit to bear, and presently the government was entrusted to a British Commissioner and his staff. It was not till 1867, a few months before the old Rajah died, that the right of his adopted heir to inherit the kingdom forfeited by his adoptive father was formally acknowledged by the home Government of India. In 1868, the new Rajah was duly proclaimed; but being then a little child, his country remained under our management, and an English tutor, Colonel Malleson, was appointed to train him worthily for his future post. For that end no pains have since been spared, and the young Rajah gives fair promise of doing credit to his able guardian. The climate of Mysore, which lies exposed both to the south-west and north-east monsoons, is very moist, and this, combined with the general height of the country above sea-level, serves greatly to temper the fierce tropical heat. All sorts of wild beasts, including tigers and elephants, abound in the wooded valleys, and some of the coffee now exported from Southern India, is grown in the highlands of Mysore. The revenue is £1,094,968. The ruler has a salute of twenty-one guns.

Cochin.—To the south of Malabar lies the little Native State of Cochin, which, in spite of Portuguese and Dutch inroads, and of wars with Malabár, maintained for many centuries its old independence under its own Hindoo sovereigns. At last, however, it fell under the yoke of Hyder Ali, from whom, in 1791, it was delivered by British help. Subsequent treaties bound the Zamórin of Cochin to pay us tribute in return for the British guarantee.

Travancore.—From the southern frontier of Cochin to Cape Comorin extends the kingdom of Travancore over an area of 6,600 square miles, about five times the size of Cochin, with a population of two million and a quarter. Before the middle of the last century, Travancore was ruled by a number of chiefs, whose subordination to one head was begun by Rájah Mastanda, and completed by his successor. The latter proved our staunch ally against Hyder Ali and his son Tippoo. In 1793 he bargained to supply the Bombay Government with pepper in exchange for arms and European goods. Two years later he too entered into that system of subsidiary alliances which issued in establishing our supremacy over all India. In Travancóre, as well as Cochin, exists the custom, handed down by the Nairs, the ruling class in those countries, by which the succession to the *guddee* descends invariably in the female line. In other words, the Rajah's next heir is never his own son, but the son of his sister or his daughter, or, failing these, of some near kinswoman whom he may have adopted. Besides various classes of Hindoos and Mussulmans, Travancore owns many thousands of Native Christians, chiefly of the old Syrian Church. In this State, also, the heat is largely tempered by the heavy rains, the sea-breezes, and in many parts by the height of the land above the sea. Under the wise management of Sir T. Mádhava Ráo and the present minister, Travancóre has become a model Native State, with a large yearly balance saved from its handsome revenues, while its schools, roads, reservoirs, and other public works, will bear comparison with those of many under our own rule. The Rajah is a G.C.S.I. His salute is seventeen guns.

Padukátta.—On the eastern side of Southern India, between Trichinopoli and Madura, is the little State of Padukátta, whose ruler, commonly known as the Tondimán Rájah, belongs, like most of his subjects, to the Kullan or Thief Caste. His ancestors were our oldest and truest allies in the fight for empire last century with the French, and in our subsequent wars with Mysore.

Among lesser chiefs on the Madras side, we may mention the Rájah of Vizianágram, who claims descent from an old Rájpoot family, and receives a salute of thirteen guns, but retains no kind of Political independence.

Petty Hill-Chiefs.—In the Jeypore Agency (Madras) which once formed part of Orissa, a wild, rugged country, peopled thinly by aboriginal Konds, there are a number of petty chiefs, whose power over their own tribesmen is limited by the general control of the Political Agent. In the Central Provinces there are eighteen feudatory chiefs, ruling about a million of people, over an area of 28,000 square miles, and paying a fixed tribute yearly to the

Indian Government. They are free to govern according to their own laws, so long as they keep the peace and refrain from oppression. Like conditions govern our relations with a number of petty chiefs in Orissa, in Chota-Nágpore, on the west of Bengal, in Tipparah, to the south of Silhet, and in the hill districts of Assam, peopled by rude tribes of Nágas, Khásias, Gáros, Abors, and so forth. The outlying State of Munipore, on the Cachár frontier, with an area of 7,584 square miles, is ruled by a Rájah whose ancestors, with English help, threw off the Burman yoke in 1823, and who now enjoys a qualified independence under our guarantee. A small part of Kúch Behár, on the northern frontier of Bengal, is still governed by its own Rájah.

We have now gone through the list of Native States and Chiefships, which owe direct allegiance to the Imperial Crown. Their total revenue amounts to £14,500,000, of which only about £742,000 accrues as tribute to the Paramount Power. Among them they can muster an armed force of 64,172 cavalry, 241,063 infantry, and about 9,390 trained gunners, with 5,252 pieces of ordnance. A great many of these troops would probably count for little beside our own Sepoys, some of them being merely picturesque ruffians in old world link mail; but Scindia's infantry are highly disciplined and carefully drilled, and the Nizám's troops are not to be despised. Each of the larger States moreover counts its guns by hundreds, such as they are, and it appears that some of the Native Princes, especially Scindiah, are beginning to adopt the short-service system, as a means of evading the rules which limit the numbers of their standing armies.

Thus there is an army, more or less effective, of above 300,000 men and over 5,000 guns in the service of the native princes of India. This enormous force is certainly not required for internal tranquillity or for display on state occasions. As for external purpose there is none, as the Imperial Power both restrains these vassal potentates from aggression upon each other and from every possible enemy from without. What, then, is the meaning of this immense standing army, which is being better armed and disciplined year by year, and notably in the case of Scindiah augmented by the short service system?

It would be well to demand from H.H. of Gwalior some explanation of his evasion of the rules which define the number of his troops; and the costly and useless armies of the other feudatories should be either greatly reduced or a portion of them used for imperial purposes.

Is what is now felt to be an inconvenience to be allowed to grow to a menace? This playing at soldiers on a large scale by the feudatory princes of India, the at present loyal subjects of Her Majesty, should cease, and the sooner the better for them and for us.

Far be it from us to think that the opportunity we have given them of meeting at the imperial assemblage and elsewhere,—bringing tribes and nations together that never met before face to face, or if they did in times past it was too frequently for mutual destruction

—can be turned to evil, or that, having made them to know each other and enabled them to take counsel together and to estimate each other's strength, that they would be tempted to use the telegraph and the railway to communicate and combine against us and misuse the very means which we have introduced for their and our own advantage.

Yet as the Paramount Power in India we owe a duty to those who live under the shadow of our protection, to put an end to arrogant assumption, or evasion of treaties, and to curb these inflated useless armaments, so fraught with future danger, especially to the feudatory princes themselves.

The British force in India consists of 65,000 Europeans and 125,000 Native troops under British officers, 190,000 in all, numerically less than two-thirds of the forces of the Native Princes. The troops of the feudatories would as a rule be useless against an external enemy, however well they might enact the part of Bashi-Bazouks in provinces which might be left unprotected by the withdrawal of our troops on any emergency. The contribution of £750,000 paid by the feudatory princes is much too small for the immunity they enjoy from internal disturbances and external aggression, while their exchequer would be improved and the burdens on their people lightened by the enforced reduction of armies who have no foe to fight with, unless they turn their arms against their friends and protectors.

The heroic and loyal conduct of some of the feudatory

princes of India, especially during the Mutiny, has been done justice to in former chapters.

From the foregoing sketch it will be seen that within the boundaries of our Indian Empire, no such thing as an independent Native State exists, or has for many years past existed. From the time, indeed, when Lord Hastings dealt the death-blow to Mahratta ascendancy, the English have virtually remained Lords Paramount of all India. In 1819, says Captain Trotter, "the last of the Peishwas had ceased to reign, the Rája of Berár was a discrowned fugitive, the Raja of Satára a king only in name, while Sindia, Holkar, and the Nizám, were dependent princes, who reigned only by the sufferance of an English Governor-General at Calcutta. The Mogul Empire lingered only in the palace of Delhi; its former Viceroy, the Nawáb of Oudh (afterwards king) was our obedient vassal, the haughty princes of Rájputána bowed their necks, more or less cheerfully, to the yoke of masters merciful as Akbar, and mightier than Aurangzebe. Ranjít Singh himself cultivated the goodwill of those powerful neighbours who had sheltered the Sikhs of Sirhind from his ambitious inroads." The conquest of the Punjáb, Scinde, and British Burmah, the absorption of Oude, and the final extinction of the Delhi dynasty, completed the process begun by Clive. The Royal Proclamation of November, 1858, followed up by the Sunnads or Letters-Patent, in which Lord Canning guaranteed to the Native Princes and Chiefs their old treaty rights, enlarged in some cases by new concessions, may be said to have formally reasserted the supreme powers which the servants of the East India Company had for half a century wielded without dispute. The degrees of vassalage may vary widely, from the kind of sovereignty still enjoyed under the German Kaiser by the King of Saxony or Bavaria, to the very limited powers of an English land-owner acting as a Justice of the Peace. But of the vassalage itself there is no doubt whatever. The most powerful of Indian princes holds his dominions by a tenure, differing only in degree from that of the smallest Feudatory who, within certain limits, rules over a few square miles of country in accordance with the rights transmitted from his forefathers.

The Proclamation of the Queen at Delhi as Empress of India on the 1st of January, 1877, while confirming the princes and people in the possession of their rights and privileges, made it plain to all that their Empress was not only the fountain of honour and beneficence, but of power also; that the destinies of India and England are one; the Empress-Queen being as much the Sovereign of India as of England.

"The native Chiefs command collectively 5,252 Guns, 9,390 trained Artillerymen, 64,172 Cavalry and 241,063 Foot soldiers." They are cantoned as follows:—

Names of Divisions.	Guns.	Infantry.	Cavalry.
Rajputana	2,003	69,028	24,287
Central India	893	55,664	15,321
Central Provinces		2,115	140
Western India	1,083	32,770	9,331
Southern India	734	38,401	8,262
Eastern India	109	5,264	404
Northern and North Western India ...	428	37,799	6,407

"The appended List will show how these forces are distributed among the more important States:"—

I.

	States.	Guns.	Infantry.	Cavalry.
I.	Udaipur	538	15,100	6,240
II.	Jaipur	312	10,509	3,530
III.	Jodhpur	220	4,000	5,600
IV.	Bundi	68	2,000	200
V.	Kota	119	4,600	700
VI.	Jhalawar	90	3,500	400
VII.	Tonk	53	2,288	430
VIII.	Karauli	40	3,200	400
IX.	Kishugarh	35	2,000	150
X.	Dholpur	32	3,650	610
XI.	Bharatpur	38	8,500	1,460
XII.	Alwar	351	5,633	2,280
XIII.	Bikanir	53	940	670
XIV.	Jaisalmir	12	400	500
XV.	Sirohi		350	375
XVI.	Dongarpur	4	632	57
XVI.	Banswara	3	500	60
XVI.	Partabgarh	12	950	275

II.

	States.	Guns.	Infantry.	Cavalry.
I.	Gwaliar	210	16,050	6,068
II.	Indur	102	5,500	3,000
III.	Bhopal	39	4,766	1,194
IV.	Dhar	4	790	370
V.	Dewas	—	—	—

III.

	States.	Guns.	Infantry.	Cavalry.
	Rewa	35	2,000	905
	Other States in Bundelkhund.	421	22,163	2,677

IV.

	States.	Guns.	Infantry.	Cavalry.
I.	Barodah	30	11,000	3,098
II.	Kolhapur	258	1,502	154
III.	Kachh	38	600	300
IV.	Kathiwar	508	15,306	3,033

V.

	States.	Guns.	Infantry.	Cavalry.
I.	Haiderabad	725	36,890	8,202
II.	Mysore	6	1,000	35
III.	Travankur	6	1,211	60
IV.	Kochin	3	300	—

VI.

	States.	Guns.	Infantry.	Cavalry.
I.	Cis-Satlaj States	141	7,185	3,191
II.	Kashmir	96	18,436	1,393
III.	Trans-Satlaj States	27	3,275	300
IV.	Bhawalpur	80	2,484	360

VII.

	States.	Guns.	Infantry.	Cavalry.
	Petty States	302	18,000	4,000*

* Malleson's "Native States of India."

CHAPTER XXXI.

FOREIGN EUROPEAN SETTLEMENTS IN INDIA.

Portuguese—Dutch—Danish—French.

The Portuguese.—To the Portuguese belongs the honour of having been the first of modern European nations to carry its arms and trade into any part of India. The fifteenth century, famous for the discovery of America by Columbus and his successors, saw also in 1486 the successful rounding of the Cape of Storms—the name first given to the Cape of Good Hope by the brave Portuguese captain, Bartholomew Diaz. Twelve years later the yet more famous Vasco da Gama, the discoverer of Natal, cast anchor off Calicut, on the Malabar coast. His efforts to establish a peaceful trade with the subjects of the well-disposed Zamorin, or Tamuri of Calicut, were thwarted by the intrigues of Moorish rivals from Egypt and Arabia, who begrudged a share of their profits to the strangers and infidels from the far West, and tried, but in vain, to capture Vasco's three ships on their homeward voyage.

In 1500 the attempt to establish trade with Calicut was renewed by Pedro Cabral, with a larger fleet. Moorish jealousy again stood in the way, and a Portuguese factory at Calicut was carried by storm. After plundering and burning some Moorish vessels by way of reprisal, Cabral found a friendlier welcome at Cochin and Cannanore. Further insults to the Portuguese flag were requited two years later by Vasco da Gama himself, who bombarded Calicut and hanged a number of native fishermen by way of a warning to their rulers. At Cochin, however, he found his countrymen fairly established as traders, under the protection of a rajah who refused to obey the orders of his suzerain, the now hostile Zamorin of Calicut.

In the next few years the Portuguese fleets at Chaul, Diu and elsewhere, fought winning battles against numerous, and sometimes formidable foes. Under the far-famed Albuquerque, the Portuguese ere long carried their arms from Ormuz, in the Persian Gulf, to Malacca, and Goa itself became the seat of his viceregal sway. Some years after his death, in 1515, the port of Diu, on the southern coast of Kattywar, fell at last into Portuguese hands. Its capture was shortly followed by that of Damán, on the coast between Surat and the Northern Concan. Attacked in vain by the fleets and armies of neighbouring rulers, Diu for some time flourished as the chief seat of Portuguese trade in the Gulf of Cambay.

During the sixteenth century the Portuguese reigned supreme on the seas, and along the coast of Western India. A great league of native princes warred for ten months in vain against the splendid city of Goa, defended only by 700 soldiers and 1,300 monks, with the help of their armed slaves. The chief seat of Portuguese rule in India had already become the great stronghold of Roman Christianity in the East, governed by an archbishop whose influence was strengthened by a large body of monks, and secured by the terrors of the Inquisition. There is a noble cathedral, and a church which contains the shrine of St. Francis Xavier, Rome's first and noblest apostle to the East.* The churches founded by him are still conspicuous, with their Christian villages nestling under palm-trees, to the traveller as he passes the southern shores of the peninsula. Monasteries, churches, palaces and other

* "The road to the cathedral passes under a large arched gateway. In a niche over the arch, beneath one of St. Catherine, stands a painted statue of Vasco da (not de) Gama, and we were told that it was of necessity that each Governor of Goa should go under this archway—"Aliter Gubernator not potest fieri." There was one of the smooth, well-bred, amiable ecclesiastics, who are ever to be found *in situ*, to show the Prince round and explain everything. The cathedral inside is of vast and noble proportions, very plain and massive outside. It contains shrines and chapels, and much gilding, many middling pictures, fine old silver work. There were only seven worshippers—all women, all natives—all before one shrine; at least, *they* were real, for the visit was a surprise. What had become of the worshippers for whom these churches had been erected? Or were they the work of Faith and Hope? From the cathedral the Prince went to the Bom Jesus. On the steps a musical performance welcomed the Prince, which he never heard or saw the like of before. One tall, lanky native gentleman, whose principal raiment was a big drum slung from his neck, belaboured that instrument with one hand, and with the other held to his mouth a fearful tube of brass, from which he compelled the most dreadful sounds. A boy beside him, without the benefit of drum, clanged two cymbals, and a couple of youths joined in, one on a kettledrum the other on a drum simple, Above this din rose the ding dong of the small, and the sonorous roll of the great, bells of the church, and the barking of noisy curs. There were no beggars, and that for the reason that there were no people to be begged of. The Bom Jesus is chiefly noted for the shrine of St. Francis Xavier, a man whom the churches of the world may unite in accepting as a true apostle. It is certainly one of the most beautiful and one of the richest objects of the kind which can be seen anywhere. But it is placed in a very small, dark chapel, and can scarcely be conveniently examined. The treasuries, full of gold and silver cups for the sacred elements, were opened, and their contents and many curiosities were exhibited."—"The Prince of Wales's Tour," by W. H. Russell.

public buildings still attest the former greatness of a power now hastening to decay. The middle of the same century (the sixteenth) saw the Portuguese established also in the valley of the Ganges, at a place since known as Hooghly, on the river of that name. In Ceylon, also, they soon obtained a footing. Of the seaborne trade of India, the countrymen of Albuquerque enjoyed, if not quite a monopoly, at least the lion's share. No foreign ship in these waters could hope to trade in peace without a Portuguese passport, or was free to trade at all if a Portuguese vessel remained unloaded. But, with the first years of the seventeenth century, new rivals began to assert their strength. To the daring Dutchmen, fresh from their revolt against Spain, the Portuguese gradually yielded Ceylon and Malacca. English fleets drove them out of Ormuz, and wrested from them the trade of Surat. Chimnajee, brother of the Mahratta Peishwa, Bájee Rao, drove them in 1739 out of Bassein and Salsette.

Long before then, in 1632, their settlement at Hooghly had been stormed by Shah Jehán's Moguls, with heavy slaughter of its brave garrison, and the almost utter destruction of a very large fleet of merchantmen. Thenceforth the Portuguese never rose again to power on the side of Bengal.

By the middle of the eighteenth century the glory had departed from the Portuguese possessions in Western India also. A Portuguese viceroy still rules over a province forty miles long by twenty wide, and inhabits a huge palace in New Goa, overlooking a harbour second only to that of Bombay. But Old Goa is now little more than a cluster of splendid ruins; and the trade of the modern city, built largely of materials brought from Old Goa, has dwindled down to a mere nothing before the advance of its great English rival on the same coast. Diu and Damán have both shared in the same decay, although the former affords good anchorage, while Damán can still boast of its docks and its appliances for building ships. At Goa the Prince of Wales met with an interesting and impressive reception.

The Dutch.—The first appearance of the Dutch in Indian waters was ere long followed by the establishment of trading factories at Surat, Balasore, Chinsurah, and other places along the coast. In the early part of the seventeenth century the Hollanders seem to have entered into a sort of trade-alliance with their English cousins in the East; but after the collapse of their Portuguese rivals, the jealousies which sprang up between the two Teutonic nations bloomed forth at last in the massacre under judicial forms of twelve Englishmen at Amboyna, in 1623, and the closing of the Moluccas to English trade. A temporary revival of the old concert took place in 1627, when a fleet of Dutch and English ships sailed together from Surat to form a settlement in Bombay. That scheme, however, came to nought, and a bitter spirit of rivalry marked the subsequent career of the Dutch and English merchant-companies. During the war between England and Holland, which broke out in 1652, the Dutch wrought much damage to our trade in the East, especially at Surat. In 1656, three years after the peace, they retook Colombo from the Portuguese, and gained possession of Calicut. Again in 1673, towards the close of another war which left England supreme at sea, a strong Dutch fleet threatened Bombay, and afterwards sunk or captured several of our merchantmen off Masulipatam.

From that time, for many years to come, the Dutch and English in India held their several ways in peace and comparative friendliness, the power and interests of the former being centred rather in Java than in India itself, where the only troubles the English encountered arose from the aggressions of native princes in Bengal and Maharashtra, on the Malabar coast, on the opposite side of the Peninsula. At last, in 1759, the intrigues of Meer Jaffier, the new English-made Nowáb of Bengal, with the Dutch at Chinsurah, led to a sharp but short struggle between the latter and the countrymen of our gallant Clive, fresh from the victories which had avenged the disaster of the Black Hole. In requital for outrages done to English shipping in the Hooghly, Commodore Wilson, with his three men-of-war, attacked and captured twice their number of the Dutch ships. On the plain of Bidára, outside Chinsurah, a force of Dutchmen and Malays was heavily routed by about half as many Englishmen and Sepoys under Clive's best officer, the bold Colonel Forde, who had been told by Clive to "fight immediately," and the Order in Council should be sent him on the morrow. Thoroughly humbled by these defeats, the Dutch were glad enough to accept peace on Clive's own terms, and to resume the footing on which they had hitherto traded in Bengal.

In 1781, when Holland and England were again at war, Sir Hector Munro, the hero of the splendid victory of Buxar in 1764, attacked and captured the strong Dutch settlement of Negapatam at the mouth of the Cavery. This success was followed early in the next year by the capture of several Dutch settlements in Ceylon. Later wars resulted in fresh victories, and before the end of the 18th Century the Dutch had lost all their possessions in India and Ceylon. In 1811 their losses were crowned by the conquest of Java under Sir Samuel Achmuty; but after a few years of English rule that island was finally restored to its former masters in 1816. Chinsurah itself, which still remained in Dutch keeping, was made over to England, with Malacca and some other places in the Eastern seas, in exchange for our possessions in Sumatra.

The Danes.—Denmark also played its part among the pioneers of European trade with India. About 1619 the agents of a Danish company made their way from Ceylon to the coast of Tanjore, and with the countenance of its Rajah founded their first settlement at Tranquebar, whose old Danish fort, the Dansborg, still gleams white and picturesque as viewed from the sea. In the course of a century of peaceful trade broken by few quarrels with neighbours of either colour, the Danes had carried their settlements, few and far between, up the Bay of Bengal into the Hooghly. A few miles above Calcutta, on the opposite bank, they founded Serampore, "a handsome place"—wrote Heber in 1825—"kept beautifully clean, and looking more like a European town than Calcutta." Here, towards the end of the last century, Messrs. Carey, Marshman and Ward founded a Baptist Mission, whose work, though hindered for a time by the

English masters of Bengal, was destined to smooth the way for other labourers in the same field. Long before then, in the first years of the same century, Tranquebar itself became the seat of a Danish Protestant Mission, ere long to be rendered famous by the life and labours of its greatest leader, Christian Frederic Swartz, the Protestant Xavier. From 1750, for more than thirty years, did Swartz pursue his self-denying career among the natives of Southern India, winning reverence for his spotless worth, even from the fierce Hyder Ali. On one occasion, when the Madras Government sought to treat with the formidable ruler of Mysore, he refused to receive an envoy from their own service. "Let them send me the Christian" (meaning Swartz), "he will not deceive me." On his deathbed the Rajah of Tanjore begged the great missionary to undertake the guardianship of his son and heir. Nearly to the middle of this century the Danes contrived to keep their footing on Indian ground. But meanwhile, the British colour had been spreading over the map of India, and the Danish settlements had become more of a burden than a gain to the mother country. Thus it happened that in 1845 Serampore and Tranquebar were handed over to the East India Company in exchange for a goodly sum of ready money.

The French.—Last but not least conspicuous of the European candidates for a share of India's wealth, were the French, whose first settlements at Pondicherry on the Madras coast, and Chandernagore on the Hooghly, date only from the latter half of the seventeenth century. It was in 1664 that the first French "Company of the Indies" was started under the auspices of the great minister, Colbert. Four years later the first French factory was established at Surat. The Grand Monarque had declared "that it was not beneath the dignity of a gentleman to trade with India," and ere long the French had gained a footing at Masulipatam and St. Thomé, or Milapore, on the Madras coast. On their expulsion from the latter place by the Dutch in 1674, some of its defenders under the gallant Martin set forth to found a new settlement on the sea-coast, about 80 miles south of Madras, on a piece of ground obtained from Sher Khan Lodi, Governor of the Carnatic for the King of Beejapore. After a struggling infancy, imperilled by the movements of the famous Mahrátta, Sivajee, the new settlement of Pondicherry, as it came to be called, in 1679 became the freehold of the French Company, and Martin set to work at fortifying the future capital of French India. But the Dutch at that time were too strong for him, and in 1693 Pondicherry, after a stout resistance, passed into their hands.

Four years afterwards it was restored to its former owners under the Treaty of Ryswick. Martin resumed his old post, and with the aid of his countrymen soon made Pondicherry safe from ordinary risks of capture. The town itself grew into a handsome city, defended by a strong French garrison, and important as the chief seat of French power in India.

In the first half of the 18th century Mahé on the Malabar coast, and several other places were added to the French Company's rule.

Chandernagore prospered under the management of Dupleix, whose talents were soon to display themselves on a wider theatre. In 1741 he became Governor of Pondicherry. Five years later the capture of Madras by the high-souled but ill-starred Labourdonnais encouraged Dupleix to carry out a scheme of conquest, which at one time bade fair to place France, not England, at the head of all India. His trained Sepoys taught our own countrymen how to win victories against any number of ill-led native troops. The peace of Aix-la-Chapelle in 1748 involved the surrender of Madras to the English, but it set Dupleix free to make his power felt over all the neighbouring princes, to control the destinies of the Deccan under a ruler of his own choosing, and to win for his masters the virtual lordship of the Carnatic.

Dupleix was at this time a power in India. He dominated over the native princes, and, disdaining the feeble action of the English, cherished the idea of founding for his country a vast empire in the East, and for himself he had the wildest visions of future power and glory. He was gorgeously arrayed and held great state, in strange contrast to the simple attire and modest appointments of his English rivals. Princes were his vassals and the revenues of provinces flowed into his exchequer. He was a master in intrigue and without a rival in resource, and never faltered in his diplomatic resolves; but he required others to fight his battles. He was not a soldier, and disliked the noise and turmoil of war as unsuitable to his genius. He required tranquillity for the elaboration of his plans, and this course he defended in language worthy of Captain Bobadil. Dupleix was a great man nevertheless.

He reckoned however without that sturdy force of English rivalry which was soon to bear fruit in the victories of Clive and Lawrence, bettering the lessons they had learned from the French. His own recall in 1755 proved perhaps a yet deadlier blow to schemes which his weaker successors lacked the means or the energy to carry to successful issues. In 1757, the year of Plassey, Clive became master of Chandernagore. His best subaltern, Forde, drove the French, in Bussy's absence, out of the Northern Circars. In vain did the brave but hot-headed Lally attempt to stay the tide of England's fortunes by the capture of Fort St. David, and the siege of Madras. On the road to recover the former "lay the city of the victory of Dupleix, and the stately monument which was designed to commemorate the triumphs of France in the East. Clive ordered both the city and the monument to be razed to the ground. He was induced, we believe, to take this step, not by personal or national malevolence, but by a just and profound policy. The town and its pompous name, the pillar and its vaunting inscriptions, were among the devices by which Dupleix had laid the public mind of India under a spell. This spell it was Clive's business to break. The natives had been taught that France was confessedly the first power in Europe, and that the English did not presume to dispute her supremacy. No measure could be more effectual for the removing of this delusion than the public and solemn demolition of the French trophies."* Eyre Coote's crushing defeat of the French at Wandi-

* "Critical and Historical Essays," by Lord Macaulay, and "Life of Clive," by Sir John Malcolm.

wash was crowned by the capture of Bussy, the only Frenchman who had seemed to approach the genius of Dupleix. With the fall of Karical in 1760, nothing remained of Dupleix's empire save Pondicherry. In the following January Lally himself was starved into surrendering the stronghold which, with failing means and ever-darkening hopes, he had defended against a close siege of four months.

With the fall of Pondicherry the French power in India may be said to have passed away. On the peace of Paris in 1763 the French regained possession both of Pondicherry and Chandernagore. But never again could they make head against the growing power of their English rivals. In 1778, when the two nations were again at war, and Warren Hastings was Governor-General of India, both these places were recaptured by our troops, and the fortifications of Pondicherry once more destroyed. A few months later not an inch of ground in India remained to the French. Twice again, with returning peace, was Pondicherry restored to its first owners, only to fall again, after a brief interval, into our hands.

Meanwhile the old rivalry between French and English was maintained into the beginning of this century by a succession of French officers who placed their swords at the disposal, now of Hyder Ali and Tippoo Sahib, now of the Nizam of Scindia, or of any prince strong enough to strike a blow for the sovereignty of India. But it was all in vain. His French allies failed to avert the doom which overtook Tippoo under the gateway at Seringapatam; Raymond's Sepoy brigades were disarmed by Malcolm, and disbanded at Hyderabad.

Perron was glad to retire from Scindiah's service, "when every hereditary prince, from the Sutlej to the Nerbudda, acknowledged him as master, and he enjoyed an income equal to that of the present Viceroy and Commander-in-Chief of India combined ; at this climax of his fortune when he was actually believed to have sent an embassy to the First Consul of the French Republic." *

The famous Savoyard General De Boigne's trained battalions were nearly annihilated by Lake's Englishmen and Sepoys at Laswari.

After the peaçe of Paris in 1814, Pondicherry, Chandernagore, Mahé, Karical, and Yanaon on the Orissa coast, were finally restored to France. Of these places Pondicherry alone retains any of its old importance. The city and surrounding country cover an area of 107 square miles, peopled by about 140,000 souls, of whom less than half are contained within the town itself. Described by Lord Valentia in the beginning of this century as the handsomest town he had seen in India except Calcutta, Pondicherry with its well-built streets, shady boulevards, and white-stuccoed public buildings, still retains much of its former beauty ; and its lighthouse, 90 feet high, throws its friendly warning many miles out to sea. But the city has no harbour, and its declining trade now barely exceeds the value of £200,000 a year.

Chandernagore also has seen its best days, and the Hooghly, which once bore the largest vessels thither, now flows in shallow volume past its lonely quays and grass-grown streets. The Prince of Wales was received here with much simplicity and cordiality.

* The Fall of the Moghul Empire, by H. G. Keene.

The rivalry of the English and French for Empire in India has been very remarkable and the contrast of the treatment of the officers of the two countries at the hands of their governments on their return home, will be found not less so.

"The equitable and temperate proceedings of the British Parliament (respecting Lord Clive's conduct in India) were set off to the greatest advantage by a foil. The wretched government of Louis the Fifteenth, had murdered directly or indirectly, almost every Frenchman who had served his country with distinction in the East. Labourdonnais was flung into the Bastille, and after years of suffering left it only to die. Dupleix, stripped of his immense fortune, and broken-hearted by humiliating attendance in antechambers, sank into an obscure grave. Lally was dragged to the common place of execution with a gag between his lips. The Commons of England, on the other hand, treated their living captain with that discriminating justice which is seldom shown except to the dead."* When thus praising ourselves for the treatment of our public men, let us not forget Sir Walter Raleigh, Warren Hastings and Governor Eyre, lest we become too proud.

* Critical and Historical Essays by Lord Macaulay.

CHAPTER XXXII.

COMMERCE OF INDIA.

Cotton—Effects of Civil War in America—Cotton Manufacture revived in a new form in India.

Commerce.—From the very earliest times, India has been a great commercial country, and to trade with the Indies was the ambition of each European nation as it rose in the scale of civilization and power. To the Portuguese belong the credit of the first successful trade operations between Europe and India by sea, as has been already stated, and to their intrepid Navigator, Vasco da Gama, are we indebted for the discovery of the Cape of Good Hope route, by which for three centuries and a half the vast bulk of the traffic was conveyed.

Our own Commercial relations with this great country date from the year 1600, when Queen Elizabeth granted a charter to a number of London Merchants, and from this small commencement developed the powerful East India Company, which not only displaced the commerce of Portugal, Holland, and France, but became the political ruler of India until absorbed by Her Majesty's Government in 1858.

Since the days of the Company's Factories or trading establishments, the trade of India has undergone, not only gigantic growth, but many changes. The varied climate of India and her abundant population enable her to produce almost everything that is necessary or agreeable to man. As the Crimean war stopped the trade in Russian hemp, and developed the growth of cotton and jute, and the American war further enriched the cotton growers of India, so whilst under the peaceable and beneficent rule of Great Britain, India will always gain by the cessation of production in other parts of the globe, from war or any other calamity. India is eminently an agricultural country, two-thirds of her dense population live by the cultivation of the soil, and the land tax still yields the chief part of the revenue.

To develope the resources of a country is to utilize its soil and climate for the growth of the products most suited to them, and to provide easy transit for the exchange of commodities from one district to another. This simple truism, too often neglected, is becoming more apparent to the Government of India and to the people, and to this we are indebted to a great extent for the large annual outlay upon roads, railways, and canals.

The industry of the Indian Cultivator is ably seconded by the Merchant, and trade both Home and Foreign is steadily growing, but large as its proportions now are, it may be regarded only as yet in its infancy.

The Home trade consists of the exchange of products from one province to another; for instance, since the extended growth of cotton in Western India, and of coffee in Ceylon and the Malabar Coast districts, grain and sugar have had to be imported from Bengal in large quantities to supply the wants of these districts. Under the head of

Home trade may also be included the barter or exchange of commodities with the countries bordering upon India, though it is known to be very extensive, no reliable statistics exist by which its value can be gauged. The Home coasting trade is estimated at 25 millions sterling per annum, 15,000 vessels and native craft of all kinds are employed upon it. The value of the Foreign trade is more readily arrived at by the Custom House returns, and the following figures from the Government Blue Book show the progress that has been made.

FOREIGN TRADE OF INDIA, INCLUSIVE OF THE PRECIOUS METALS AT 2s. PER RUPEE.

Yearly average during each half decade for forty years, ending 31st March, 1875, with the average yearly excess of Imports over Exports, or Exports over Imports for each period.

Average of Five Years.	Import. £	Export. £	Total. £	Excess of Import over Export. £	Excess of Export over Import. £
1836-1840	7,640,428	11,951,620	19,592,048		4,311,192
1841-1845	11,799,600	15,525,320	27,324,920		3,725,720
1846-1850	12,047,407	17,112,846	29,160,253		5,065,439
1851-1855	16,066,186	20,399,270	36,465,456		4,333,084
1856-1860	32,022,778	27,586,461	59,609,239	4,436,317	
1861-1865	42,841,401	51,285,802	94,127,263		8,444,401
1866-1870	48,788,346	54,473,089	103,261,435		5,684,743
1871-1875	39,511,389	58,696,784	98,208,173		18,185,395

* Trade of Bombay.—The trade returns of British India for the twelve months from 1st April, 1876, to 31st March, 1877, show that the imports of merchandise amounted to Rs. 37,26,13,219, and of treasure to Rs. 11,43,61,197; total, Rs. 48,69,74,416. The exports of merchandise were valued at Rs. 61,07,65,941, and of treasure to Rs. 4,02,98,978; total, Rs. 65,10,64,919. The share of Bombay, exclusive of Scinde, in this trade, was as follows:—

	Imports.
Merchandise	Rs. 12,74,72,244
Treasure	8,29,61.582
Total	Rs. 71,04,34,826

During these forty years the above figures show that there has been an excess of exports over imports amounting to £226,500,000, or at the rate of £5,650,000 per annum. During the last fifteen years, commencing three years after the Mutiny, the excess export has averaged £10,777,000 per annum.

The import of gold and silver during the four decades included above, amounted to £342,360,546, whilst the export only reached £43,192,463 during the same time; showing the enormous absorption of £300,000,000 in round numbers, or at the rate of £7,500,000 worth of these durable and universally valuable commodities per annum.

England of course occupies the place of first importance in the trade with India; China is next in rank, but all civilized countries to a greater or less extent are steady and increasing consumers of her products.

The principal exports are cotton, opium, rice, grain, jute, tea, coffee, timber, indigo, saltpetre, tobacco, seeds, shellac, gums, oils, wool, cocoa-nut, and cocoa-nut fibre,

---

	Exports.
Foreign Goods	Rs. 1,79,15,882
Indian Produce and Manufactures ...	20,62,48,065
Treasure	3,29,06,758
Total ... ... ∴	Rs. 25,70,70,705

That is to say, the trade of Bombay amounted to more than 40 per cent. of the whole trade of India. The figures of the trade of Scinde stand thus:—Imports of merchandise, Rs. 32,04,621: treasure, Rs. 28,610; total, Rs. 32,33,231. Exports of merchandise, Rs. 1,64,60,787; treasure, Rs. 1,87,950; total, Rs. 1,66,48,737. The whole volume of Indian trade was larger last year than in any previous year since the American War. The value of the wheat exported rose from Rs. 90,10,255 in 1875—76 to Rs. 1,95,63,325 in 1876—77.

shawls, and other valuable fabrics. In exchange India imports cotton and woollen goods, and other manufactured goods of all kinds, machinery, clothing, stationery, railway materials, wines and spirits, besides metals, salt, coals, and other raw products, and many other articles.

Cotton.—Of the above articles of export cotton is first in value and from time immemorial has been one of India's staple products. The beautiful gossamers, the woven air muslins of Dacca and the calicoes of Southern India, soft in texture and tasteful in design, enjoyed a world-wide renown when the textile productions of Europe were rude and undeveloped.

In the earlier years of trade with India it was these fine manufactured goods which were sent to Europe, and not the raw material, and the hand loom weavers in every Indian village supplied serviceable cloths for the wants of their neighbours and had to spare for other countries. The invention of steam machinery coupled with the cheapening of freight which followed the extensive growth of our mercantile marine brought about a gradual change. England in turn became the manufacturer of cotton goods for consumption in India, receiving back the raw material; and extensive cotton fields grew up in all parts of India, the chief seat of production being in the western provinces for which Bombay is the outlet. The civil war in America in 1861 gave a new and powerful impulse to the growth of Indian cotton, and in a few years it rose in value from 6 to 37½ millions sterling. The producing districts for a moment became rich beyond the dream of avarice, and the formerly poor Ryots became men of substance, independent of loans from the usurious money lenders, and able to deck out their wives and daughters in costly ornaments of gold and silver. With the close of the civil war this flush of prosperity began to wane, American cotton gradually assumed its old ascendancy in the English markets, and the value of raw cotton exported from India consequently fell in 1872 to about 14 millions sterling.

Another change is now taking place. India is again resuming the manufacture of cotton goods, and in the neighbourhood of Bombay and Calcutta many spinning mills supplied with the best machinery of the day have been erected. It is found that the supple fingers, quick intelligence and patient habits of the natives of India make them the best of mill hands, and bearing in mind the cheapness of their labour as compared with that of Europeans, and the fact that the raw material is at hand and that there is a ready sale for the goods when made, it is evident this comparatively new industry, or more properly speaking, old industry revived in a new form, must rapidly grow, and it is well that we should be prepared for its competing with our home manufactures, not only in the Indian markets but elsewhere.

CHAPTER XXXIII.

COMMERCE OF INDIA—*continued.*

Rice—Jute—Cereals—Seeds—Tea—Sugar—Opium—Coffee—Indigo—Saltpetre—Timber—Tobacco—Agriculture—Primitive method of Natives—European Planters.

Rice.—Next to cotton, rice ranks in quantity though not in value as an export, and few trades have grown with the extraordinary rapidity of the Indian rice trade. From Calcutta and the ports on the Madras coast rice is extensively shipped to Bombay and the ports on the West coast of India, to Muscat, the Persian Gulf, the Red Sea ports, Mauritius and Australia. It is from British Burmah, however, that the rice trade has developed in the most remarkable degree. Little more than twenty years have elapsed since the first cargo of rice was exported from a Burmese port, and now the exports thence exceed half a million of tons annually to all parts of the globe. This very cheap and nutritious article of food is growing in favour, particularly on the continent of Europe, and it is to be regretted that the people of England do not sufficiently appreciate it.

Jute.—How little is known to the public at large of this most useful article of commerce! To many well-informed persons the name even is unknown, and yet what a conspicuous place it occupies in the manufactures of the United Kingdom and India! The jute or Indian hemp trade received its first important start in 1854, during the war with Russia, but the Civil War in the United States gave the strongest impetus to it. Before the year 1853 the export of jute from Calcutta was only about 20,000 bales; in 1863, the exports were 800,000 bales, and in 1872 the shipments of jute and jute cuttings actually exceeded 2,000,000 bales. Of this quantity the United Kingdom took about a million and a-half bales, America 450,000, and the Continent the remainder. But in addition to the large quantities of raw material thus exported, there is a considerable local consumption of jute cloth and extensive export of manufactured articles; in the year 1872, above referred to, there were 106,000 pieces of gunny cloth and 28,500,000 gunny bags exported from Calcutta. Jute is used for sacking, sail-cloth, carpet manufacture, paper making and many other purposes. This one article of commerce has built up the prosperity of the town of Dundee, and the trade between Calcutta and that port employs a splendid fleet of iron sailing ships, of which the nation may be proud. The quantity of jute imported into the United Kingdom now exceeds 200,000 tons per annum. Some excellent jute mills have recently been erected in the neighbourhood of Calcutta, but the manufacture is at present chiefly confined to sacking and gunny bags which are exported to China, Australia and all parts of the globe.

Efforts are being made to establish the manufacture of the finer descriptions of cloth, and with reasonable prospects of success.

Cereals.—Hitherto India has not been a large grain-exporting country; wheat, maize, barley and pulse have been chiefly grown for home consumption, and the exports have been comparatively limited owing to grain deteriorating during the long sea voyage round the Cape to Europe; but the opening of the Suez Canal and the construction of railways and roads in India having accelerated the transport to Europe, wheat has been shipped in annually increasing quantities from Calcutta, Bombay and Kurrachee to London and Liverpool. Last year 5 per cent. of the British imports of wheat came from India, and there can be little doubt the trade will grow rapidly. The valleys of the Nerbudda, Upper Ganges, Indus and other large rivers in India are capable of producing an almost unlimited supply of wheat, and demand will speedily ensure it. The average annual importation of wheat into England at the present time is about 12,500,000 quarters, and with our rapidly-increasing population and decrease of arable land, the deficiency of home-grown breadstuffs must increase. The knowledge of this fact has long occasioned more or less anxiety. It has been stated that the great wheat-producing countries have only to combine to withhold their supplies to starve us into submission. It is improbable that such a state of things could be brought about, but admitting the possibility, why should not India in this respect largely provide for our requirements? The exportation of wheat would enrich her, by forcing a larger importation of the precious metals which would tend to diminish the losses in exchange with Europe, which have of late been sustained by merchants who have had to remit money from the East, and by servants of the Crown whose incomes are derived from India.

Lord Lawrence, in his report on the Punjaub when Lieutenant-Governor, states, that 500,000 tons of wheat might be exported annually from that province alone,* without interfering with the wants of the people, and the *Times* recently drew attention to the following remarkable growth of the Calcutta wheat trade:—In 1870 the quantity of wheat exported from Calcutta was 2,000 tons, in 1873 it was 10,000, and in the first eight months of the last year (1876) no less than 120,000 tons were shipped to England, which came chiefly from the Punjaub, and it only requires the completion of the Indus Valley Railway to export wheat in greater abundance at a cheaper rate, from this province. The quality of Indian wheat is much liked by millers because of its extreme dryness.†

* *Vide* "The Indus and its Provinces," by the Author.

† "Since the report was published advices had also reached them from India that arrangements had been made with Scinde, Punjab and Delhi Railway Company, by which purchasers of grain in the Punjab would be able to send it down to Calcutta from Umritsur—a distance of about 1,245 miles—at the remarkably low cost of about 12s. 9d. per qr.—Speech of Mr. R. W. Crawford, Chairman East Indian Railway, *Jan.* 4, 1877.

The *Dundee Advertiser*, under date 8th February, 1877, states:—"the following figures show the extraordinary rapidity with which the shipments of wheat from Calcutta to Great Britain have extended. It will be seen that while the clearances were only 500 tons in 1870 and 14,370 in 1874, they sprang up to 49,930 tons in 1875 and 141,715 last year. The shipments through the Suez Canal were equal to the freight of forty steamers of 2,000 tons. The total quantity of wheat shipped from Calcutta in 1876 was equal to the entire crop grown in Scotland. The following are the figures:—

Seeds.—Collectively seeds form a huge item in the commerce of India—linseed, rape, gingelly, castor and other oleaginous seeds are largely shipped from India to Europe. In utilizing these seeds, the oil is first extracted and the refuse (in the form of oil cake) is then used for cattle feeding and artificial manures. A large quantity of rape and linseed goes forward to the south of France and to Italy, where the oil by careful refining is used for adulterating olive oil, and for preserving fish, &c. The use of oil cake in England for cattle feeding is extending. The production of meat for the increasing necessities of our large population cannot be overtaken by grazing or feeding upon farm produce, consequently

CLEARANCES OF WHEAT TO GREAT BRITAIN DURING 1876.

	London.		Liverpool.		Hull.	Dundee.	Falmouth.	
	Canal. Tons.	Cape. Tons.	Canal. Tons.	Cape. Tons.	Canal. Tons.	Cape. Tons.	Cape. Tons.	Total. Tons.
Jan.	2,735	16	...	100	...	100	...	2,951
Feb.	3,330	...	...	...	...	...	...	3,330
March	4,270	...	...	...	...	100	...	4,370
April	5,250	100	200	...	...	...	...	5,550
May	9,060	7,052	200	1,185	...	...	...	17,497
June	12,352	3,870	...	600	1,700	...	...	18,522
July	10,240	7,515	500	1,600	...	...	...	19,855
Aug.	6,752	1,700	...	1,350	...	...	...	9,802
Sept.	7,376	4,150	...	1,500	...	...	...	13,026
Oct.	10,325	3,400	2,300	...	2,210	...	325	18.560
Nov.	7,550	2,425	400	1,125	2,650	...	...	14,150
Dec.	2,557	9,195	50	600	...	...	1,700	14,102
Total	81,797	39,423	3,650	8,060	6,560	200	2,025	141,715

Clearances during	1870	500 tons.
„ „	1871	12,315 „
„ „	1872	2,195 „
„ „	1873	11,445 „
„ „	1874	14,370 „
„ „	1875	49,930 „
„ „	1876	141,715 „
„ Jan. to Oct.,	1877	236,633 „

farmers have to seek elsewhere for food for their stock, and oil cake has proved so far to be the best procurable, and when fed upon it cattle and sheep fatten quickly and give back valuable ingredients for enriching the soil. A trade once established with England in any article of food, whether for man or beast, must of necessity increase, and the products and uses of the Indian seeds are so varied and necessary to the wants of civilized society, that we may fairly assume that the trade in them will steadily continue to increase.

Tea.—In connection with the introduction and growth of the various commodities which India produces, the progress of tea cultivation is perhaps of all the most interesting to record. As recently as the year 1832 Lord William Bentinck, Governor-General of India, proposed active measures to introduce this most useful plant into India. Previous to this the cultivation had been recommended by several persons, by some who possessed scientific knowledge because they believed the climate and soil of the hill districts were suitable to it, and that the culture would be a profitable one, and by others because they felt that the world at large ought not to be solely dependent upon China for this highly-valued product. The Chinese being then as now strangely exclusive, few facilities and many obstacles were put in the way of foreign trade by their government, and for this reason it was considered to be of national importance to England that some better field should be provided for the supply of tea. Hence the Directors of the East India Company sanctioned a liberal expenditure upon experiments. Seeds and plants were imported from

China, as well as persons accustomed to the cultivation; but, as in all such attempts, there were many difficulties at first to contend with and many failures. In 1834 it was discovered that the tea plant, somewhat different to the China plant, but nevertheless the tea plant, was growing wild in Assam, and some of the leaves having been manufactured into tea, which was highly approved of by the London tea brokers, hopes were entertained that it might be produced in sufficient quantities to become a staple article of commerce. Experiments continued to be made by Government with the indigenous plants, and with seeds and plants imported from China, nurseries being established in Assam, the Himalayas, Neilgerries and elsewhere with more or less success. In 1839 the first Joint Stock Tea Company was formed in London, "The Assam Company," with a capital of one million sterling, and the fortunes and reverses of this Company furnish an excellent illustration of the fluctuations experienced in tea culture in India. At one time their £20 shares were sold for less than 2s. each. Tea cultivation at that time was at its lowest ebb; Government had abandoned the work to private speculators, and owing to mismanagement all hope of successfully producing tea in India was well nigh abandoned. The shares thus sold at 2s. are now worth £64, and the Assam Tea Company, once so near ruin, is at present a most prosperous undertaking. Tea agriculture and manufacture may now be deemed to be well-established industries of India. At the present time there are numerous joint-stock tea undertakings, and still more gardens in private hands, and the importation into

England in 1875 amounted to no less than 25 million lbs., equal in value to £2,200,000: but this does not represent the whole; for India with her large population is herself a consumer of the leaf. Year by year the growth is extending, more care and experience are introduced into the cultivation and manufacture, and the problems which exercised the minds of the far-seeing Governor-General and others forty years ago are now happily solved. It is estimated there are 160,000 acres of land now under tea cultivation, which within a few years should yield 50,000,000 pounds weight per annum.*

* Tea of China and of India.—Sir W. H. Medhurst, in his last Consular Report from Shanghai, recently laid before Parliament, states that the tea trade of that port showed again in 1875 a marked decline. The competition of India increases. Fifteen years ago the growth of tea in India was regarded as an experiment, but the export from Calcutta reached 25,000,000 lb. in 1875, and now it may almost be thought that unless there be some change in the mode of cultivation or packing, it is only a question of time when China will be ousted from the field. The total export of tea from China was 212,000,000 lb. in the season 1875-76, or four millions less than in the preceding season. The increase in the demand for tea in Great Britain has heretofore benefited both China and India, but the returns for 1875 indicate that the whole increase then went to the credit of India. The cause of the poor quality of Chinese tea of late years seems to lie in hasty preparation, with a view to bring teas early to market, and in the unsystematic way in which the different processes necessary to convert the raw leaf into the tea of commerce are carried on. Small proprietors, farmers, to whom the cultivation of tea is mostly a secondary object, growing from 50 lb. to 500 lb., carry it off on their backs to a neighbouring market, and even to a second, perhaps, the unfired leaf spoiling fast by exposure to the air and the long interval between the picking and the firing. The packers are speculators, who hire a house in the district temporarily, and collect the leaf in little lots from the growers. Thus, the leaf from different districts is mixed, and pure, one-flavoured tea is scarce. The packing also is defective; if wood is scarce, it is planed so thin that a cwt. chest is little better than a band-box, and the outside package splits and the inside bed gets rent and torn. Sir

Sugar—At one time this was a commodity very largely exported, as much as 350,000 tons having been shipped annually, but now, although the quantity produced is greater than ever, India imports more than she exports. This fact is worthy of notice, as indicating the increased wealth and prosperity of the people.

Opium.—Much has been said and written respecting the growth of this drug, and the immorality of the Government of India in directly encouraging and supervising a trade in many respects so injurious. It is not

W. H. Medhurst says that we must look to India for the perfection of tea culture; there planting, picking and firing are all in one hand, and the needful capital outlay to produce a good result is not spared. In China the process is in the primitive and unscientific style dear to the natives of that country. He considers that nothing but the introduction of European capital and enterprise into the tea districts can save the foreign tea trade of China from decay. Had foreigners free access to the country, not only would the leaf be systematically packed, and not left at times to grow old on the shrubs and at times to spoil after picking, while the owner is haggling for the last cent., but many a barren hillside would be cleared of its jungle, and employment given to thousands of half-starved peasants. Isolated attempts made by foreigners to perfect the system of packing tea by personal supervision in the interior have been generally unsuccessful, except in the case of brick tea made in some of the black tea districts, under the eye of Russians from Siberia, who show more readiness in adapting themselves to Chinese ways, and whose Government gives them every protection. Were permission given to foreigners to hold land in the interior, a few well-ordered plantations would in time reform the Chinese methods by example. In regard to green tea China is being ousted from the American markets by Japan, where no labour is spared in the firing and packing, and the petty economies are not attempted which a Chinaman will employ at any cost. His inland taxation also is heavy. In India the trade is free, and in Japan burdened only with a nominal tax. The Chinaman is not keeping his place in the race. Our Custom House returns for 1876 show 155,897,192 lb. of tea imported into the United Kingdom from China, but that is 5,000,000 lb. less than in the preceding year; the import from British India, 28,126,854 lb., shows an increase amounting to 2,342,000 lb.—*Times*, May 21, 1877.

our intention here to enter upon the merits or demerits of this vexed question, it is sufficient for our purpose to note the fact of its existence and to state that if the revenue of upwards of six millions sterling which the opium monopoly yields to the Government were given up, other taxes would have to be levied, to make good the deficiency. The effect of this tax is to make opium so much more costly, and consequently to diminish the consumption, and it is hard to see any reasonable grounds for abandoning so valuable a source of income and shifting a burden from the shoulders of the Chinese, who buy this baneful drug, to the backs of our poor Indian subjects. In the provinces of Behar and Benares Government supervises the growth of the poppy and manufacture of the opium, binding the ryots to sow yearly the needful amount of land, and receiving the entire produce at certain fixed prices. The opium is gathered in the early spring, manufactured and stored in the summer at Patna and Ghazepore, and sold by public auction in the following year at Calcutta to merchants who ship it to China. In Malwa, on the other hand, the opium is produced by the subjects of native princes and forwarded to Bombay for shipment where it pays a heavy export duty. The general adoption of this latter system is advocated by many who would wish to see the Government of India freed from all immediate connection with the opium trade, and we must confess our preference for it; but the Bengal system has prevailed so long that Indian financiers hesitate to interfere, lest the revenue should be adversely affected.

Coffee.—Like tea the growth of Indian coffee is comparatively recent, and the progress has been very satisfactory. The value of the exports has increased from £75,000 in 1849 to £1,250,000 in 1874; and upwards of 100,000 acres are now planted with coffee in Coorg and the Wynaad alone, besides large tracts in Travancore.

The cultivation of tea, coffee and indigo in India has been taken up by some of our retired officers, and provides occupation for a great many young men, who go out from England to superintend the plantations and manufacture.* On some of the plantations a few of the more enterprising agriculturists produce other valuable plants such as India rubber, Tobacco, Chincona, &c., which are sent forward to Calcutta, Bombay and Madras for shipment to Europe.

Indigo—Is chiefly cultivated in Behar and the N.W. Provinces and is exported to all parts of the world. The trade in this beautiful dye has grown in the last ten years from two to three and a-half millions sterling.

Saltpetre.—The soil of Upper India teems with "villanous saltpetre," which modern nations find so indispensable, either for peace or war. This article, which the Indian husbandman would so gladly miss from his fields, is collected and exported to Europe, America and China to the value of about half a million sterling per annum.

Timber.—The forests of British Burmah yield rich stores of teak, that most valuable timber, which is now extensively used in this country. Nearly as hard and durable as oak, it is easier to work and it can be polished

* In the beautiful valley of Kangra in the Himalayas there are more than thirty Europeans solely engaged in tea planting.

as highly as mahogany; in ship building and railway carriages it is especially serviceable, and for beauty and solidity combined no wood surpasses it. The teak ships built in Bombay, Cochin and Singapore were found after fifty years of hard work to be as tough and seaworthy as when new; and but for the changes that have taken place in naval architecture, whereby a modern iron ship is capable of carrying a much heavier cargo than the old-fashioned vessels the pride of our youth, these good old craft would still be ploughing the waters.

Other woods, such as the Himalaya pines and deodars serve many purposes of use and ornament. The Sâl forests of the Himalayas provide sleepers for our railways. The light and feathery bamboo growing everywhere in India must not be overlooked. This invaluable wood, always available, is put to every conceivable purpose; it provides the supports for the rude huts in the jungle; tipped with iron it may be used for an instrument of war or implement of husbandry; sawn off above a knot it makes a drinking cup; it is used for making pens, and for musical instruments; it forms the arms for the palanquins to carry the living, or the bier to bear the dead to the funeral pile. In Japan young bamboo stewed or preserved is esteemed a great luxury. In China and Persia old bamboo is in more frequent request, but the application is external and of a less agreeable character; it is usually applied to the back or to the soles of the feet. The fibre is worked up into mats and baskets and boats' sails. The Sissa or black wood of Bombay, the sandal wood of Southern India and ebony of the West are known to us all in the exquisite carved pieces of furniture, inlaid boxes and ornaments which so admirably exhibit the artistic taste of the workman and the beauty of the material.

Within the last sixteen years the Government of India has very properly undertaken the conservancy of the forests; on the one hand the department has to take care that timber is felled and disposed of upon prudent and safe principles, and that there is no needless waste of the valuable tracts of forest at the disposal of Government; on the other hand the cultivation of the more valuable timber needed for the construction of public works, railway sleepers and for commerce has to be attended to. The young men selected in England for this work have to undergo a special education, and are sent to Germany and other countries to study other forest conservancy systems before taking up their duties in India. The practical value of this good service cannot be over-estimated when we bear in mind not only the value of the timber but the disasters that have overtaken Eastern countries, where fertile districts have been rendered barren deserts by the reckless destruction of the forests. Through the influence of cultivation rains are now periodical in parts of Scinde where they were formerly as rare as at Aden, that barren rock garrisoned by our Indian troops. By clothing the bare hill sides with wood, and by judicious planting, not only may rains be rendered more regular and genial, thus lessening the chances of frequent drought and famine, so fearfully destructive to human and animal life in India, but something may be done to limit, if not prevent those terrible floods, which carry everything before them whilst they last; climates also may be changed and unhealthy districts rendered more salubrious. Before leaving this subject we must mention the valuable service rendered to India by the introduction of the Chincona and ipecacuanha plants. The important medicinal properties of quinine produced from the Chincona bark are well known to all, but the boon to India is especially great; with the aid of this powerful restorative travellers ward off attacks of jungle and malarious fever; and many have shewn, like the great African traveller Livingstone, how with its aid they have been able to prosecute their journeys and their work, when without it they must have succumbed to disease. Ipecacuanha is now accepted as the most efficacious remedy in the treatment of dysentery, the malady of all others most destructive to European life in India. Chincona was introduced into India in the year 1860, and Mr. Clement Markham, C.B., the courteous and well-known Secretary of the Geographical Society superintended the transport of the plants from South America to the Neilgerries, where by care they have been successfully grown; and the Indian cultivation is so far secured, that there is no longer any anxiety as to the supply of this invaluable bark. The ipecacuanha root more recently introduced, has been planted on the outer slopes of the Sikhim Himalaya, and there is every reason to hope for equal success with it.

Tobacco—Is widely cultivated for home use in many parts of India, but as yet the quantity imported into Europe has been very limited, owing to defects which are still to be remedied in the process of preparing the leaf.

Agriculture.—As before stated India is essentially an

agricultural country, and the mass of the population support themselves by husbandry, but in the tillage of the soil the ryots, or peasantry, follow the rude and inefficient methods of their forefathers, merely scratching the surface of the ground by means of a bullock-plough of the most feeble and primitive construction, using little manure or other means to aid the dormant resources of the soil, and in the absence of irrigation, trusting the coming harvest solely to the sun and rain of heaven. The ryots' mode of rearing live stock is equally antiquated.

General and scientific farming, as practised in Europe, America and Australia has never been really tried in India.

The European planters of India, unlike the native ryots, are an enterprising and prosperous class, and the increasing demands for the products before enumerated when treating of the commerce of India, necessitate the use of machinery and ever-improving modes of cultivation. Native farmers, like their brethren elsewhere, are slow to adopt changes, and do not readily take either to improved implements or a more scientific mode of working. Animal food is so little consumed by the natives of India, that the profits of raising agricultural stock are not sufficiently high to encourage expenditure in the direction of rearing improved breeds of sheep and cattle. Efforts to improve the quality of cattle and horses and to introduce foreign seeds and plants have from time to time emanated from the Government, and experimental farms have been worked in the Presidencies of Bengal, Madras and Bombay which have been of service in the selected localities and have helped to furnish statistics; but the experiments have involved considerable outlay and have led to little practical result generally. Recently agricultural exhibitions have been organized with some success in various parts of India, and the competition created for the prizes appears to be producing a beneficial effect. It is very interesting to note in the last report of the "Material Progress of India," that in British Burmah the ploughs in use numbered 383,976. Steam machinery is little used and probably not needed, because not only is manual labour abundant and cheap, but the regularity of the seasons relieves the farmer from the anxiety and haste which attend the harvesting of crops in our more uncertain climate.

In agricultural operations in India irrigation forms one of the most necessary and costly items of expenditure, and in every province the peasants patiently draw from wells and streams the life-sustaining water which under the powerful rays of the tropical sun produces rapid vegetation.

The sad effects of drought have more than once lately been painfully illustrated. The native rulers have an adage that "to attempt to relieve a famine is to water the branches when the roots are dead;" thanks however to roads, railways and steamers, it has been proved that relief can be given. Still, such calamities as the Orissa and Bengal famines and that subsequently prevailing in Madras and Bombay are terrible to contemplate, and to prevent rather than to cure them, the rigorous prosecution of irrigation works should always be kept prominently in view with improved means of communication.

CHAPTER XXXIV.

INTERNAL COMMUNICATIONS.

Roads—Railways—Telegraphs.

Communications.—Under this head a volume might be written. The communications, external and internal, comprise lines of ships and steamers, telegraphs, railways, roads, canals, &c., &c., representing many millions of money and employing thousands of persons. Like the Romans of old, the British may now fairly be said to make road-making the first of their duties, and throughout the provinces of India this necessary work is diligently prosecuted. In the neighbourhood of large towns the responsibility of providing good roads devolves upon the municipalities, &c., in the provinces the means are provided by the presidency funds apportioned to such local works. For information concerning the postal and telegraphic services and railways the reader interested in such matters should peruse the Government reports, which furnish precise and valuable details, and alone can properly explain the gigantic character of the work which is embraced under these three heads. The postage of a letter from and to any place in India is half an anna, equal to three farthings, and except England no country in the world possesses a more efficient postal service.

Telegraphs.—In telegraphy India is little if anything behind Europe. From Europe to India there exist the deep sea cable through the Red Sea, and two distinct land communications through Turkey, Russia and Persia; these are connected with a sub-marine cable by the Persian Gulf to Kurrachee. It also possesses telegraphic communication with China and Australia, and an efficient internal service is maintained with the principal military and commercial centres. Had these complete services been in existence in 1857, on the outbreak of the mutiny, many valuable lives might have been spared, and it is apparent that our tenure of India is greatly strengthened by the facilities now existing. The wide extent of territory spanned by the wires necessarily renders the services costly to organise and maintain, and not only is the material liable to damage by storms, floods and robbery, but the distance from observation gives facilities for dishonest tampering. A curious instance of this occurred some time ago; some telegraph clerks, at the instigation of a wealthy native, dealing largely in opium, proceeded to a solitary spot, where they cut the wires, read off all the messages, and transmitted them to Bombay with such alterations as enabled their employer to reap the unfair advantage which he sought.

Railways.—In railway communication a good commencement has been made, but much remains still to be done in this respect. At present there are five or six great trunk lines intersecting the country: the East India Railway extending from Calcutta for 1,000 miles along the valley of the Ganges and Jumna to Delhi, to meet the Indus Valley line from Kurrachee, and thus to form the great steam arch connecting the Bay of Bengal with the Arabian Sea, and which at Allahabad throws out a branch to Jubbulpore to meet the Great Indian Peninsular Railway, placing Calcutta and Bombay in immediate connection; the Bombay and Baroda Railway running from Bombay almost in a direct northerly line to Surat, Baroda and Ahmedabad, and tapping the cotton districts; the Scinde, Punjaub and Delhi Railway commencing from Kurrachee and proceeding *viâ* Lahore to Delhi, which with its proposed branches to the Bolan and Kyber, will be the great political line of India, by providing the means of transport of troops and material for the defence of the frontier, and enable us to meet Russia in the markets of Central Asia on more than equal terms, and which at the same time will open up the great grain-producing districts of the Punjaub; the Oude and Rohilkund; the Southern of India; the Madras and minor lines;—altogether in 1877 there were 8,142 miles open, of which 1,729 miles are of the metre 3ft. 3⅜in. gauge, the remainder being on the normal gauge of 5ft. 6in.

That there should be two gauges in India is much to be regretted, as a branch might speedily become a trunk line. The principal portions of these lines have been constructed and are being worked by Companies and Boards of Directors under Government supervision. A few have been made by Government officers, and the question of the future regarding Indian railways is, whether they should pass wholly into the possession of the

State and be worked from one central point, or whether the several Companies should maintain their distinctive commercial character and be managed as at present. Those in favour of the former system, with some show of reason, maintain that as the Government guaranteed interest is what the shareholders chiefly look to for the return on their capital, there can be no objection to the lines being entirely under the control of the State. But, on the other hand, it is clear that our English railways could never have arrived at their present efficient and profitable condition, nor could they meet the ever-varying wants of the public were it not for the character of the management and its freedom from the hard and fast regulations of the public services. The capital of the railway companies of the United Kingdom in 1876 reached the sum of 658 millions, and the yield of the gross revenue from this immense investment was 62 millions, the net revenue being 29 millions. These figures will give some idea of the cost of providing railways for our great Indian dependency, and it is not too much to say that no single department of Government can possibly do justice to these gigantic works, and that the best that can be done is to continue and perhaps strengthen the present system of supervision.

Further, the progress of this necessary and national work ought not to be left to the mere question of a surplus or deficiency in the Budget. In India we possess a magnificent estate needing capital for its development, and we have a tolerably sure guarantee that money advanced will be honestly expended; but instead of advancing money for railways, canals, roads, &c., in

India, for bringing produce from the interior to the coast, we lend millions to foreign countries to be squandered, or perhaps to be spent in arms and war vessels to be used against ourselves. One word more before leaving the question of railways. It is proposed in some places to make lines parallel with the coast. In the present condition of the country it appears questionable policy to use state funds for the construction of lines of railway, which would compete with and tend to cripple the sea traffic now maintained by private enterprise. It would be much better to encourage the development of that traffic by improving the existing harbours and constructing new ones where they may be most required, at a reasonable outlay, and confining the extension of railways and roads to lines into the interior for the free exchange of commodities.

All must concur in the opinion recently expressed by Lord Salisbury, and that is, "that the best and surest means of developing the resources of a colony is to improve the means of communication."

It is expected that in 1879 the net revenue of the guaranteed railways will be equal to the amount of the interest guaranteed by the State.

CHAPTER XXXV.

EXTERNAL COMMUNICATIONS.

Ancient Routes of Commerce—Shipping—The Suez Canal—The Euphrates Railway—Harbours.

FEW facts bear more conclusive testimony to the sagacity of the ancients, when the limited amount of their geographical knowledge is remembered, than the tenacity with which commerce adhered to the direction given to it by them, and the readiness with which it returns to any of those channels when temporarily diverted by political events or geographical discoveries. The overland route from Europe to India, by the Isthmus of Suez and the Red Sea, is certainly as old as the days of the early Phœnician navigators. The navigability of the Euphrates was tested long before Trajan ever sailed on its waters, and was revisited by the Italians in the eleventh century, and our own merchants in the days of Elizabeth as the best way to the East;* whilst the value of the

* "Various causes concurred in restoring liberty and independence to the cities of Italy. The acquisition of these roused industry and gave motion and vigour to all the active powers of the human mind. Foreign commerce revived, navigation was attended to and improved. Constantinople became the chief mart to which the Italians resorted. There they not only met with favourable reception, but obtained such mercantile privileges as enabled them to carry on trade with great advantages. They were supplied both with the precious commodities of the East, and with many curious manufactures, the product of ancient arts and ingenuity still

Indus, as the shortest and easiest route for the commerce of India, not only with Central Asia and the north of Europe, but with the whole of the West, was fully recognised by the later Romans in the seventh century. Necessity, in their case, was the mother of invention. When the rapid progress of the Mohamedan arms had wrested Egypt from the Byzantine power, and thus closed the overland route of Suez to the Greek merchants, they forthwith turned to other means and sought out a new channel, by which the productions of the East might be transmitted to the great emporium of the West. The route thus discovered was that by the Indus. The rich and easily-stowed products of India were carried up the great river as far as it was navigable; thence transported to the Oxus, down which stream they proceeded as far as the Caspian Sea. There they entered the Volga, and sailing up it, were carried by land to the Tanais (the Don), which conducted them into the Euxine Sea, where ships from Constantinople waited their arrival. The discovery of the long, but easy route, by the Cape of Good Hope, combined with the deadly feuds between the

subsisting among the Greeks. As the labour and expense of conveying the productions of India to Constantinople, by that long and indirect course which I have described (the route by the Indus, the Oxus, the Caspian, and the Volga) rendered them extremely rare, and of an exorbitant price, the industry of the Italians discovered other methods of procuring them in greater abundance and at an easier rate. They sometimes purchased them at Aleppo, Tripoli, and other ports on the coast of Syria, to which *they were brought by a route not unknown to the ancients.* They were conveyed from India by sea up the Persian Gulf, and, ascending the Euphrates and Tigris as far as Bagdad, were carried by land across the desert of Palmyra, and from thence to the towns on the Mediterranean." —Robertson's "America," quoting from Ramusio.

Christians of the West and the Mahomedan nations that held the countries of the Nile and the Euphrates, for a time diverted the stream of commerce from those routes. It has not been so, however, with the Indus, to the same extent. If the revival of the overland route and the hoped-for re-opening of the Euphrates as the highway to the East, are evidences of a return to old paths, the continuance of a commerce with Central Asia and northern Europe, by way of the Indus, and the two great gates of India, the Khyber and Bolan Passes, is a pregnant proof of the tenacity with which trade adheres to its old channels, and of the sagacity which originally selected that direction for the produce of the East. However great may have been the changes of masters and manners in the territories between the Indus and the Bosphorus, a portion of the tide of commerce has flowed, and does still flow, as it did in the seventh century.*

With respect to its shipping, India has experienced great changes since the pioneer expeditions of the old East India Company in the 17th century. At that time, it would appear, the carrying trade by sea, with the exception of the very few British, French, Portuguese and Dutch vessels trading with Europe, was in the hands of the Arabs, who have ever shown themselves bold and skilful seamen. These were superseded by the fine old ships of the East India Company, half frigate and half merchantmen, and some still living relate with pride how the perils of the voyage to India in their vessels were often enhanced by successful encounters with hostile men-of-war and with pirates.

* "The Indus and its Provinces," by the Writer.

It is however during the last fifty years that the greatest changes have taken place. The rapid growth of the Indian trade about half a century ago necessitated an extension of the marine, and private shipowners one by one then entered the field, and continued sending their ships in increasing numbers to the ports of Calcutta, Madras and Bombay.

In 1834, through the energy and heroic perseverance of Richard Waghorn, the route through Egypt, better known as the Overland Route, was adopted for the carriage of letters, thereby shortening the passage to India by at least half the time occupied by a Cape voyage. This mail service by the Isthmus was conducted between Suez and India by steam vessels of the Indian Navy until the year 1840, when the Peninsular and Oriental Steam Company contracted with the Government of India to carry it on; and from that time until 1869 when M. Lesseps' great work of cutting through the Isthmus was completed, this Company, with the Messageries Maritimes, enjoyed a virtual monopoly of the most valuable part of the Indian trade. Immediately however upon the Suez Canal becoming a *fait accompli*, the enterprise of British shipowners was brought into full play, and large and powerful steamers were constructed for the new route. Steam vessels now run regularly from London, Liverpool, Glasgow, Hull and Southampton to Kurrachee, Bombay, Madras and Calcutta: while the number of sailing vessels by the Cape does not diminish. Round the coast of India and Ceylon to Burmah, the Straits Settlements, China, Australia, Java, in the Persian Gulf and Red Sea and on the East Coast of Africa there are lines of steamers under the British flag trading regularly from the principal ports of India. The officers and engineers of these ships are British—the crews chiefly natives of India. As recently as 1857, on the outbreak of the Sepoy War, the Government of India were in extremity for steamers to bring troops from Mauritius, Ceylon and China to the assistance of their hard-pressed and greatly outnumbered forces. At the present time, it would be easy for that Government to have promptly available, chiefly by means of the Suez Canal, 80,000 to 100,000 tons of steam shipping for such a purpose. An additional security for the safety of the Empire, is thus afforded, the value of which it would be difficult to estimate.

But, in congratulating the nation upon this great additional security, it must not be overlooked that it is dependent upon access to the Suez Canal being always available. Should that route be closed, which might easily occur by accident or design,* or by A COMPLICATION OF EVENTS IN EUROPE, our extensive steam fleet would be rendered useless, either for purposes of trade or for transports,† and as the commerce of India extends, so that country becomes more identified with the interests

* *See* Appendix E., "Evidence of Select Committee of the House of Commons on Euphrates Railway, 1871-1872," &c.

† On a recent occasion Sir Garnet Wolseley declared at a numerously attended meeting at the Royal United Service Institution, that the largest ironclads could not pass by the canal, and it was evident that it would be the easiest matter in the world to stop the traffic on that canal. It might be done by a few barges, by one good large torpedo, by a vessel laden with dynamite or powder and taken to certain positions in the canal well known in our Intelligence Department, and where they would do enough damage

of Great Britain. The necessity for the alternative route by the Euphrates Valley becomes more than ever apparent. Twenty years have elapsed since the largest and most influential deputation that ever waited upon a Minister urged the importance of this subject upon Lord Palmerston, and in 1871-1872 the Select Committee of the House of Commons, presided over by the present Chancellor of the Exchequer, fully confirmed the opinions then expressed,* and recommended the construction of the Euphrates Valley Railway connecting a port on the Mediterranean with the head of the Persian Gulf, to the consideration of Government, based on the evidence of Lord Stratford de Redcliffe, Lord Strathnairn, Sir Bartle Frere, Sir Donald Macleod, Sir Henry Green, Mr. S. Laing and Sir Henry Tyler; of General Chesney, the original explorer of the route, and of two officers of the expedition, Admiral Charlewood, R.N., and Mr. W. Ainsworth; of Sir John Macneill, Mr. Telford Macneill and Mr. Maxwell, C.E., who surveyed and reported on the most difficult portion of the design, and of Captain Felix Jones, who surveyed the entire route, from the head of the Persian Gulf to the Mediterranean. If this line were in other than British hands, in those of Russia, for instance, the Suez Canal could be turned, and the railway could be extended through Persia and Beloochistan to India, notwithstanding all the ironclads of England being in the Persian Gulf.

to stop the canal for a year. Or a simpler method might be adopted by taking out a few heavy vessels and scuttling them. So we could not depend upon the canal.

* *See* Appendix E, Euphrates and Indus route.

In seaports and harbours of refuge India is less favoured by nature than most other parts of the globe, but efforts have been, and are being made to supply the deficiency. It is far, however, from being destitute of such natural advantages. The harbour of Bombay is probably one of the safest and most picturesque in the world, and would accommodate shipping far in excess of the trade of the port, present and prospective. Calcutta, approached by a noble, though somewhat treacherous river, is admirably situated for trade, and the long rows of stately Indiamen moored along the banks was a sight not to be surpassed elsewhere. Madras is unfortunately, at present possessed of no harbour, and the loss of shipping, lives and property at that place has been very great; in bad weather vessels have to slip their cables and run out to sea to prevent stranding. Cochin possesses a good little harbour, but the bar is only to be crossed by vessels of small tonnage and light draught. Within six miles of Cochin, however, is Narrakal, where ships discharge and load in perfectly smooth water in the heaviest weather; this harbour is an open roadstead, and how it happens to have its peculiar immunity has never been satisfactorily explained; passengers and cargo landed there are conveyed by back water to stations on the Madras Railway. At Carwar, on the Malabar coast, and Kurrachee, a port 500 miles north of Bombay, excellent harbours have been constructed, easy of access and provided with accommodation for a large trade, which is finding outlets at these ports.

Besides the above-named, there are the smaller ports of Pooree, Gopaulpore, Vizagapatam, Coconada, Masulipatam, Negapatam, Tuticorin, Colachel, Aleppy, Calicut, Tellicherry, Cannanore, Mangalore, Vingorla, Rutnagherry, Surat, Gogah, Porebunder and Verawa, as well as the ports in British Burmah, Arracan and the Malay Peninsula. All of these places have of late years greatly increased their imports and exports, and some of them being the terminal ports for the railways, will doubtless be far better known in the future.

Between the southern ports of India and Ceylon there is a very considerable trade, which deserves a better communication than now exists; it has been proposed that the Paumbaum Channel, which divides India and Ceylon, should be deepened, in order that large steamships to and from the East Coast of India may be saved the extra distance of going round the island of Ceylon.

CHAPTER XXXVI.

FINANCE.

Revenue—Land Tax—Opium Tax—Salt Tax, Customs, &c.—Indian Budget—Lord Northbrook on Famines—Depreciation of Silver.

The revenue of India at the present time (1878) amounts in round numbers to fifty millions sterling a year, or nearly double the figures of 1850, and higher by ten millions than the sum total of 1860. As compared with the revenues of England or France, these fifty millions may appear a small sum to raise from so large a population, but the great mass of the people is very poor, living from hand to mouth in the most simple, frugal and primitive manner possible, consuming little that can legitimately be taxed; and it should further be remembered that a foreign government cannot tax its subjects to nearly the same extent as a native government: for what in the one case is submitted to as a necessary evil, is in the other resented as extortion, and pointed to as an aggravation of the drawbacks of foreign rule. One such drawback of an undeniable character in connection with the collection of revenue is the petty tyranny which corrupt native officials are prone to wield in the name of their foreign masters, too few to supervise personally what is going on and keep the rapacity of subordinates in check. In trying to reach the wealthier classes we are liable to provide lucrative employment for a large number of native underlings, who render themselves extremely obnoxious to all classes of their countrymen and bring discredit on our rule, without producing much benefit to the public revenue. The fiscal arrangements in connection with the now happily abolished, the odious and inquisitorial income-tax, may be cited in illustration of this.

The chief sources of revenue in India are the land-tax, opium and salt monopolies, excise, customs and stamps. The first of these yields two-fifths of the whole amount raised, or about 21 millions sterling, and is the tax best known to the people of India, every successive dynasty having imposed it. Under Hindoo and Mahomedan Governments the tax levied on the landholders represented about two-thirds of the gross produce of the land. Under British rule, in those provinces where the land is subject to re-assessment at stated intervals, the contribution to the State is estimated at about half the net rental of each estate; but in Bengal, where the land revenue was permanently settled by Lord Cornwallis in 1793, the increased value of the land and its products has rendered the tax comparatively insignificant.

The Land Assessment has always been troublesome and many proposals have been put forward with the view of adopting a more uniform system, and have from time to time been hotly debated; but the varying circumstances of climate and long existing habits and customs in the different localities, render it a most difficult subject to grapple with. In Madras the settlement is made yearly direct with each ryot. In the North-West Provinces the settlement is fixed for thirty years, the revenue officer dealing through the village head-men. A similar process is pursued in the Punjaub, while in Oude the Talukdárs, or landholders, have to pay the Government demand. Bombay has a thirty years' settlement based on the Madras or Ryot wárí system.

The Opium-Tax, which yields about eight millions a year, has already been described.

The Salt-Tax comes next, which swells the revenue by about six millions. This tax upon one of the first necessaries of life can only be justified by necessity; it presses hardly upon the poor by preventing them from using enough salt to keep their households and their cattle in proper health. An effort is being made to lessen the evils of the tax by abolishing a long line of inland custom stations throughout the country, and this, with reduced carriage, will facilitate the distribution of the commodity; but, so soon as the finances of India will admit of it, the tax should for sanitary reasons be abolished.

Customs yield about two and a-half millions, derived from a number of imports and a few articles of export. Except those levied on wines and spirits, the duties now in no case exceed 5 per cent. *ad valorem.* Until recently the import duty on manufactured cottons and woollens was 7 per cent., but on the strong representations of the Manchester manufacturers that they were unable to compete with the growing manufactures of India, Lords Salisbury and Northbrook agreed to reduce it to 5 per cent. Stamps and excise each yield a sum about equal to the customs: and the post-office, telegraph, forests, justice, and a few other items make up the balance of India's revenues.

The above revenue of 50 or 51 millions sterling is fairly balanced by the expenditure, of which the army absorbs upwards of 15 millions, and the interest on the debt nearly five millions. Of late years an increasing interest has been shewn in Indian finance, and in the discussion of the question we have two distinct parties, one predicting utter ruin and discomfiture from the growing expenditure, the other pointing to the increasing prosperity of the country and the elasticity of the revenue. It is not our intention to take part on either side; each is doing a good work, and if the British public generally would manifest a yet deeper concern in the affairs of our great Indian Empire, we should not have to complain of lukewarmness in the House of Commons when Indian subjects are debated. It is to be feared, however, that the people of England do not sufficiently realize how much of their country's wealth, power and glory are derived from the possession of India, and how much of all these we should lose if deprived of the government of that noble dependency. We have already pointed to the poverty of the masses of the Indian population and the peculiarities of our foreign rule, as powerful arguments in favour of a minimum taxation and restricted expenditure, and in the serious depreciation of silver, which has hung like a black cloud over Indian finance for the past two years, we have a further incentive to economy. At the same time, with our experience of the past, are we not justified in somewhat discounting the future? Although the people of India are poor, India is not poor in her soil and climate; with her teeming population, peaceful and industrious, she might be made a mine of wealth; and how much more judiciously might not the surplus earnings of England be spent in India than squandered in foreign loans! Roads, railways and canals for opening up and irrigating the country, would be excellent investments and help the people to bear a heavier taxation.

Our Indian Budget has hitherto been exposed to the disturbing elements of the opium-tax and small wars, to which must now be added famines and the depreciation of silver. Public opinion has fixed upon the Government of India the responsibility of meeting famines with relief, and in quick succession they have had to contend with the Orissa and Bengal famines, and as would appear from the recent despatches, an enormous expenditure has been required to relieve the late distress in the Madras and Bombay Presidencies.

The experience derived from famines in the past proves that they do not extend at one time over the entire continent of India, but on the contrary a scarcity in one province is generally (we might almost say invariably) compensated by an abundant harvest in another. For instance, during the Orissa famine there was a large surplus of grain in Bengal and Burmah. During the Bengal famine upwards of 500,000 tons of rice were contracted for by the Government of India from Burmah, Madras and Saigon; and lately, in view of the scarcity prevailing in the Madras and Bombay Presidencies, it was a matter of sincere congratulation to learn that the rice fields of Bengal and Burmah were blessed with an abundant harvest.

That portion of the public press which most strongly insists upon the Government of India directly protecting the people from the scourge of famine, insists also upon the necessity for limiting the expenditure upon public works to an amount which may annually be spared from the revenue. Would it not, however, be more prudent to increase, rather than to diminish the expenditure upon roads, railways and canals, thus expediting the opening up of the country from the coast to the interior and from one district to another, in order to facilitate the operations of trade and enable it in its natural course to provide for the scarcity of one province from the surplus in another, instead of throwing the onus of this upon the Government, as well as that of providing work at periods of need.*

* On this subject the following extract from a speech by Lord Northbrook at the Society of Arts, on 16th February, 1877, is of interest, and corroborates the views above expressed.

"Lord Northbrook said, that in dealing with famines in India, the extension of railroads was the most effective manner of guarding against any such calamity. It was only the existence of railroads in India which made it possible for any government to meet these famines (hear, hear) In the recent famine in Rajpootanah it was perfectly impossible, owing to the difficulties of transport, to have conveyed the food, of which there was plenty, to the famished district, the distance between the two places being so great. At the present time the government of India was doing its utmost to prevent a repetition of calamities that had overtaken some parts of the country. It would be successful, because the railroads now traversed the whole area of the recent famine, and enabled the country to send on demand food-grain to districts that required it (hear, hear). Although the cost of the famine in Bengal was six millions and a-half sterling, the surplus of three years was sufficient to produce a sum equal to the whole of the expenditure—a fact which showed the sound condition of Indian finances" (cheers).—*Times, 17th February*, 1877.

Depreciation of Silver.—But how is the silver difficulty to be surmounted ? At first sight it would appear there can be no relief, but in truth the "silver dilemma" and the "famine question" have practically to be met in the same way. The communications which would facilitate the distribution of grain, would also facilitate the transport of the produce of India, and, whilst lessening the chances of scarcity of food for the people, would tend to equalise the balance of trade with foreign countries.

To interfere directly with the silver currency itself is next to impossible, but it does not appear there are grounds for much despondency. Heavy as has been the fall in the value of silver, it is improbable that it should all at once and permanently lose its place. The demonetizing of silver by Germany and the alleged greatly-increased production of the American mines have certainly produced a marked decline in its value, but it has already recovered 8 per cent. from the lowest point. The sensitive state of the market, however, has opened the door to speculation, and not only the Government of India but all who are trading with the East, find their calculations for the present at the mercy of bullionist speculators.

There can be no fixity of exchange between two countries, one of which has a gold and the other a silver standard, because setting aside all other considerations it is impossible that parallel lines of cost should be preserved between these or any other two substances, and this would be the first necessity for such fixity. With regard to a metallic currency India's primary requirement is to possess that which is the most suitable for her internal transactions. If this be silver then of necessity her international transactions must be chiefly settled in that metal, which as an import would alone yield a certain return. The bitter experiences of the past resulting from the operations of unsound currency views are not likely to be repeated in India; and we may be confident that if it is found expedient to change the standard from silver to gold, it will only be done in common justice to our fellow subjects in India by the government calling in the silver currency and issuing a new gold currency for the same.

But it would appear that India is still far from requiring such a change. That the fluctuation in the price of silver will continue for some time to be a source of anxiety to those directing the finances of India is probable, but on the other hand there are fair grounds for believing that silver will not permanently fall very much below its present value. The reported yield of the American mines is proved to have been greatly exaggerated, and whilst some countries are exchanging silver for gold, there are others as yet without a metal currency, and to these silver is becoming more acceptable. Africa, for instance, only now being opened up to the commerce of the world, will doubtless take a portion, when the rich lands described by Livingstone, Burton, Grant, Speke, Baker, Cameron, Stanley, and other travellers, have been freed from the iniquitous slave trade and brought under cultivation.

The high protective duty in Great Britain of eighteen pence per oz. (about 33 per cent.) upon manufactured silver, has greatly diminished the use of the pure metal for such purposes during the past twenty-three years, notwithstanding the enormous growth of the wealth of the country. In the present position of the silver market, the wisdom of retaining this exorbitant tax is very doubtful.

CHAPTER XXXVII.

OUR NEIGHBOURS.

Beloochistán—Afghânistán—Persia—Turkistán—Russia.

Having treated in previous chapters of the various provinces and principalities or vassal States owning allegiance to the Empress of India, and of the settlements of European Powers, let us briefly survey the different countries which girdle the frontiers or affect the fortunes of her Indian empire.

Our relations with Russia may be powerfully influenced by our relations with Cabul, and our relations with Cabul may modify our treatment of the intervening hill tribes on our north-west frontier.

So that, whatever disturbs and excites one or other of the States named in the heading of this chapter, will affect or influence the others more or less remotely.

Beloochistan.—To begin with Beloochistan. This country, spreading from the Arabian Sea to the borders of Afghanistan, forms the western boundary of Scinde. It is a land of hills and deserts, with here and there a cultivated valley, inhabited by a number of pastoral tribes who obey no government but that of their several chiefs. Of these the most considerable is the Khán of Khelát, who wields among his neighbours a kind of lordship as unstable as that which the earlier kings of France wielded over the Dukes of Burgundy and other powerful vassals of their day. It is difficult to say what the Beloochees are by race, for they vary greatly among themselves in ethnical traits. Semitic or Aryan, however, they all speak some Aryan tongue, and profess some form of Mahomedanism. The country is said to be rich in minerals, especially copper and sulphur. Such trade as it boasts is carried on by caravans, or káfilas, which make their way across the Hála Range into Scinde through the long winding gorges of the Bolan Pass, liable occasionally to attacks from the robber tribes who infest the border. The chief carriers of the trade are the Lohanee merchants, a pastoral race of Afghans, who occupy the country eastward from Ghuzni to the Indus.*

* Lohanee merchants. The following is an extract from an interesting letter from Sir Bartle Frere, when Commissioner in Scinde, to the Author: —"These men are the great carriers of the Afghan trade. They have their homes about Ghuzni, where they spend the summer. Since the trade *viâ* Tatta and the Indus was extinguished in the latter end of the last century, these people have supplied themselves with seaborne goods *viâ* Calcutta. They descend the passes before they are blocked up by snow, between Ghuzni and the Indus, in vast caravans of eight or ten thousand souls—the whole tribe, moving bodily—men, women, children and cattle—their goods being on camels and ponies. Arrived in the Derajat, they leave the aged men, women and children in black felt tents, with their flocks and herds in the rich pastures bordering on the Indus, while the able-bodied men push across the Punjaub with their goods for sale, either in that province or on the banks of the Ganges. The leading merchants precede the main body on dromedaries, taking with them a few samples, letters of credit, &c., &c.—make their purchases at Delhi, Agra, Allahabad, Cawnpore, Mirzapoor, and even Calcutta, and return with them express—collect their families and flocks, and force their way up the passes. Their numbers generally enable them to compound with the tribes of the mountains for a reasonable amount of black mail; but they have sometimes to fight their way. I have heard of the wife of an eminent merchant of this tribe, whose husband had been detained longer than he expected at Delhi, offering the "Kaffila-Bashee (head of the caravan)

It was along the sandy wastes of southern Beloochistan that part of Alexander's army plodded their weary way back to Babylon from the plains of Scinde, while Nearchus and the fleet proceeded by the Arabian Sea and Persian Gulf. Great, too, were the hardships which Sir John Keane's soldiers had to endure in their successful march through the Bolán Pass to Candahar and Ghuzní, in 1839. In 1843 bravely did the Belooch troops of the Ameers of Scinde fight against Sir C. Napier at Meanee and Hydrabad.*

Afghánistán.—North of Beloochistán are the rugged highlands of Afghánistán, the land of a Semitic race with a varying admixture of Aryan blood, and a common devotion to the creed of Islám. Their language Pushtu, belongs to the same Aryan stock as Sanskrit, and is nearly allied to the Beloochee. The country, which is about as large as the Punjáb, Oude, and the North-Western Provinces together, is divided from the Punjáb by the Suleimán Hills, while the lofty Hindoo Koosh, the supposed cradle of the Aryan races, sweeps with many spurs across its northern provinces. Far away towards the Amu or Oxus lies the province of Balkh, the ancient Bactria, once ruled and largely colonised by Alexander's Greeks. In later times Afghánistán became the prize of successive conquerors from Persia and

demurrage at the rate of 10,000 rupees a day, to defer the upward march of the caravan, and enable her husband to rejoin, as she knew that if left behind he would be unable to follow them through the passes, except at great risk of his life and the property he might have with him."—"The Indus and its Provinces."

* "Conquest of Scinde," by Sir W. Napier.

Turkistán, and the eyrie whence successive invaders swooped down upon the Punjáb and Hindústán. From thence in the beginning of the 11th century issued the terrible Mahmud of Ghuzni, followed nearly 200 years later by Mahomed Ghóri, founder of the Patháu kingdom of Delhi. At the close of the 14th century the merciless Tímur passed like a bloody meteor from the Indus to the Ganges, and back again to Samárkhand. In 1526 the adventurous Báber led his hardy Turks and Afgháns from Cábul to the field of Páneeput. A later victory of Páneeput, won by another warrior from Afghánistán, Ahmed Shah, failed to rescue from impending ruin the splendid dynasty of Baber Akbar and Aurungzebe.

It was a grandson of the last named conqueror whom Sir John Keane's Army of the Indus set forth in 1839 to replace on the throne whence he had been driven by the powerful Dost Mahomed. The brilliant storming of Ghuzni was followed by Shah Sujah's triumphant return with the help of British bayonets to Cábul. Dost Mahomed fell into our hands, and under British protection the new king reigned for a time in peace. But in 1841 the flames of insurrection burst out on all sides, and the British troops cantoned at Cábul found themselves helpless, for want of a capable leader, to meet the growing danger with a bold front. At last in the bitter January of 1842, Elphinstone and his doomed followers, of whom only 4,000 were fighting men, passed out from their surrendered post, as Sir Hugh Wheeler afterwards did from Cawnpore, under promises of safe retreat. Afghan treachery and the snows of the passes leading to Jellálabad soon did their worst, and one man only, Dr. Brydon, struggled on to the place where the gallant Sale and his "illustrious garrison" still upheld the honour of our flag. Of the rest only a few score men and women escaped the general massacre by becoming prisoners to Akbar Khán, the son of Dost Mahomed.

A few months later, however, General Pollock was forcing his way through the far-famed Khyber Pass, which had so often baffled the efforts of larger armies led by the best generals of Akbar and Aurangzebe. Jellálabad was relieved, and Pollock marched on through every hindrance to Cábul, where he was joined by Nott, the heroic defender of Candahár. With the recovery of the prisoners, and the burning of the great bazár at Cábul ended the work which Pollock and Nott had to accomplish. On the return of the victors to Ferozepore, Dost Mahomed was set free; and thenceforth for many years the great Barukzai chief held firm sway over the country still ruled by his son Shére Ali. In the second Seikh War a body of Afghans fought against us and shared the defeats of the Kalsa leaders Shére and Chuttur Singh; but during the Mutiny, thanks to Sir John Lawrence and Sir Herbert Edwardes, our old enemy Dost Mahomed proved himself a wise and forbearing neighbour, if not a faithful friend. His son, who after some years of chequered fortune, fought his way into his father's throne in 1868, has hitherto kept the mastery over his unruly and turbulent subjects, with, until lately, the countenance and occasional help in arms or money of the Indian Government.

Along the rugged hills that bar Afghánistán from the Punjáb dwell a number of fierce warlike tribes, who scarcely owe a nominal allegiance to the neighbouring rulers, and prefer a life of fighting and plunder to the regular pursuit of trade or husbandry. Their quarrels with each other are varied by raids across the border, which have brought them one after the other into more or less disastrous collision with our troops. For many years after the conquest of the Punjáb a British force had to go out against one or another of these robber clans, burning their villages, carrying off their cattle, or clearing off old scores by well-aimed discharges of shrapnel and rifle-balls. Now and then a refractory tribe has been starved into submission by a well-planned blockade. Sometimes, as in the Ambeyla campaign of 1863, the offending tribes have only been brought to terms after inflicting heavy losses on their assailants. Of late however the peace of the frontier has only been broken by smaller raids by these restless hill-men, a good many of whom have taken service among their kinsfolk in the regiments of our Punjab Frontier Force, as the highlanders did in Scotland when they enrolled themselves in the Black Watch.

The two border countries of Beloochistán and Afghánistán should be conciliated by us by the establishment of friendly commercial relations, while we should abstain from provoking their hostility by interference in their internal affairs. To advance beyond the mountain barrier is to abandon a strong position for a weak one, and convert those who might be our friends into treacherous and vindictive foes.

With a railway along the valley of the Indus from

Lahore to Kurrachee, with branches TO the Khyber Pass and the Bolan, AND NO FURTHER, with our resources close at hand we can await the advance of aggression with tranquillity, while we promote the prosperity and comfort of our wild and restless neighbours, subduing them through their interests, by affording them a ready and certain market for their horses, their fruit, their silk and their wool.

In 1857, when the writer formed part of a deputation to Lord Palmerston regarding steam communication to the north-west frontier of India *viâ* the valleys of the Euphrates and Indus, he pointed out the importance of a railway along the valley of the Indus with branches to the two great passes of the Khyber and the Bolan in the following words, "The grand object was to connect England with the north-west frontier of India by steam transit through the Euphrates and Indus Valleys. THE LATTER WOULD RENDER MOVABLE TO EITHER THE KHYBER OR THE BOLAN THE TWO GATES OF INDIA, THE FLOWER OF THE BRITISH ARMY CANTONED IN THE PUNJAUB and connected by the Euphrates line by means of steamers, the flank and rear of any force advancing through Persia towards India would be threatened. So that the invasion of India would by this great scheme be placed beyond even speculation."*

In order to strengthen the hands of those entrusted with the management of our frontier policy, the writer also twenty years ago advocated the union of the Punjaub and Scinde.

"The union of the Punjaub with the Meerut and Delhi territory for political and military purposes, has been so

* *Vide* Letter to Viscount Palmerston, K.G., by W. P. Andrew, 1857.

plainly marked out by recent events, that their political connection under one distinct government appears inevitable, and the fortunes of these extensive and important regions are inseparably connected with that of Scinde." *

"The two provinces (Scinde and the Punjaub) have been connected by the fortunes of the great empire to which both belong. They are *the provinces of the Indus*, as Bengal and Behar are *the provinces of the Ganges.* They constitute one section of the empire, and are separated from every other part of it by rivers, mountains, the sea, or broad belts of sandy desert. Their commercial interests are inseparably united." Both must ultimately depend upon the traffic of the same railway system.

"Both depend for their communication with the external world upon one and the same port. The Punjaub has no outlet towards the north, but an imperfect outlet towards the west, and a long, difficult, and expensive, though open outlet towards the east. Would the Government place Bengal under one authority, and the Hooghly, under the commissioner of Pegu? Yet that is exactly what we have done with our north-west possessions. Our Danube has its mouth occupied, not by enemies, it is true, but by allies, owing allegiance to a different authority.

"Again, the physical, political, and social characteristics of the two countries are identically the same. Physically, the districts of Mooltan, Dhera Ghazee Khan, and Khangurh might be districts of Scinde. The soil is the same, the products are the same, the people are the

* "The Indus and its Provinces."

same. Politically, both have the same disadvantages, and the same military necessities. Both have a turbulent frontier to be guarded, which is identical in character from one end to the other, and which should be arranged on one principle, and be obedient to one head. The vast chain of military forts which stretch along the Scindian and Punjabee frontiers, depend upon one head. Both have populations whom it is necessary to disarm and overawe, and in both an enormous military force requires an energetic central administration. The system, too, of the Punjaub, would suit the province of Scinde better than that of Bombay. It is less regular, and better adapted to the fierce passions and uncontrolled habits of a wild Mohammedan people. The revenue settlement, too, is more in consonance with the ancient ideas of the population."

"It (the union) would strengthen, not root up, the system already successful; and on every other ground it is indispensable." The presidency of the Indus would be the first in political importance of the great divisions of British India. This immense territory, extending from Kurrachee to Peshawur and Delhi, would cover an area of 130,000 square miles,* and is occupied by a population of nearly thirty millions.

Our most dangerous foreign relations, with Central Asia and with the Beloochees and with the innumerable warrior chieftains of the highlands, must be conducted at Lahore. Whoever may be the final authority, every word of the Lieutenant-Governor reverberates among the hills, every blunder is bitterly resented in Cabul.†

* Great Britain covers 53,300 square miles.

† "The Friend of India" and "The Indus and its Provinces."

In these border lands to have a rival in prestige and power would be dangerous—to have a superior would be impossible—and every act in the great drama of the Russo-Turkish war as affecting the fortunes of the Sooltan of Room and the white Czar will be minutely canvassed and well remembered in Central Asia as well as in the bazars along the length and breadth of India.

Persia.—On the west of these two border countries, stretches the kingdom of Persia, or Iran, still largely peopled by the same old Aryan race which once sent forth a Darius and a Xerxes on bootless errands against the Greeks of Marathon and Salamis, and afterwards fought in vain under another Darius against Alexander's sturdy Macedonians. Between that monarch's fall and the victories achieved by Othman's Arabs, successive dynasties, Greek or Persian ruled the land of Cyrus the Great, and carried on a frequent struggle with the Byzantine Emperors.

As related in a previous chapter, the Parsees, descendants of the old Persian fire-worshippers, left their native land in the early days of Mahomedan conquest to find shelter from persecution, first in Gujerat, and afterwards in Bombay. Though few in number, they are at once among the wealthiest, most enlightened, and most energetic citizens of the western capital.

The official designation of the sovereign is Shah-in-Shah, or King of Kings. He holds in his hand the lives and property of his subjects, but, unlike the Sultan of Turkey, has no spiritual supremacy.*

* The Sultan is the Caliph or spiritual head of the Soonees, who adhere to the successors of Mahomet Aboobukhr, Omar, and Osman, while the Sheahs are the followers of Ali, the son-in-law of Mahomet and his sons, Hoossein and Hassan, whose memories they revere, and annually lament their death by public mourning.

One of the greatest kings of modern Persia was Shah Abbas, a contemporary of Akbar and our own Elizabeth. In the early years of this century the first Napoleon sent a mission to Tehran, which was received with extraordinary distinction, in order to further his designs on India, and for several years French influence was all powerful at the Court of the Shah.

Before anything was accomplished to the detriment of England, her great and implacable enemy was removed from the arena in which he had enacted so great a part, and Persia fell again into the coils of a more sinister and abiding influence.

Russia from the time of Peter the Great sought under one specious pretext or another to despoil Persia of whole provinces, having recourse to violence when other means failed. This state of things continued until about the middle of the eighteenth century, when the ferocious but mighty conqueror, Nadir Shah, compelled the Muscovite and the Turk to restore the territory they had wrested from the ancient dominions of the Shah.

On the death of Nadir Russian designs were renewed. Russia interfered to settle the claims of rival princes of Georgia, which owned allegiance to the Persian crown, and settled the matter by absorbing the province in the mighty spunge of Russian ambition.

War was declared, and Persia was defeated, and more territory was annexed by her powerful and relentless foe, until at last, fearful that the Colossus of the North would seize in his iron hand the entire kingdom of Persia, the British interfered diplomatically and obtained a respite for the enfeebled and hard-pressed king, who agreed to give up more territory, and to have no armed vessels on the Caspian.

Regarding the insidious movements of Russia towards the East, Sir Justin Sheil, late British Envoy at the Court of Tehran, made some years ago the following pregnant and suggestive remarks:—

"The Caspian Sea washes the coasts of the Persian provinces of Talish, Geelan, Mazenderan, Asterabad, and Persian Toorkomania. The inhabitants of these spacious territories carry on an extensive commerce, in part with the Persian ports on that sea, in part with the Russian districts on its northern and western shores. With a far-seeing policy, which anticipates all the possibilities of futurity, when Persia was gasping almost in the last throes, Russia humbled her to the dust, by forcing on her the renewal of a stipulation contracted at the treaty of Goolistan, by which she bound herself not to maintain any vessel of war in the Caspian Sea. Upwards of a hundred years ago, an Englishman named Elton, a man of wonderful ability and resource, who had been brought up to a seafaring life, and who had previously been an officer in the Russian navy, was in the service of the Shah (Nadir), and not only commanded his naval forces in the Caspian Sea, but built ships for him on European models. The most unnautical nation in the world, with an Englishman as their leader, became dominant on the Caspian; and, as the author of the 'Progress of Russsia in the East' says, '*forced the Russians to lower their flag*,' and the banner with the open hand* floated triumphantly

* "The banner of Persia is surmounted by an open hand, of which the five fingers are said to express Mahommed, Ali, Fatma, Hassan, and Hoosein."

through the length and breadth of the Caspian. To preclude a revival of this discomfiture, Persia was forced to sign her degradation, and the Caspian became a Russian lake."

"Not a boat is allowed to move without a passport, under heavy penalties, and even Persian boats are under the same restriction; this, too, on the coast of their own sea!"

In the early part of this century the British envoy concluded a treaty with the Shah of Persia, which brought Persia and India for the first time into close political relations, with the view of thwarting the ambitious designs of Buonaparte against our Eastern possessions. Some years afterwards an embassy from England reached Ispahan, and since then English influence has been always brought to bear on Persian politics. In 1839 Lord Auckland's forward movements in the Persian Gulf and Afghánistán compelled the Shah to recal his troops from the siege of Herát, so gallantly defended by the young Englishman, Eldred Pottinger. Another attempt in the same direction in 1856 had to be checked by force of arms, and Sir James Outram's brief but successful campaign along the Persian Gulf, ended in a peace which has never since been broken. Rumour gave Russia the credit of suggesting these moves, but which were promptly disavowed.

The revenue of Persia is less than £2,000,000, and as there is generally a surplus, it is paid to the private treasury of the Shah, who is supposed to be enormously rich, while his people are miserably poor and diminishing in number from misgovernment. The area of the country is above 600,000 square miles, with a population of 4,000,000, or about seven to the square mile.

The present Shah, Nasr-ud-din, visited Europe in 1874, taking England on his way from Berlin to Paris. To judge from his diary, which was afterwards published, he was particularly struck with the populousness, the general well-doing, the busy traffic, and the vast resources of this fortunate country. Tehran, his present capital, is in telegraphic communication with Bombay, London and St. Petersburg, and he is said to be anxious to introduce railways and other modern improvements into his dominions.

It is to be hoped the Shah may be allowed to cultivate the arts of peace, and that he may not have to play the part of Roumania or Servia in Central Asian politics.

Turkistán.—Along the northern frontier of Persia, Afghánistán, and Cashmere, stretches a vast expanse of rolling table-land, crossed here and there by rugged hills, and watered mainly by two rivers, the Sír and the Amú, better known to classical scholars as the Jaxartes and the Oxus. Túrkistán, or as it was once called, Tartary, extends from the Caspian to the borders of China, and is peopled for the most part by roving tribes of Turkomans, Uzbeks, Kurghiz, and other branches of the great Mongol race. Of this vast region the only settled parts are the three "Khanates," or kingdoms of Khiva, Khokán, and Bokhára, with the country lately ruled by Yákúb Beg, the strong-handed Ameer of Káshgar. The terrible Tartar, Chingiz Khán, carried his iron sway over the greater part of Central Asia, and his famous grandson Tamerlane (Timur the lame), ruled over a wide dominion from his splendid capital of Samarcand in Bokhára. From the neighbouring province of Khokán, or Firghána, Timur's illustrious descendant, Báber, made his way, after many strange turns of fortune, across the Indus to found the Mogul Empire of Hindustan. Khiva, the ancient Khárizm, was also in its time a powerful kingdom ; but its greatness had long decayed, before the marauding habits of its people provoked the Russians, in 1874, to invade their country, and reduce their Khán to the state of a tributary prince.

One after another, each of these three khánates has felt the weight of Russia's victorious arms, and paid with loss of territory for its raids on Russian ground, or its vain resistance to Russian ambition. The work of conquest, begun about twenty-five years ago, has already stripped them of half their former territories, and the Kháns who still nominally rule the remainder, have sunk into the position of weak and obedient vassals to the "White Czar." Kashgar, on the other hand, under the strong sway of the late Yákub Beg, the successful soldier from Audiján in Khokán, has in the last twenty years risen from an outlying province of Western China, into a powerful Mahomedan State, connected by commercial treaties alike with Russia and British India. The encouraging reports of English travellers to Yarkand, one of the Amir's chief cities, were followed up in 1874 by the despatch of an English mission under Sir Douglas Forsyth, who brought back with him a treaty securing favourable terms of trade between the two countries. It would appear, however, that no profitable trade can ever be established with a country divided from India and Cashmere by dreary and difficult mountain passes of tremendous height, open only for a few months in the year, and even then unfit for the passage of anything but lightly laden mules and ponies. The Chinese, moreover, who have so lately crushed the Mahomedan revolt in Yunnan, seem little disposed to let Kashgar slip for ever from their grasp; while the close neighbourhood of Russia, with her known dislike of all commercial rivals, bodes ill for the hopes which Sir D. Forsyth's mission raised in the hearts of English cotton spinners, and Indian dealers in tea, kinkobs (or gold brocades), piece-goods, and shawls, even were it possible to overcome the physical difficulties.

But Yakoob Beg is dead, and a striking actor is removed from the scene of Central Asian politics, leaving his kingdom to be absorbed once more in the overgrown empire of China, which has been for years slowly advancing to resume its old dominion. Or, if the Celestials are too tardy, Russia is ready with her *protection*, like as in the other Khanates, even although the people may be Mahomedan fanatics; and their late prince received titles of honour from holy Bhokara and the Sooltan of Room. No man in Central Asia can wield the sword of Yakoob Beg.

"If Kashgar were permitted to fall into the Czar's possession, we should lose our *prestige* with the Mahomedans in Central Asia; whilst the occupation of Kashgar would prove a disagreeable thorn in our side, and give rise to endless intrigues."

"We have learnt how much trust can be placed in a Russian statesman's promises."*

* "A Ride to Khiva," by Captain Fred Burnaby.

How methodically and steadily, if slowly, the task enjoined upon his successors by Peter the Great has been pursued, let history attest.

The old southern boundary of Russia in Central Asia extended from the Ural, north of the Caspian, by Orenburg and Orsk, to the old Mongolian city of Semipolatinsk, and was guarded by a cordon of Cossack outposts. In 1716 Peter the Great sent a force, commanded by Prince Bekovich, to take possession of part of the eastern shore of the Caspian. Three forts were then built, though subsequently abandoned, after an unsuccessful expedition against the Khivans. More recently, since 1834, Russia has succeeded in firmly establishing herself on the eastern shore of the Caspian, where she has now four permanent posts, Fort Alexandrovsk, Krasnovodsk, at the mouth of the Balkan Gulf; Chikishlar, at the mouth of the Atreck; and the island of Ashurada. To the east she has crossed the Kirghis Steppe and established herself on the Sir Daria, or Jaxartes, which Admiral Boutakoff is said to have navigated for 1,000 miles in 1863. Thus the Russian frontier in Central Asia has been pushed forward until her advanced posts on the east look down from the Tian Shan range upon the plains of Chinese Turkestan. In Western Turkestan, also, she has gradually extended her boundary, and has annexed or subjected Tashkend, Kokand, Khojend, Samarcand, Bokhara and Khiva. In thus pursuing her career of annexation, Russia but follows the natural policy of a great military empire, being forced, moreover, as Sir John Malcolm said, by an impelling power which civilisation cannot resist when in contact with barbarism. She may indeed stop short of absolute and entire annexation, but there can be no doubt that by bringing Khiva under the same yoke as Bokhara, has established her influence on the Oxus, as she has already established it on the Jaxartes. The Oxus, or Amu Daria, is a noble river, not easy of navigation, but, it is believed, capable of being made so. It will furnish a ready means of carrying the tide of Russian annexation eastward until it finds a barrier in the Hindoo Koosh. When Russia shall have established herself along the Oxus, her position will be at once menacing to Persia and India. From Chardjuy on the Oxus there is a road to Merv, distant about 150 miles, and from Merv a direct road runs along the valley of the Murghab to Herat, the "key of India." Merv is historically a part of the Persian Empire, but in these countries it is notoriously difficult to define boundaries with any precision. Should Russia succeed in occupying Merv, as there is too much reason to fear she ultimately will, and in converting the neighbouring tribes into friends or allies, her position would be one which we could not regard without the gravest apprehension.

Surely, in the face of such facts as these, the time has arrived when England should rouse herself from the apathy of the past, and take steps to secure the incalculable advantages which would accrue to herself and her Eastern dependencies from the opening up of the Euphrates route.

The military and political value of the Euphrates Line is a matter of extreme moment, and has a far more decided bearing on the defence, not only of Turkey, but of Persia and the whole district lying between the Mediterranean, the Caspian, and the Indian Ocean than might at first be supposed.

So long ago as 1858 Field-Marshal Lieutenant Baron Kuhn von Kuhnenfeld, Austrian War Minister, predicted that Russia would in future probably try to satisfy her craving for an open sea-board by operating through Asia. '"She will not," says this distinguished authority, "reach the shores of the Persian Gulf in one stride, or by means of one great war. But taking advantage of continental complications, when the attention and energy of European States are engaged in contests more nearly concerning them, she will endeavour to reach the Persian Gulf step by step, by annexing separate districts of Armenia, by operating against Khiva and Bokhara, and by seizing Persian provinces. . . . .

'"The most important lines which Russia must keep in view for these great conquests are,

'"1. The line from Kars to the Valley of the Euphrates and Mesopotamia.

'"2. That from Erivan by Lake Van to Mossul in the Valley of the Tigris, to Mesopotamia, and thence, after junction with the first line, to Bagdad.

'"3. That from Tabreez to Schuster, in the Valley of the Kercha, where it joins.

'"4. The road leading from Teheran by Ispahan to Schuster and thence to the Persian Gulf. . . . .

'"Once in possession of the Euphrates, the road to the Mediterranean, *viâ* Aleppo and Antioch, and to the conquest of Asia Minor and Syria is but short.

'"It is clear that all these lines are intersected by the

line of the Euphrates, which, running in an oblique direction from the head of the gulf north of Antioch to the Persian Gulf, passes along the diagonal of a great quadrilateral which has its two western corners on the Mediterranean, its two eastern on the Caspian and Persian Seas, and so takes all Russian lines of advance in flank.

'"From this it is evident that the secure possession of the Euphrates Line is decisive as regards the ownership of all land lying within the quadrilateral. It must therefore be the political and strategic task of Russia to get the Euphrates Line into her hands, and that of her enemies to prevent her doing so at any cost.

'"The great importance of a railway along this decisive line which connects Antioch with the Persian Gulf follows as a matter of course. It is the only means by which it would be possible to concentrate, at any moment, on the Euphrates or in the northern portion of Mesopotamia, a force sufficiently strong to operate on the flanks of the Russian line of advance and stop any forward movement. . . . .

'"It is true that, at first, the aggressive policy of Russia in the East will only threaten the kingdoms of Turkey and Persia, but as neither one nor the other, nor both combined, would be strong enough, without assistance, to meet the danger successfully, England must do so; and it is certain that she must, sooner or later, become engaged in a fierce contest for supremacy with Russia. . . . .

'"The Euphrates Valley Railway becomes therefore a factor of inestimable importance in the problem of this great contest. Even now the construction of the line will counteract the Asiatic policy of Russia, for it will strengthen the influence of England in Central Asia and weaken that of Russia. . . .

'"The growth of Russia in the East threatens, though indirectly, the whole of Europe, as well as the States named above, for, if she were firmly established in Asia Minor, the real apple of discord, Constantinople, would be in imminent danger, all the commerce of the Mediterranean would fall into her hands, and she would command the canal through the Isthmus of Suez.

'"Whatever the commercial value of the Suez Canal to Central Europe, there is no doubt that it is secondary in importance to the Euphrates Railway, which affords the only means of stemming Russian advances in Central Asia, and which directly covers the Suez Canal."

"Yet the establishment of this route has been pressed for twenty years in vain on the attention of the Government of this country; and even the high recommendation of the Select Committee of the House of Commons has failed to awaken the Government to a sense of the gravity of the issues involved."*

* "The Euphrates Valley route to India, in connection with the Central Asian Question," by W. P. Andrew. A Lecture delivered at the Royal United Service Institution, May, 1873.

CHAPTER XXXVIII.

OUR NEIGHBOURS—*continued.*

Tibet—Nepaul—Sikhim—Bhutan—Burmah—Siam.

Tibet.—The great table-land of Tibet, lying between the Kuen Lun Range and the Himálayas, is still for the most part a land unknown to Europeans, whom Chinese jealousy has long and persistently shut out from even a passing acquaintance with the country ruled in their name by a succession of Buddhist Lamas, or incarnation, of the great Buddha himself. Of these Lamas, whose sanctity is upheld by large bodies of Buddhist monks dwelling in strong convents picturesquely perched on steep hill-tops, the most important is the Lama of Lhasa, the capital of Tibet, in the valley of the Sánpee or upper course of the Brahmapútra. It was to one of his predecessors that Warren Hastings, in 1784, sent Mr. Bogle on a friendly mission which was welcomed in a friendly spirit. For a few years an Indian agent lived at the Lama's capital, and trade with Bengal was carried on by way of Bogra. But little came of a movement which succeeding Governors-General were unable or unwilling to follow up, and fear of Nepaulese aggression united with orders from China to close the door which Warren Hastings had opened. Early in this century another

Englishman, Mr. Manning, made his way as far as Lhása, but he too had to leave the country. Of later years Lhása has been visited and parts of Tibet surveyed by some of Colonel Montgomerie's "Pundits," travelling in disguise as Buddhist pilgrims. Hitherto, however, all attempts to open Tibet, the country of the shawl goat, of gold, silver, and precious stones, to our regular Indian trade, have been baffled by the vigilance of the Chinese soldiers along the frontier.

Nepaul.—Along the southern frontier of Tibet lie the Himálayan States of Nepául, Sikhim, and Bhután. Of these the westernmost is the independent Kingdom of Nepául, which stretches for about 500 miles along the Himálayas overlooking Rohilkund, Oude, and Northern Bengal, and is peopled mainly by races of Tibetan or Chinese descent, with a certain admixture of Hindoo or semi-Hindoo immigrants who form the governing race. The highest mountains in the world furnish a snowy background to this Indian Switzerland without its lakes. The Nepaulese mostly dwell in the valleys, the largest of which is twelve miles long by nine broad. Through these valleys which are fairly cultivated, flow the Gogra, the Gundak, and the Kosi, on their way down to the mighty Ganges. Catmandoo, the capital, lies in one of the valleys, along the bank of a small stream, and is reckoned to have a population of 50,000. Most of the people are Buddhists in religion and Mongol in speech, but the ruling classes speak a kind of Hindí. Copper, iron, and brass articles are manufactured in the country, and form with timber, hides, rice, ginger, and honey, the chief objects of trade with other countries.

In the beginning of this century an English Resident was established at Catmandoo, where the Gúrkha dynasty had reigned for about forty years past. But in a few years the Resident was recalled, and in 1814 the continued encroachments of the Nepaulese on British ground led to a war in which, after a brave resistance, they were finally beaten by Sir David Ochterlony; and the Gúrkha Government had to purchase peace by forfeiting part of their possessions. From that time an English Resident has always lived at Catmandoo; but to this day no other Englishman is allowed to enter the country.

Ever since 1846, when the famous Jung Bahádur marched his way to power by the destruction of all his rivals, the government of the country virtually rested in his hands, under a Rajah who retains the mere show of kingly power. During the Mutiny Sir Jung Bahádur proved so useful an ally, that he was rewarded with some forest-lands on the Oude border, and made Grand Commander of the Star of India.* He gave the Prince of Wales a princely welcome within the borders of Nepaul, and treated him to some days of rare and exciting sport among the elephants and tigers of the Terai, or jungle, at the foot of the Népaulese hills. Sir Jung having died rather suddenly, a son appears to have succeeded to his power.

Sikhim.—The little State of Sikhim divides Nepául from Bhután, of which latter it may be called an offshoot. Our relations with the Sikhim Rajah began apparently in 1817, when his little territory in the Tista valley was

* Previous to this Sir Jung was a G.C.B.

placed under a British guarantee. In 1835 he made the Darjeeling district over to the Indian Government for a few hundred pounds a year. His seizure of Dr. Campbell and Dr. Hooker in 1849, in revenge for the refusal of the Government to send back his runaway slaves, was punished by the forfeiture of his lowland domains and the temporary stoppage of his allowance. But the latter was afterwards restored to him, and has lately been doubled as a reward for his co-operation in our efforts to open a trade with Tibet through his country.

Bhután.—Bhután, on the east of Sikhim, covers the northern frontier of Assam. The Bhutias, who people its rugged highlands are of a kindred race to their Tibetan and Burmese neighbours. They too are Buddhists if they are anything in creed, and are governed in spiritual things by a Dharm Rajah, and by a Deb Rajah in things temporal. Their chiefs are called Penlos. In the time of Warren Hastings their raids into Kooch Behar were checked by British interference; and since then they gave us no further trouble until after our conquest of Assam. Subsequent raids into Assam provoked reprisals, followed by the despatch of Mr. Ashley Eden's embassy to Punákha. He was received with coldness and insolence which brought on a war ending in the annexation of the Duárs, or passes from Bhután into Dharangu and Kamrúp.

In the highlands to the east of Bhután and round the north-eastern frontier of Assam, are a number of wild tribes, Abors, Daflas, Mishmis, Singphos, Kámptis, and so forth, all of the same Chinese type, and more or less prone to raiding across the frontier. By means of small yearly payments in money, they are generally kept from indulging their lawless habits at the cost of their peaceful neighbours; but the desire for plunder sometimes gets the better of their prudence, until they have learned the sharp lesson of a close blockade.

Burmah.—The Patkoi and Yomadung Hills form the western boundary of Burmah Proper, whose southern frontier marches with Pegu and Siam. It is bounded on the east by Yunnan and on the north by offshoots from the Himálayas. Its area of 42,000 square miles, watered by the Irawáddy and the Salwín, is supposed to contain about 3,000,000 souls. Mandalay, the present capital, lies on the Irawaddy, not far from the ruins of two former capitals, Ava and Amerapura. In the days of Alompra a successful military adventurer and his earliest successors, the Burman empire extended over Assam, Arakan, Pegu, and other provinces now subject to British rule. But Burman arrogance came into conflict with British power, and the braggart King of Ava paid dearly for his rash invasion of Bengal with the loss of several provinces in 1826. In 1853 another war provoked by another King of Burmah ended in the forfeiture of Pegu and the remainder of the Burman seaboard. A British Resident is now firmly established at Mandalay, a city of wooden buildings, which contains about 80,000 inhabitants, and is the seat of a considerable trade with British Burmah, and Western China. Within and about the Burman frontier are a number of hill-tribes, Sháns, Khákyens, and Karéns, over whom the King of Burmah has little, if any direct control. Higher up the Irawáddy is the town of Bhámo, whence Major Sladen led an exploring party in 1868, across the hills to the borders of Yunnan, with the view of opening up a regular trade-route from Western China to Rangoon. Burman jealousy and the Panthay revolt from China combined to mar the success of his undertaking, and a more recent mission led by Colonel Horace Browne was driven back by a sudden onset of hill-men and Chinese, with the loss of one of its leading members, the brave young Margary, who had just before made a successful journey overland from Pekin to Bhamo.

Siam.—On the southern frontier of Burmah is the kingdom of Siam, peopled by a kindred race to the Burmese, with features yet more expressive of their Mongol origin. They, too, like their neighbours, are Buddhists in religion. The western frontier of Siam marches with that of Tenassarim. Its chief river, the Meinám, flows southward into the Gulf of Siam, past Bankok, the seaport of the capital itself, which lies forty miles higher up the river. Siam the capital, is surrounded with water, and intersected with canals, spanned by numerous bridges. The houses are mostly built, like those in Burmah, of timber and bamboo, thatched with palm-leaves; those nearest the river being raised some feet from the ground on strong wooden piles. Outside the city is a floating town of boats, each the home of two or three families. Elephants, rhinoceroses, tigers, boars, and other wild beasts abound in the woods and marshes of Siam. Its mines yield gold, copper, tin, lead, and antimony, and the rich soil of the plains needs little help from art to grow anything suited to a tropical climate. In the animal kingdom the most celebrated is the famous white elephant, and the edible swallow, whose nest is the delight of Chinese gourmands. The present king of Siam is an able and enlightened ruler, well stored with Western learning, and of a marked turn for scientific pursuits. His goodwill to the rulers of India has shown itself in various ways, and the help he gave our astronomers in the process of observing the recent transit of Venus, would have done honour to the most civilised of Western States.

The foreign trade is in the hands of Chinese, and centres at Bankok, the capital. In 1874 the exports amounted to £1,225,864, the chief article being rice. The imports were of the value of £964,128, comprising textile fabrics, hardware and opium, all from India.*

* "Area ... ... about 250,000 square miles.
Population ... ... „ 11,800,000=47 to sq. m.
Revenue ... estimated at £3,145,000.
Expenditure is stated to be within receipts."*

* "Statesman's Year Book," for 1878.

CHAPTER XXXIX..

OUR NEIGHBOURS—*continued.*

Malay Peninsula—Singapore—Java—Sumatra—Borneo—Spice Islands —New Guinea.

The Malay Peninsula.—South of Tenassarim stretches the long, narrow Malayan Peninsula, inhabited by people chiefly of the original Malay stock, from which the native populations throughout the Eastern Archipelago have sprung, but containing also Indian, Chinese and other elements. The greater part of the peninsula is divided into small States, each ruled by an independent chief or Sultan, whose power over his vassals varies with his ability and their own means of resistance. English rule, however, prevails in the district of Malacca, bordering the Straits between the Peninsula and the island of Sumatra. Malacca, its chief town, lies at the mouth of a small river, and has long been the outlet for a considerable trade. In the last two centuries this province has passed successively under Portuguese, Dutch, and English rule; the last-named transfer dating from 1824. The other English settlements in this quarter are Penang, a small island off the Malayan coast, near the northern entrance of the Straits, the province of Wellesley, a narrow strip of seaboard opposite Penang, and the island and town of Singapore.

Singapore is a place of considerable importance, serving as an *entrepôt* for the commerce of Europe, India, China and the Eastern Archipelago. Its admirable position and the entire absence of any restrictive dues or vexatious regulations have combined to raise it within a comparatively brief period to a centre of great activity. The climate though hot is remarkably healthy.*

These "Straits Settlements," as they are called, were for many years ruled from India, in the name of the East India Company; but after the transfer of India to the Crown, they were disjoined from the Viceroy's government and administered by the Colonial Office.

Java.—Of the three large islands that fringe the Malay Peninsula, Java, the smallest and southernmost, is the most important. It is about 575 miles long and varies in breadth from about 48 to 120 miles. The soil is for the most part extremely fertile, and it produces large crops of coffee, sugar, rice and spices. Tobacco and tea are also cultivated with success, though at present on a small scale. The climate is generally healthy. The island contains several volcanoes, and earthquakes are consequently not uncommon. It is, as is well known, under the dominion of the Dutch, whose system of administration has been very successful in securing the prosperity of the European settlers and tranquillity among the native tribes. As in Hindostan, the Government is the principal landowner; but, unlike our sovereignty, it derives large direct trade profits from

* Area, 1,350 square miles; population, 308,097.

its possessions, which go to swell the revenues of the mother country. In the five years between 1811 and 1816, the island passed under British rule, and Sir Stamford Raffles was appointed Lieutenant-Governor, under the authorities at Calcutta. While occupying this position, he instituted many reforms and greatly ameliorated the condition of the native races, by whom his memory was long gratefully cherished. The original population of Java is Malay, but there are numerous admixtures from neighbouring countries. The Chinese are well represented, and many of the settlers from the "Flowery Land" have achieved wealth and position as planters or traders. The religion of the natives is chiefly the Mahomedan. There are still several native princes exercising a certain amount of authority, and some of them maintaining considerable state, but their rule is always under the direction of the agents of the Supreme Government. It is in Java that the fabled Upas tree was said to flourish which destroyed all life that came within the influence of its deadly exhalations.*

The Dutch claim authority over most of the other islands of the Eastern Archipelago, the chief seat of Government for the whole of their possessions being at Batavia, the capital of Java, from which place a well-conducted steam service keeps up regular communication

* The word *Upas* in the Javanese dialect signifies poison, and it has been applied to a large forest tree, the *Antiaris Toxicaria*, which yields a juice of dangerous quality, which the natives used in former times to poison their arrows. The operation of the poison, however, is slow, and it can be easily counteracted. This appears to be the origin of the Upas tree of tradition, and the reality, as usual, affords a very slender basis for the absurd superstructure of fiction.

with the outlying territories. Batavia was formerly very insalubrious, having been built in the old Dutch style on a low, marshy site, with numerous canals running through it; but some few years ago the canals were filled up and other improvements were introduced, and it is now considered as healthy as any town in the East. Of the other towns in Java, Samarang and Sourabaya on the north coast are by far the most important. The places on the south coast are few and small, but regular communication has recently been established between them and Batavia, and the usual results of increased facilities of intercourse may be expected to follow.*

Sumatra, the large island north-west of Java, has still its native rulers, but all of them are now under Dutch control. Till lately the Sultan of Atjeh, or Acheen, occupied an independent position as sovereign of a small but valuable district at the north-west end of Sumatra, but, hostilities having broken out between him and the Dutch in 1872, the result has been that he and his feudatories after a stubborn resistance are now practically reduced to subjection. Sumatra has many large tracts still unexplored, some of which are believed to contain valuable mineral deposits. It is the country from which black pepper is mostly obtained, and this was the principal article of trade of the subjects of the Sultan of Atjeh. Other tropical products such as coffee and sago are profitably cultivated, and at Deli and Langkat on the

* "Area ... ... 51,336 square miles.
Population ... 18,125,269—or 353 per square mile.
1874—Imports ... £7,874,416.
,, Exports ... £12,017,666."
—"Statesman's Year Book," 1878.

eastern coast tobacco plantations have lately been much extended. Padang, the capital of Sumatra, is on the western coast, and since the commencement of military operations at Atjeh has greatly risen in importance.

Borneo.—In this large island—the largest in the world next to Australia—the Dutch have extended their sway over about two-thirds of its space, and they have several settlements on the east, west and south coasts, from whence their influence extends over the rule of the native chiefs. Borneo is a mountainous country, but the coasts are bordered by extensive plains, the soil of which well repays the cultivator. Its native inhabitants are of a fiercer and more intractable character than those of the neighbouring islands, and owing to this, among other causes, European settlement has not made the rapid progress which from the natural advantages of the island might have been predicted. Here we find innumerable species of the Simia tribe, including the orang outang. On the north-east coast of Borneo is the province of Saráwak, which some thirty years ago was granted by the Sultan of Borneo to Sir James Brooke, as a reward for assistance rendered in suppressing the piratical raids of the Dyaks, a fierce and sanguinary tribe of his own subjects.

Spice Islands and New Guinea.—To the east of Borneo are the beautiful Spice Islands, the most important, though not the largest of which are Amboyna and Banda, the nutmeg and clove plantations of which are widely celebrated, and the tawny and robust inhabitants, once among the most warlike, are now subdued and peaceable. Eastward again of the Spice

Islands, the magnificent island of New Guinea claims attention. At present it is but little known, although doubtless before long European enterprise will succeed in establishing a footing there, to the advantage both of its promoters and of the now uncivilized inhabitants of the island. The exquisite birds of Paradise, whose plumage has been so frequently borrowed to grace the head gear of ladies, find their chief home in New Guinea.

CHAPTER XL.

OUR NEIGHBOURS—*concluded.*

Muscat—Zanzibar—Ceylon.

Muscat and Zanzibar.—Muscát or Omán on the South Arabian, and Zanzibár on the East African coast, should also be mentioned in a list of India's neighbours. The Arab rulers of both countries are of the same family, Zanzibar formerly paying tribute to Muscat. But fourteen years ago on the death of the last Imaun, Zanzibar became independent. Oman forms the south-east extremity of the Arabian peninsula, washed partly by the Indian Ocean and partly by the Persian Gulf. The surface is varied by mountains and woods, wildernesses and fertile oases; the latter produce dates, grain and lofty trees yielding the true gum arabic (acacia vera.) Muscat and Mattra are the chief towns and ports of the country ruled by the Imaun or Sultan; the former is the capital, and is situated near the entrance to the Persian Gulf, with a population estimated at 60,000. The harbour is completely sheltered from the prevailing winds or monsoons. The town is built along the shore in the form of a horseshoe, encircled by hills crowned with forts. The houses are mean; even the Sultan's palace is no exception. The streets are so narrow, that palm leaves laid across from house to house form a perfect protection from the sun, whose rays are here unusually powerful. The town of Mattra is near Muscat, is connected with it by a good road, and has about the same number of inhabitants ; has docks for ships and a seafaring population. There is an extensive transit trade with Arabia, Persia and India ; cloth and corn being the principal imports. The exports consist of dates, horses, salt fish, hides and madder to India; sharks' fins to China, and asses, &c., to Mauritius ; besides pearls, and gums and other products. In addition to the native Arab inhabitants there are, attracted by the hope of gain or barter, Persians, Hindoos, Syrians, Kurds, Afghans, Beloochees, Negroes and other races.*

Zanzibar.—The Suahele or Zanzibar coast, is commercially the most important portion of the east coast of Africa. Facing it, and close to the main land are the islands of Pemba, Zanzibar and Mafia, which, together with the adjacent coast, are subject to the Sultan of Zanzibar, though his rule does not extend far inland.

"The extreme limits of his rule are the settlement of Warsheikh on the southern Somâli coast north of the Juba, and the village of Tunque immediately south of Cape Delgado (10° 43′ S.) where his dominions touch those of Portugal."†

According to Stanley, "Zanzibar is, of course, the place from which travellers bound for East Central Africa start. It is forty-five miles long by about fifteen miles average width. It is interesting to the explorer, as the point where he organises his forces."

* "Universal Gazetteer," by W. F. Ainsworth, F.R.G.S., &c.

† "Africa," by Keith Johnston.

The island of Zanzibar is "2,400 nautical miles from the southern point of India, and about the same distance from the Cape of Good Hope and the Suez Canal."*

The town of Zanzibar has a handsome appearance, being built of white stone; and the streets present an animated aspect, from the motley crowds of natives and foreign merchants from all the neighbouring coasts engaged in the commerce of this rising port, which is the centre of the trade of the eastern shores of Africa. From the apathy of the native races the trade is almost entirely monopolised by Hindoo as well as Mahomedan merchants from India, who deal not only in English goods, but in those of the continent of Europe and America. Notwithstanding the great acuteness and perseverance of these Indian traders, the vast resources of the east of Africa are far from being developed. Ever since the British India Steam Navigation Company in 1873 established a monthly line of steamers between Aden, Zanzibar and Madagascar, a considerable impulse has been imparted to commerce. The slave trade has been for years chiefly in the hands of the natives of India, but in 1873 Sir Bartle Frere, as the representative of England, concluded a treaty with the Sultan of Zanzibar for its suppression in Eastern Africa which was considered at the time a diplomatic victory; as yet, however, the chief result obtained has been that of giving the traffic a new direction by longer routes to other ports, leaving the old familiar roads and depôts for shipment on the coast encumbered and defiled with the skeletons of a bygone trade.

Slowly it begins to appear that, so long as the demand

* "Africa," by Keith Johnston.

for slaves all over the East continues, this inhuman traffic cannot be effectually put down. Domestic slavery in Egypt has not diminished, and the demand for slaves in Arabia, Persia and Madagascar is now as great as ever, and a new slave market on the Somali coast, near Cape Guardafui, was recently established for local wants.

Besides, in the interior there are no means of preventing the Africans themselves from taking part in the purchase and sale of slaves; and in many regions the horrors of a revolting superstition and the hideous practice of cannibalism reign supreme. In regarding the various races in the dark continent, it is melancholy to think that the man-eating barbarian excels his fellow barbarians, both in physical attributes and mental force.

Commerce under European guidance will, it is hoped, gradually penetrate into the darkest recesses of this benighted land, bringing in its train the humanizing and elevating influences of the religion and enlightenment of the west, rending asunder the dark cloud of cruelty and barbarism with which its face has been covered for centuries as with a funeral pall. It may be long, but it will surely come, when, instead of internecine war there shall be peace; when the sound of the hammer shall ring in the solitude, and the desert shall blossom as the rose. Ages must elapse before the African is free, but in the meantime the good work is progressing.

The present Sultan of Zanzibar, Seyd Burghash,* is

* "ZANZIBAR AND THE SLAVE TRADE.—Having only recently returned from the east coast of Africa, where I had been employed organizing a colony of freed slaves on behalf of the Church Missionary Society at Frere Town, Mombas, I wish to add my testimony to the sincerity and good faith of His Highness the Sultan in the part he is taking for the suppression of the traffic. His last scheme has been to raise a force

giving effect to the treaty for the suppression of the slave trade with sincerity and good faith, and when His Highness visited this country not long ago he made a very favourable impression, by his dignified demeanour and the anxiety he evinced for the improvement of his country. During the prevalence of the slave trade, the valuable resources of the country were undeveloped and legitimate trade entirely neglected, but now the energies of the merchants are directed of necessity to the establishment of a trade in ivory, cinnamon, cloves, sugar, cocoa, coffee, nutmegs and other spices; indigo, cotton and other products, and the Sultan has set a good example by the establishment of thriving plantations. He has also an extensive and valuable stud for rearing horses, the entrance to which is said to be guarded by an enormous sow, as a charm against evil spirits playing pranks on the horses.

The population of the island and town of Zanzibar "is estimated at from 300,000 to 350,000, or about 375 to the square mile, and of this number about 60,000 live in the city. During the north-east monsoon, the arrival of

consisting entirely of freed slaves, to take the place of the mercenaries from the north, who are directly interested in keeping the trade alive. These men are well drilled by European instructors, and are ready at any time to be landed where their services may be required. My object in writing you, Sir, is to suggest that something should be done to recognise the efforts of Seyd Burghash in having done his part well. No better time than the present could be found to send His Highness 400 Snider rifles, with a good supply of ammunition, as his troops are principally armed with the old matchlock. As his new yacht will sail shortly for Zanzibar, the arm racks on board should not be empty.

I remain, Sir, your obedient servant,

W. F. A. H. RUSSELL, Commander, R.N.,

Temple Club, Arundel Street, Strand, *March* 25."—*Times*.

foreign traders increased the population by 30,000 or 40,000. The basis of the population is formed by the Arabic owners of the soil and the numerous half-castes of mixed Arabic and African blood."*

Ceylon.—One of India's nearest neighbours is the island of Ceylon, divided at one point from Southern India only by a narrow sea with rocks and sand-banks, one of the latter, of considerable magnitude, being denominated Adam's bridge, between two parallel ridges of rock, leaving, after several attempts at improvement, a passage for vessels of light draught. Taprobané, under which name it was known to the ancients, the great island, the fame of which has exercised such an influence over men's minds for many centuries—"the mother land of fables—the country which to the Greeks, the Romans, the Egyptians and the Arabs offered the same mysterious attractions that the East long did to the people of Western Europe." The mountain range which forms the backbone of Ceylon, varies in height from two to eight thousand feet, and undulates into fair and fertile valleys, while great tracts of forest afford shelter to elephants and many other wild beasts. Ceylon, or Lanka, its old Hindoo name, is about the size of Ireland, and is supposed to contain over two million people, mostly Buddhists, who speak a language akin to the Támil of Southern India. In the northern parts are various races of Indian origin, while Mahomedan Arabs are found everywhere, and a few aboriginal Veddahs still linger in their native forests and hills. The Indian element has of late been fed by a steady flow of immigrants from the

* "Africa," by Keith Johnston.

mainland. Rice, coffee, cotton, sugar, tobacco, cinnamon, and cocoa-nuts, form the staple produce of the island, which also yields many kinds of minerals and precious stones.

The interior is remarkable for possessing some of the grandest and most lovely scenery in the world, the hill sides being clothed with the most exuberant and magnificent of tropical vegetation, mingled with trees of a sterner climate. Side by side with the oak there are the banyan and iron-wood trees, the satin-wood tree and the acacia, rhododendron and magnolia, with mighty creepers, while mountain and valley glow with every variety of flower and colour. All this is still to be seen in full bloom and beauty, in defiance of the inroads of the rice and coffee planters.

Kandy, in the middle of the island, was the seat of a long line of native kings. Since the final capture of Kandy in 1815 there have been several uprisings and rebellions, one, the most formidable, in 1817; the latter in 1848, which Lord Torrington stamped out with a vigour which nearly brought on him the fate incurred by Governor Eyre in later years.

"All we had heard," says a recent traveller, "of the beauty of the situation of Kandy and of the character of the scenery, was fully sustained. In a deep ravine at one side of the plateau, or, more properly speaking, of the broad valley surrounded by hills, overlooking a still deeper depression, on which the town is situated, the Mahawelli Ganga river thunders in its rocky bed. The small lake by the side of which part of the city is built lends a charming repose and freshness to the scene, which is mirrored in its waters. Wherever the eye is turned rise mountain tops, some bare masses of rock, others clothed with vegetation. There is no idea of a town or of a 'city' to be realized in what one sees: it is all suburb—verandahed pavilions and bungalows stretching in lines bearing the names of streets; here and there the native houses packed more closely may be termed lanes; but the whole place is as diffused as Balham, or Clapham, or any other rural quarter of the great Metropolis. Kandy was once a stronghold of kings; but it was not till the end of the sixteenth century that it became the capital. When that dignity was conferred on the city, it was forbidden to the common people to have windows, or white walls or tiles to their houses, as these were luxuries for royal use alone. Public buildings, properly so called, there are none; but in lieu of these was one of the most picturesque crowds ever seen."

The English capital, Colombo, is a flourishing town on the western coast. Point de Galle, at the extreme south-west, has a large though rocky harbour, and is still the meeting place for mail-steamers plying between Suez and the far East. The pearl fishery in the Gulf of Manár, still employs a good many divers during the season, which is of short duration, commencing towards the end of February, and terminating early in April. Colombo, although a rising town and the chief port of the island, is an open roadstead always difficult of access, and the last act of the Prince of Wales before leaving Ceylon was to lay the foundation stone of a breakwater.

"The undertaking is a great one, and worthy of all success, and the breakers which thundered close at hand spoke very eloquently of the necessity for such a work, which will illustrate the administration of Sir W. H. Gregory,"* the then Governor, leaving at the same time a fitting and lasting memorial of the Prince's visit.†

Having thus glanced at the past and present of India, and of the nations which surround her, or influence her fortunes, the author concludes with the hope that he may have in some degree excited an additional interest in our great Eastern Empire, and with the sincere wish that its inhabitants may realise to the fullest extent the beneficent desires conveyed in the grand and simple words of the Queen, addressed in 1858 to her people in India: "IT IS OUR EARNEST DESIRE TO STIMULATE THE PEACEFUL INDUSTRY OF INDIA, TO PROMOTE WORKS OF PUBLIC UTILITY AND IMPROVEMENT, AND TO ADMINISTER THE GOVERNMENT FOR THE BENEFIT OF ALL OUR SUBJECTS RESIDENT THEREIN. IN THEIR PROSPERITY WILL BE OUR STRENGTH, IN THEIR CONTENTMENT OUR SECURITY, AND IN THEIR GRATITUDE OUR BEST REWARD. AND MAY THE GOD OF ALL POWER GRANT TO US, AND TO THOSE IN AUTHORITY UNDER US, STRENGTH TO CARRY OUT THESE OUR WISHES FOR THE GOOD OF OUR PEOPLE."

* Russell's "Tour of the Prince of Wales."

† Ceylon.

Area	24,454 square miles.	
Population	2,128,884.—1870.	
Revenue	£1,375.888	1876
Expenditure	£1,276,930	

—"Statesman's Year Book," for 1878.

APPENDIX.

APPENDIX A.

LIFE IN THE JUNGLE.

MOONDIA GHAUT THE PARADISE OF SPORTSMEN.

A Correspondent, says *The Times*, who has resided and hunted in the district writes to us:—

Moondia Ghaut is the place whence the telegrams relating the sporting adventures of the Prince of Wales have recently been despatched. No doubt many have searched for it unsuccessfully on the map, so a short account of its position and physical characteristics may not be without interest. The word 'ghaut,' or 'ghat,' bears several analogous meanings. We daily hear it applied to the scarped and terraced hills overlooking Bombay and the Concan. The bathers' ghaut, or flight of steps at Benares or Hurdwar, is familiar to every reader of Indian travels. So hereafter Moondia Ghaut, or ford, will be remembered as the spot selected as the head-quarters of the Prince's sporting excursion in India.

'It is the sport of kings,' was the remark made by a distinguished officer, brother to one of the Prince's most trusted companions, as we put our elephants in line to beat from the little river Choka to Moondia Ghaut, one brilliant October morning twelve years ago. The sport of kings! Little thought we then how his words would be verified!—how the pathless plain over which the line slowly but irresistibly swept would become historic, as the meeting place of the heir to the British Empire and the ruler of proud Nepaul.

Moondia Ghaut is the name of a ford over the Sarda, a river of which the left bank belongs to Nepaul and the right bank to the Province of Rohilkund. The territory opposite the Ghaut, and for many miles to the eastward along the foot of the lower ranges of the Himalayas, was conferred upon Nepaul by Lord Canning, after the Mutiny, in reward for the assistance given by the Goorkhas to our arms at Lucknow and elsewhere. The policy of that step has been warmly debated, but it would seem discourteous to raise the discussion at a time when the Prince has been enjoying the unique hospitality of what may be called the Goorkha State on the very ground in question.

Even after the cession of the Nepaulese Terai, the actual boundary was long in dispute, and it was during the determination of the boundary question that we first had the opportunity of becoming acquainted with this paradise of sportsmen.

Moondia Ghaut, till about ten years ago, was included in the district of Shahjehanpore, but it was then transferred to Phillibeet, a sub-magistracy connected with Bareilly. The Ghaut lies 70 or 80 miles to the north of Shahjehanpore, and only about 30 miles north-east of Phillibeet.

For a considerable part of the year the vicinity of Moondia Ghaut is almost deserted. Lying as it does in the heart of the Terai, a district notorious for malaria, it is only habitable in the cold season. From the end of November till the middle of March, not only is there no danger of fever, but the climate is most enjoyable. After March till the rains commence the atmosphere in the Terai is very hot and muggy, but at that season the danger to health lies in the temptations to injudicious exposure to the sun, rather than in any miasma peculiar to the locality. From the beginning of the rains till some time after they have ceased, residence in the Terai is fatal to most constitutions. Englishmen, hill-men, and Hindostanees alike flee. The villagers of the Phillibeet district speak of even the very southern fringe of the Terai with bated breath, and call it Mar, or Death. Not a soul remains save the Taroos (so called from their being the inhabitants of the Terai), a distinct race, squalid, feeble and timid, but singularly truthful, which has struggled on for ages against adverse physical influences. It is wonderful that they should live where all others die. They seem to use no special prophylactics against illness, but rather to have inherited from their ancestors comparatively fever-proof constitutions. Many fall victims to wild beasts. They have, indeed, little wherewith to protect themselves, except the voice, on which they place great reliance. It is often impossible to induce a Taroo to go alone through his native wilds, though he will start readily enough if he has a companion. They do not seem to care about being in close proximity to one another. As long as they can give an occasional halloo and hear the answer faintly resounding through the giant tree trunks they are satisfied. Their dislike to solitary journeying is, however, attributable as much to horror of evil spirits as to fear of bear or tiger.

To the sportsman and naturalist, if not to the statesman and administrator, the abundance, the bewildering variety of animal life, amply compensate for the deficiency of population.

'You have never killed a crocodile? Well, there are a dozen lying on that sandbank, and you can have your pick if you hold straight. I would not try the largest of all, he is lying directly end on, and at this angle the bullet would glance. Take the third from the left. He is very nearly as large, and you can clearly see the patch of pale, soft skin just behind the foreleg. Put your bullet right in the middle of that patch, and he will never move again. You cannot get near enough to him or sufficiently above him to shoot him through the brain. If he once wriggles into the water you will lose him, though his carcase may, perhaps, be picked up ten miles down the river.'

'Are you a fisherman?—Just below the throat of that rapid, where you see that naked dusky imp holystoning a prostrate elephant in the shallow water, you are sure to hook a mahseer before breakfast. If he will not take a fly, you can try a phantom minnow or a live bait. Be sure that your tackle is strong and your line long, for you never can tell how far a big one will go in his first rush, though he is apt to sulk afterwards. They are not as large here as in the Ganges or the Jhelum, but we shall expect some steaks for breakfast from the tail of a 20-pounder at least.'

'Are you eager to slay the brindled monarch of the forest? Hark! Did you hear that dull grunting roar on the river bank? Pshaw! Merely some wretched buffalo moaning for her calf. Again! Listen! A hundred yards further up the river. No! There is a vibration in that sound once heard never forgotten. Low and distant though it be, yet it seems to thrill the very ground beneath your feet. Don't you notice how the mumbling conversation of the camp is suddenly hushed? All are listening. I hear a Dhummer mutter outside the tent, 'Sher bolta, kat zacur milega' There is a tiger calling; we are sure to get him to-morrow.'

The Sarda emerges from the Himalayas at Burrumdeo. Moondia Ghaut is about twenty-five miles to the south of that place. From the debouchure at Burrumdeo down to Moondia Ghaut the Sarda is a bright, sparkling, merry mountain stream, often broken into two or three channels. It flows through grassy glades and emerald sissoo forests, swells here over deep sunken rocks, and there forms a tail below a shoal of glittering gravel, which makes the fisherman's eye glisten as it recalls to memory happy days on the Spey or the Findhorn. But here and there a backwater still as death runs back far into a ghastly swamp, where the water is never rippled, save by the silent plunge of the weird snake-bird, or the stealthy waddle of a gorged alligator. Huge ungainly fish and bloated carrion turtle glide far below the surface, round the skeleton roots of bleached and barkless trees, a phantom forest lichen-shrouded. On the stark framework of bonelike branches sits motionless the gaping, lockjawed cormorant, with half-spread stiffened wings—a living parody of taxidermy; or the foul vulture, its livid neck smothered in fluffy feathers, like some shapeless Caffre kaross, the only sign of life a dull, deceitful eye. On a dead willow, stretching far over the inky pool lies twined a python, limp, semi-rotten. The head is gone; the muscles of the neck blanched and torn into strings are hanging a few inches above the water, jagged by resistance to the tug of the turtle teeth. Here and there the scales have separated, and the glairy sodden skin hangs flabby and ruptured. Can you believe that you are within earshot of a babbling, rattling mountain torrent on whose floods the mightiest tree trunks are but as straws, a torrent irresistible, ever living, ever fitful? A few miles below Moondia Ghaut the river loses its rocky and rapid character, and rolls slow and turbid through fulvous unvarying plains.

It is a few minutes before sunrise, and the bank overhanging the river at this spot faces nearly north-east. Below there is the river bed, perhaps 300 yards broad, but the water does not cover the whole of it. The largest channel is just below our feet, and there is another considerable stream under the opposite bank, while two or three smaller rivulets ripple over beds of shingle, or flow silently under the ephemeral banks of crumbling islets. On yon dry sandbank lies a mighty tree, in shape uninjured, but ever and anon a light flickering tongue of flame shoots up through some minute crevice in the bark, or a filmy curl of smoke wreathes itself into nothingness in the still chill air. That tree is hollow from end to end, the core eaten out by a mouldering fire. For weeks trunk and branches have been charring internally under its ravages, though the traces of destruction are scarcely visible. A few days more—a puff of strong cold wind from the mountains—and that mighty shell—trunk, root and branch—will gradually sink away with a dull crash into a mere heap of white ashes outlined on the golden sand.

Nor are these tiny gray ripples the only signs of fire which add still life to the landscape. On the right where that crowded promontory juts out into the river, you can see the lurid furnaces of the rust-coloured catechu-burners. Here and there along the distant bank a faint column of smoke betrays where the gold washers are pursuing their miserable avocation. Immediately opposite signs of matutinal cookery taper upwards far above the low acacia trees, in which the huts of the Nepaulese outposts nestle, and far away to the north and east faint gauzy lines are traced on the high hills. At this distance they look like mere floating, fading films of mist. In truth they are the evidence of forest fires involving the vegetation of whole mountain sides in one common destruction.

By what a curious perversion of language Anglo-Indians speak of those mountains as 'the hills.' 'Do you realize that those peaks which the sun is just illumining with the brightest, most glittering gold, are the virgin summits of some of the highest mountains in the globe? Look at the isolated pyramid of Nunda Devi! Watch the bright sunbeams kissing successively the three points of the trident of Trisul. 'Enough! You will see no more sunlight effects until the beams light up that black thunder cloud at the foot of the mountains with dazzling fringe. For at least 100 miles over many a sleeping valley and many a haughty range a dark veil of mist clouds the lesser mountains. From the gleaming snow peaks, which are already fast changing from gold to silver, right down to that serrated line of gigantic pines which bristle on the crest of the nearest chain, there is nothing but a lava-like sea of the densest fog. Here and there you can see it slowly swirling out of the transverse ravines in huge burly masses almost down to the level of the Terai itself. Every valley under that stupendous pall is still in darkness. Were you standing on a lofty peak jutting up through the mist, you would fancy yourself in some glassy ocean studded with wooded reefs and atolls, a sail-less silvern archipelago, fit foreground for the home of eternal snow, the holy Himalaya.'

Even in the winter an Indian sun soon makes itself felt, and though the whole orb has scarcely freed itself from the eastern hills, there is a perceptible change in the temperature, and a flickering breeze wafts the tinkling of many bells along the river bank. From a sandy ravine, half hidden in billowy grass, with long and stately tread comes the lord of a hundred herds, a milk-white Gujerati bull, of height and girth enormous, with satin skin and gentle eyes that almost cause one to sympathize with a Sikh's religious feelings and forswear beef for ever. On his head a fillet of cowrie shells, on his brawny chest a flattened bell, and on his back behind the vast hump, half drooping with its own weight, a Banjara baby boy clad in his mother's favourite colours of blue and crimson, and so laden with jewels that of skin you can see little but a nutbrown face lighted up by two sparkling, wondering black eyes and ten chubby little fingers, of which five are twined lovingly in the loose skin of his giant steed. No load ever desecrates the broad back of this majestic bull save this child, the hope of the wandering Banjara tribe, and perhaps occasionally his mother, though rarely does her proud and lissome form acknowledge fatigue.

Behind the bull the herd—and what a herd!—a long, fan-shaped surging mass, of which the rear is completely concealed by dust, cattle of every shape and colour, of every age and every condition. No struggling, jostling Smithfield crowd. With solemn peaceful step 2,000 head debouch upon the strand and slake their thirst among the shallows. And this herd is only a drop in the ocean compared to the number of horned cattle that annually depasture the Terai. From the fertile plains of Oude, from the arid wastes of Allyghur or Gourgaon, from the far-off eyries of the Kymore hills, pour annually countless myriads of half-starved quadrupeds to revel in the succulent herbage of the great northern jungles.

APPENDIX B.

SCINDIAH, A GENERAL IN THE BRITISH ARMY.

That the descendant of Ranojee Sindia should be a British General must seem very strange to the class of old Indians who only remember old India. The story of the rise of the slipper-bearer of the Peishwa, who became one of the most famous of Mahratta Chiefs, has been discredited by recent writers; but there can be no doubt that before 1725 very little was known of Ranojee, and that, at the best, his family belonged to the Chumbi, or cultivator class.* But these were fine times for daring men, and the Mahratta sword was busy cutting slices off the Empire of the Mogul and carving them into kingdoms. When Ranojee died in 1750, he had founded a dynasty. His legitimate sons did not succeed; but Madhajee, an illegitimate son, by craft as much as by courage, established himself in such a position that he became the master of the Peishwa, and restored Shah Alum to his throne in Delhi. He it was who inflicted one of the greatest blows and most bitter disgrace ever endured by a British force in India at Wargaum, baffled Goddard's attempt to force him to give battle by masterly manœuvres, and, forcing him to seek the seaboard, secured at his leisure a large part of Central India. In a subsequent campaign he forced Carnac to retreat and ratified a treaty with the British, by which he was recognised as an independent prince, secured all Gwalior except the fortress, and bound us to recross the Jumna. His usurpation at Delhi, with which we did not interfere, was one of the boldest acts of his extraordinary career. He was neutral in our first war with Tippoo. Finding we were too busily engaged to interfere with his ambitious projects, he conceived the idea of becoming master of the Peishwa himself, and of establishing himself at Poona, but he died just as he was about to realise his magnificent conception, which would have brought him into collision with our growing power under circumstances which would place the greatest strain on all our resources and power. The conflict came when we were able to dictate terms, and well for our rule was it that Lord Ellenborough in 1844 rose superior to the instincts of conquest and annexation, for it was the gratitude and attachment of the present ruler of Gwalior which in 1857 exercised a most potent influence on the course of the insurrection. His fidelity can only be appreciated at its true value by those familiar not so much with the facts as with the local colour and all the material incidents of the crisis. He had been well rewarded, and now there is an increment to his honours, but we fear he would freely give up

* Ranojee was Pateil, beadle or headman of his village, and the designation of Pateil was greatly affected by his descendant Madojee in the plenitude of his power.

ribands, medal, uniform, army rank and all, for that rock from which British sentries look down on his city, and British guns point at his palace. Above all things, however, he is fond of soldiering, and when the Prince of Wales asked him to ride down the line at the Delhi Review, it was said that the act was worth a million of money. Sindiah was once a splendid horseman—now he has lost his nerve. His manners are uncouth, his voice harsh and vulgar, but he has a fine eye and a very earnest, honest look, nor has he any power of dissimulation. Therefore, we should like to know how he received his appointment. The other General is a man of very different type. He is essentially of a British-made dynasty, but it is said that he rules his people with much severity, and that, seat of pleasure as it is, Cashmere is inhabited by a very wretched population. It would be very interesting to learn what the new officers think of their honours.—*Army and Navy Gazette.*

APPENDIX C.

EXTRACTS FROM TREATIES BETWEEN THE EAST INDIA COMPANY AND THE NIZAM OF HYDERABAD, AND BETWEEN THE QUEEN OF ENGLAND AND THE NIZAM.

Extract from a Treaty between the East India Company and the Nizam, dated the 21st May, 1853. (*See* Aitchison's "Treaties, Engagements and Sunnuds," vol. v., pages 104, 105.)

ARTICLE 6.

For the purpose of providing the regular monthly payment to the said contingent troops, and payment of Appa Dessaye's chout and the allowances to Mohiput Ram's family and to certain Mahratta pensioners, as guaranteed in the 10th Article of the Treaty of 1822, and also for payment of the interest at six per cent. per annum of the debt due to the Honourable Company, so long as the principal of that debt shall remain unpaid, which debt now amounts to about fifty lakhs of Hyderabad rupees, the Nizam hereby agrees to assign the districts mentioned in the accompanying Schedule marked A, yielding an annual gross revenue of about fifty lakhs of rupees, to the exclusive management of the British Resident for the time being at Hyderabad, and to such other officers, acting under his orders, as may from time to time be appointed by the Government of India to the charge of those districts.

ARTICLE 8.

The districts mentioned in Schedule A are to be transferred to Colonel Low, C.B., the Resident, immediately that the ratified Treaty shall be received from Calcutta; and that officer engages on the part of the British Government that the Resident at the Court of Hyderabad for the time being shall always render true and faithful accounts every year to the Nizam of the receipts and disbursements connected with the said districts, and make over any surplus revenue that may exist to His Highness, after the payment of the contingent and the other items detailed in Article 6 of this Treaty.

Extract from a Supplemental Treaty between Her Majesty the Queen of Great Britain and the Nizam, ratified by Lord Canning on the 31st day of December, 1860. (*See* Aitchison's "Treaties," &c., vol. v., pages 115 and 116.)

ARTICLE 2.

The Viceroy and Governor-General in Council cedes to His Highness the Nizam in full sovereignty the territory of Shorapore.

ARTICLE 3.

The debt of about fifty (50) lakhs of Hyderabad rupees due by the Nizam to the British Government is hereby cancelled,

ARTICLE 4.

His Highness the Nizam agrees to forego all demand for an account of the receipts and expenditure of the assigned districts for the past, present, or future. But the British Government will pay to His Highness any surplus that may hereafter accrue after defraying all charges under Article 6 and all future expenses of administration, the amount of such expenses being entirely at the discretion of the British Government.

ARTICLE 5.

The Viceroy and Governor-General in Council restores to His Highness the Nizam all the assigned districts in the Raichore Doab and on the western frontier of the dominions of His Highness adjoining the Collectorate of Ahmednuggur and Sholapore.

ARTICLE 6.

The districts in Berar already assigned to the British Government under the Treaty of 1853, together with all the Surf-i-khas talooks comprised therein, and such additional districts adjoining thereto as will suffice to make up a present annual gross revenue of thirty-two (32) lakhs of rupees currency of the British Government, shall be held by the British Government in trust for the payment of the troops of the Hyderabad Contingent, Appa Dessaye's chout, the allowance to Mohiput Ram's family, and certain pensions mentioned in Article 6 of the said Treaty.

ARTICLE 7.

The Surf-i-khas talooks and additional districts mentioned in the foregoing Article are to be transferred to the Resident as soon as this Treaty is ratified.

APPENDIX D.

DEATH OF PRINCESS KISHNA, THE FLOWER OF RAJAST'HAN, TO SAVE HER COUNTRY FROM CIVIL WAR.

KISHNA KOMARI BAE, the 'Virgin Princess Kishna,' was in her sixteenth year: her mother was of the Chawura race, the ancient kings of Anhulwara. Sprung from the noblest blood of Hind, she added beauty of face and person to an engaging demeanour, and was justly proclaimed the 'flower of Rajast'han.' When the Roman father pierced the bosom of the dishonoured Virginia, appeased virtue applauded the deed. When Iphigenia was led to the sacrificial altar, the salvation of her country yielded a noble consolation. The votive victim of Jephtha's success had the triumph of a father's fame to sustain her resignation, and in the meekness of her sufferings we have the best parallel to the sacrifice of the lovely Kishna: though years have passed since the barbarous immolation, it is never related but with a faltering tongue and moistened eyes, 'albeit unused to the melting mood.'

The rapacious and bloodthirsty Pat'han, covered with infamy, repaired to Oodipoor, where he was joined by the pliant and subtle Ajít. Meek in his demeanour, unostentatious in his habits, despising honours, yet covetous of power,—religion, which he followed with the zeal of an ascetic, if it did not serve as a cloak, was at least no hindrance to an immeasurable ambition, in the attainment of which he would have sacrificed all but himself. When the Pat'han revealed his design, that either the princess should wed Raja Maun, or by her death seal the peace of Rajwarra, whatever arguments were used to point the alternative, the Rana was made to see no choice between consigning his beloved child to the Rahtore prince, or witnessing the effects of a more extended dishonour from the vengeance of the Pat'han, and the storm of his palace by his licentious adherents:—the fiat passed that Kishna Komari should die.

But the deed was left for women to accomplish—the hand of man refused it. The Rawula* of an eastern prince is a world within itself; it

* Harem.

is the labyrinth containing the strings that move the puppets which alarm mankind. Here intrigue sits enthroned, and hence its influence radiates to the world, always at a loss to trace effects to their causes. Maharaja Dowlut Sing, descended four generations ago from one common ancestor with the Rana, was first sounded "to save the honour of Oodipoor;" but, horror-struck, he exclaimed, "accursed the tongue that commands it! Dust on my allegiance, if thus to be preserved!" The Maharaja Jowandás, a natural brother, was then called upon; the dire necessity was explained, and it was urged that no common hand could be armed for the purpose. He accepted the poniard, but when in youthful loveliness Kishna appeared before him, the dagger fell from his hand, and he returned more wretched than the victim. The fatal purpose thus revealed, the shrieks of the frantic mother reverberated through the palace, as she implored mercy, or execrated the murderers of her child, who alone was resigned to her fate. But death was arrested, not averted. To use the phrase of the narrator, "she was excused the steel—the cup was prepared," and prepared by female hands! As the messenger presented it in the name of her father, she bowed and drank it, sending up a prayer for his life and prosperity. The raving mother poured imprecations on his head, while the lovely victim, who shed not a tear, thus endeavoured to console her: "why afflict yourself, my mother, at this shortening of the sorrows of life? I fear not to die! Am I not your daughter? Why should I fear death? We are marked out for sacrifice* from our birth; we scarcely enter the world but to be sent out again; let me thank my father that I have lived so long!† Thus she conversed till the nauseating draught refused to assimilate with her blood. Again the bitter potion was prepared. She drained it off, and again it was rejected; but, as if to try the extreme of human fortitude, a third was administered; and for the third time nature refused to aid the horrid purpose. It seemed as if the

* Alluding to the custom of infanticide—here, very rare. * * * * * *.

† With my mind engrossed with the scenes in which I had passed the better part of my life, I went two months after my return from Rajpootana, in 1823, to York Cathedral, to attend the memorable festival of that year. The sublime recitations of Handel in "Jephtha's Vow," the sonorous woe of Sapios' "Deeper and deeper still," powerfully recalled the sad exit of the Rajpootani; and the representation shortly after of Racine's tragedy of "Iphigénie," with Talma as Achille, Duchesnois as Clytemnestre, and a very interesting personation of the victim daughter of Agamemnon, again served to waken the remembrance of this sacrifice. The following passage embodying not only the sentiments, but couched in the precise language in which the "Virgin Kishna" addressed her father—proving that human nature has but one mode of expression for the same feelings—I am tempted to transcribe:

. . . . "Mon père,
Cessez de vous troubler, vous n'êtes point trahi.
Quand vous commanderez, vous serez obéi:

fabled charm, which guarded the life of the founder of her race, was inherited by the Virgin Kishna. But the bloodhounds, the Pat'han and Ajít, were impatient till their victim was at rest; and cruelty, as if gathering strength from defeat, made another and a fatal attempt. A powerful opiate was presented—*the Kasoomba draught.** She received it with a smile, wished the scene over, and drank it. The desires of barbarity were accomplished. "She slept!"† a sleep from which she never awoke.

The wretched mother did not long survive her child; nature was exhausted. In the ravings of despair she refused food, and her remains in a few days followed those of her daughter to the funeral pyre.

Even the ferocious Khan, when the instrument of his infamy, Ajít, reported the issue, received him with contempt, and spurned him from his presence, tauntingly asking, "if this were the boasted Rajpoot valour?" But the wily traitor had to encounter language far more bitter from his political adversary, whom he detested. Sangram Suktawut reached the capital only four days after the catastrophe—a man in every respect the reverse of Ajít—audaciously brave, he neither feared the frown of his sovereign nor the sword of his enemy. Without introduction he rushed into the presence, where he found seated the traitor Ajít. "Oh, dastard! who has thrown dust on the Seesodia race, whose blood which has flowed in purity through a hundred ages has now been defiled! this sin will check its course for ever; a blot so foul in our annals, that no Seesodia will ever again hold up his head! A sin to which no punishment were equal. But the end of our race is approaching! The line of Bappa Rawul is at an end! Heaven has ordained this; a signal of our destruction." The Rana hid his face with his hands, when turning to Ajít, he exclaimed, "thou stain on the Seesodia race! thou impure of Rajpoot blood, dust be on thy head, as thou hast covered us all with shame. May you die childless, and your name die with you! Why this indecent haste? Had the Pat'han stormed the city? Had he attempted to violate the sanctity of the Rawula? And, though he had, could you not die as

Ma vie est votre bien. Vous voulez le reprendre,
Vos ordres, sans détour, pouvaient se faire entendre;
D'un œil aussi content, d'un cœur aussi soumis,
Que j'acceptais l'époux que nous m'aviez promis,
Je saurai, s'il faut, victime obéissante
Tendre au fer de Calchas une tête innocente;
Et respectant le coup par vous-même ordonné,
Vous rendre tout le sang que vous m'avez donné."

* The Kasoomba draught is made of flowers and herbs of a cooling quality, into this an opiate was introduced.

† The simple but powerful expression of the narrator.

Rajpoots, like your ancestors? Was it thus they gained a name? Was it thus our race became renowned—thus they opposed the might of kings? Have you forgotten the Sakas of Cheetore? But whom do I address—not Rajpoots? Had the honour of your females been endangered—had you sacrificed them all and rushed sword in hand on the enemy, your name would have lived, and the Almighty would have secured the seed of Bappa Rawul. But to owe preservation to this unhallowed deed! You did not even await the threatened danger. Fear seems to have deprived you of every faculty, or you might have spared the blood of Sreejee, and if you did not scorn to owe your safety to deception, might have substituted some less noble victim! But the end of our race approaches!"

The traitor to manhood, his sovereign, and humanity durst not reply. The brave Sangram is now dead, but the prophetic anathema has been fulfilled. Of *ninety-five* children, sons and daughters, but one son (*the brother of Kishna*) is left to the Rana; and though his two remaining daughters have been recently married to the princes of Jessulmer and Bikaner, the Salic law, which is in full force in these States, precludes all honour through female descent. His hopes rest solely on the prince, Juvana Sing, and though in the flower of youth and health, the marriage bed (albeit boasting no less than four young princesses) has been blessed with no progeny.

The elder brother of Juvana died two years ago. Had he lived, he would have been Umra the Third. With regard to Ajít, the curse has been fully accomplished. Scarcely a month after, his wife and two sons were numbered with the dead; and the hoary traitor has since been wandering from shrine to shrine; performing penance and alms in expiation of his sins, yet unable to fling from him ambition; and with his beads in one hand, *Rama! Rama!* ever on his tongue, and subdued passion in his looks, his heart is deceitful as ever. Enough of him: let us exclaim with Sangram, "*Dust on his head,*" which all the waters of the Ganges could not purify from the blood of the virgin Kishna.—*Tod's Rajast'han.*

APPENDIX E.

THE EUPHRATES AND INDUS ROUTE TO CENTRAL ASIA.

Deputation to Viscount Palmerston, K.G. on 22nd June, 1857—Letter from W. P. Andrew, Esq. to the Right Hon. Viscount Palmerston, K.G., June 30th, 1857—Report of the Select Committee of the House of Commons on the Euphrates Valley Railway, 22nd July, 1872 (Extracts)—Letter from the Under Secretary of State for India to Mr. Andrew regarding the completion of the Indus Valley State Railway, 15th March, 1877.

A deputation, in favour of the British Government granting pecuniary support to the Euphrates Valley Railway, had an interview with Viscount Palmerston, 22nd June, 1857.

The deputation consisted of the Earl of Shaftesbury, Mr. Andrew (Chairman of the Euphrates Valley Railway), Mr. P. Anstruther, Mr. W. F. Ainsworth. Sir F. L. Arthur, Bart., Mr. A. F. Bellasis, Sir W. Colebrooke, C.B., the Earl of Chichester, the Earl of Carnarvon, Major-General Chesney, R.A., Mr. F. Ellis, M.P., Mr. Estcourt Sotheron, M.P., the Hon. J. C. Erskine, Mr. A. S. Finlay, M.P., Lord Goderich, Mr. H. Gladstone, Mr. W. Hutt, M.P., Mr. Thomas Headlam, M.P., Mr. T. B. Horsfall, M.P., Col. Harvey, M. T. K. Lynch, Mr. John Laird, Mr. Macgregor Laird, Mr. James Merry, M.P., Sir H. Maddock, Major Moore, Sir D. Norreys, M.P., Colonel W. Pinney, M.P., Mr. F. W. Russell, M.P., Sir Justin Sheil, K.C.B., Count Strylecki, Col. Steinbach, Gen. Sabine, Lord Talbot de Malahide, the Lord Mayor (Mr. Alderman Finnis), Mr. Matthew Uzielli, Mr. W. Vansittart, M.P., Sir W. F. Williams of Kars, Mr. A. Denoon, Mr. L. W. Raeburn, Mr. Wickham, M.P., Hon. A. Kinnaird, M.P., Mr. Arthur Otway, the Earl of Albemarle, Lord Ashley, Mr. Thomas Alcock, M.P., Mr. J. E. Anderdon, Viscount Bangor, Mr. W. Buchanan, M.P., Mr. F. B. Beamish, M.P., Mr. G. Bowyer, M.P., Dr. Boyd, M.P., Major C. Bruce, M.P., Lord Colchester, Lord Cloncurry, Lord Cremorne, Lord R. Clinton, Sir Edw. Colebroke, M.P., the Hon. H. Cole, M.P., Mr. R. W. Crawford, Alderman Copeland, M.P., the Bishop of Durham, Lord Dufferin, the Earl of Donoughmore, Mr. R. Davison, M.P., Colonel Dunne, M.P., Sir James Duke, M.P., the Earl of Enniskillen, Earl of Erne, Lord Elcho, Sir De Lacy Evans, M,P., Mr. J. C. Ewart, M.P., Sir J. Elphinstone, M.P., Mr. W. Fagan, M.P., Sir R. Ferguson, M.P., Sir G. Foster, M.P., Mr. C. Fortescue, M.P., Mr. F. French, M.P., Lord Robert Grosvenor, M.P., Mr. E. Grogan, M.P., Mr. S. Gregson, M.P., Mr. G. Hamilton, M.P., Mr. J. H. Hamilton, M.P., Colonel Harvey, Mr. A. Hastie, M.P., Mr. H. Ingram, M.P., Mr. W. Kirk, M.P.; Mr. T. Longman, Lord Monteagle, the Earl of Mayo, Mr. J. R. Mowbray, M.P., Mr. R. Monckton Milnes, M.P., Sir John Macneill, Mr. H. A. Mackinnon, Sir Roderick Murchison, Mr. G.

Macartney, M.P., Mr. J. M'Cann, M.P., Mr. J. M'Clintock, M.P., Mr. M'Evory, M.P., Mr. P. W. Martin, Mr. C. W. Martin, Mr. G. G. M'Pherson, Mr. F. North, M.P., Colonel North, M.P., the Right Hon. J. Napier, M.P., Mr. C. Newdegate, M.P., Sir George Pollock, G.C.B., Mr. J. Pritchard, M.P., the Earl of Roden, Lord Rossmore, Lord Stanley, Lord Sandon, the Bishop of St. David's, Mr. R. Slaney, Mr. W. Sowerby, Mr A. Turner, M.P., Colonel Taylor, M.P., Mr. W. Tollemache, M.P., Sir H. Verney, Lord Wrottesley, Mr. Whiteside, M.P., Mr. Thos. Williams, Mr. J. A. Warre, M.P.

Lord Shaftesbury introduced the deputation to Lord Palmerston, and pointed out in forcible language, the vast importance to this country of securing an alternative route to India, and the great interest generally felt throughout the country in this great undertaking, so calculated to promote commerce, civilization, and Christianity; and stated that Mr. Andrew, the chairman of the company, would submit to his Lordship more detailed information.

Mr. Andrew, after expressing his regret for the unavoidable absence of Lord Stanley, said that for some years it had been considered a great national object to secure an alternative short route to India, but that recently the establishment of the route by the Euphrates had become more and more necessary, and more especially since it had been determined to open up the Valley of the Indus by the application of steam. The great traffic which would pour down this valley from Central Asia and the Punjaub, once flowing towards Kurrachee, would naturally seek an outlet by the sister valley of the Euphrates, at least the lighter and more valuable products as well as the mails and passengers; but the support of the Government was not sought on commercial grounds. That support was sought alone on the ground of the political importance of this ancient line of communication. The grand object was to connect England with the north-west frontier of India, by steam transit through the Euphrates and Indus Valleys. The latter would render moveable to either the Kyber or the Bolan, the two gates of India, the flower of the British army cantoned in the Punjaub; and the Euphrates and Indus lines being connected by means of steamers, we should be enabled to threaten the flank and rear of any force advancing through Persia towards India.* So

* TWENTY YEARS HAVE ELAPSED SINCE THE ABOVE REMARKS WERE MADE, AND WHAT HAS BEEN DONE? PRIVATE ENTERPRISE HAS SUCCESSFULLY, BY A LINE OF STEAMERS, CONNECTED THE EUPHRATES AND INDUS. THE INDUS VALLEY RAILWAY, IN THE HANDS OF GOVERNMENT, IS NOT YET COMPLETED. SEE UNDER SECRETARY OF STATE FOR INDIA'S

that the invasion of India, by this great scheme, would be rendered practically impossible; AND IT WOULD BE EVIDENT, THAT THE GREAT ARMY OF INDIA OF 300,000 MEN BEING UNITED BY THIS MEANS TO THE ARMY IN ENGLAND, THE MUTUAL SUPPORT THEY WOULD RENDER EACH OTHER WOULD QUADRUPLE THE POWER AND ASCENDANCY OF THIS COUNTRY, AND PROMOTE POWERFULLY THE PROGRESS, THE FREEDOM, AND THE PEACE OE THE WORLD. The countries to be traversed were the richest and most ancient in the world, and might again become the granaries of Europe, and not only supply us with wheat, but with cotton of excellent quality, and his gallant friend, General Chesney, who had recently visited these regions, would tell them that there were hundreds of thousands of camel-loads of this valuable commodity rotting on the ground for want of the means of transport. Sir W. F. Williams, of Kars, would tell them there was no difficulty in dealing with the Arabs, if they were fairly treated. The Lord Mayor, who had had intimate commercial relations with the East, and Mr. Lynch, of Bagdad, who had for many years traded with the Arabs, would speak to the honesty and trustworthiness of the Arab. As to physical difficulty there was none—the line had been surveyed and proved to be singularly easy. Her Majesty's Government had given their powerful influence and support in obtaining the firman and concession. They had placed Her Majesty's ship, *Stromboli*, at the disposal of General Chesney and Sir John Macneill, and the engineering staff; and Lord Stratford de Redcliffe had lent his powerful advocacy with the Porte. He (Mr. Andrew) was deeply grateful for the assistance thus far afforded them; but they had now arrived at that point when something more was absolutely necessary, and that was the pecuniary support of Government, to enable the capital to be raised for the prosecution of the work. It was not a matter for private individuals to undertake. If they wanted an investment for their funds, they would certainly not choose Turkish Arabia. The establishment of a steam route by the Euphrates had been placed before the public and the Government. Many Chambers of Commerce and other influential associations had already memorialised the Government in favour of granting pecuniary aid; and it was believed the country was anxious that this route should be carried out by Englishmen, and it now rested with the Government to say whether they concurred in the importance of the work, and if so, whether they would be prepared to recommend such an amount of pecuniary assistance, whether by guarantee or otherwise, as would enable this, the

LETTER, P. 379 OF THIS APPENDIX. THE BRANCH TO THE KYBER IS PROCEEDING SLOWLY, AND THAT TO THE BOLAN HAS NOT BEEN COMMENCED!

most important undertaking ever submitted to their consideration, to be proceeded with.

Sir W. F. Williams, of Kars, stated that during his long residence amongst the Arabs he experienced no difficulty in dealing with them, or in procuring, during his excavations in Susa, any number of workmen he might require; and he also pointed out the great importance of the proposed harbour of Seleucia, as there was not a single good harbour on the Syrian coast.

Count Strylecki briefly addressed his lordship on the support of successive Turkish Governments to the undertaking, viewing it as of incalculable political importance to England in relation to her Indian possessions.

Mr. Finlay, M.P., speaking from personal acquaintance with the country to be traversed, dwelt on its great capacity for development, if only the means of transport were afforded.

General Chesney gave full explanations regarding the harbour, as to its exact position, capacity, &c.

Sir Justin Sheil, late ambassador in Persia, dwelt on the political importance of the line, and said that it would shorten the distance to Kurrachee, the European port of India by 1,400 miles.

The Lord Mayor (Mr. Alderman Finnis) had had, through his agents, extensive commercial transactions with the Arabs, and had found them most reliable and honest; and he considered they were as much alive to their own interests as any other race, and would be in favour of the railway, because it would at once give them employment and afford them an outlet for their produce.

Mr. Lynch, of Bagdad, from long residence, fully confirmed the Lord Mayor's views.

Mr. Horsfall, M.P., assured Lord Palmerston that the undertaking was viewed with great interest in the manufacturing districts generally, and placed in his lordship's hands a memorial from the Chamber of Commerce of Liverpool, praying that the Government would extend the necessary pecuniary aid to the Euphrates Valley Railway Company.

Lord Palmerston assured the deputation that the Government were fully alive to the great importance of the Euphrates route, that they had supported, and would continue to support it; but he could not give an opinion as to giving the guarantee on the capital without consulting his colleagues. He requested Mr. Andrew to put his proposition in writing, and said it should have a proper amount of consideration, and that Government would be happy to aid it, if in their power.

Mr. Andrew having thanked his lordship for the courteous reception accorded them, the deputation withdrew, much gratified by the manner in which they had been received.*

* Reprinted from *The Times* and *Morning Herald*, of the 23rd June, 1857.

Letter from W. P. Andrew, Esq., to the Right Hon. Viscount Palmerston, K.G.

LONDON, *June* 30, 1857.

MY LORD,—In compliance with the desire expressed by your Lordship, when the deputation waited upon you on the 22nd instant, in favour of a guaranteed rate of interest being granted by Her Majesty's Government on a portion of the capital of the Euphrates Valley Railway Company, that the proposition should be submitted in writing, I have now the honour to state for your Lordship's consideration that the pecuniary support of Government is sought on the following grounds:—

2. The establishment of a railway from the Mediterranean to the Persian Gulf would have the effect of reducing the distance between this country and India by upwards of 1,000 miles and the time to about fourteen days, or about half the period now occupied.

3. It would be the means of consolidating the power of the Sultan in his Asiatic dominions.

4. By means of this railway, taken in conjunction with the system of steam transit now being established along the valley of the Indus from Lahore to the sea at Kurrachee,* the large force stationed in the Punjaub would be rendered of incalculable importance by steamers uniting the line of the Indus with that of the Euphrates,† for in that case any hostile force advancing towards the Indus would not only be met on the line of that river, but would be threatened along the sea-board of the Persian Gulf and the line of the Euphrates in flank and rear.

5. The Indus and the Euphrates thus united, the dangerous isolation of Persia would be at an end, and a Russian invasion of India would cease even to be speculated upon.

6. The first section of the line, from Seleucia to the Euphrates, has been surveyed by Major-General Chesney and Sir John Macneill, with an engineering staff, and has been reported as of easy construction. Copies of the reports of these able and scientific gentlemen are annexed for your lordship's information.

7. The Turkish government undertake to commence simultaneously with the railway the construction of a harbour at the mouth of the Orontes at the proposed terminus of the railway.

8. The harbour has been surveyed by Sir John Macneill, with the assistance of the officers of Her Majesty's ship "Stromboli." Plans of the proposed works have been already submitted to the First Lord of the Admiralty, and they are now forwarded for your Lordship's nspection.

* Kurrachee is not only the port of the Indus and Central Asia, but from its geographical position and other advantages, appears destined to become the European port of India.

† This has since been accomplished by the British India Steam Navigation Company. The Indus Railway is still incomplete.—Page 379 of this Appendix.

9. There being no harbour on the coast of Syria, better than the open roadsteads of Beyrout, Jaffa, Tripoli, and Acre, or the pestilential harbour of Alexandretta, the importance of having a safe and commodious harbour will be apparent for political as well as commercial purposes.

10. This harbour, connected by means of the railway with Bussorah at the head of the Persian Gulf, would give to England the first strategical position in the world.

11. The resources of England being made promptly available on any emergency in the East, Chatham and Southampton would become the basis of operations, instead of Kurrachee or Bombay, and would enable this country to anticipate or repel, whether in Europe or Asia, any attack with the rapidity and advantages of an irresistible force.

12. On an emergency in India, troops from England could be landed at Kurrachee in three weeks, and in another week at Lahore, by steam transit.

13. The Euphrates Valley Railway, in addition to its political advantages, would powerfully promote the commerce and civilisation of the world at large, and that the commercial and manufacturing communities concur in these sentiments has been shown by the addresses lately submitted to your Lordship. They are quite alive to the importance of obtaining cotton, wool, sugar, indigo, and other products from India and Mesopotamia, and the production, being effected by free labour, would of necessity tend to the extinction of slavery.

14. Through the zealous exertions of Major-General Chesney, aided by the advice and powerful support of Viscount Stratford de Redcliffe, a concession was granted by the Turkish Government in the early part of this year, guaranteeing a *minimum* rate of interest of 6 per cent. on the capital required for the first section from the Mediterranean to the Euphrates, besides affording other privileges.

15. But as these terms, from the state of the money-market and other causes, have neither been, nor are likely to be, sufficiently attractive to induce the British capitalist to embark his money in a distant enterprise, the deputation, of which I had the honour of being a member, waited upon your Lordship with the view of impressing upon your attention the absolute necessity of the pecuniary support of Her Majesty's Government being extended to the undertaking, in the event of the Government concurring in the opinion expressed by the deputation, that the Euphrates Valley Railway was a work of great national importance.

16. It was most satisfactory to the deputation to have from your Lordship the assurance that Her Majesty's Government entirely concurred with the deputation as to the great importance to this country of connecting England and India by the Euphrates Valley route, and that it would continue to receive the countenance and furtherance of Government.

17. The financial support required from Her Majesty's Government is a counter guarantee of 5 per cent. for twenty-five years, or $4\frac{1}{2}$ per cent. for fifty years, on the capital of £1,400,000 for the first section. The responsibility incurred by the Government in granting this assistance would, it is believed, be merely nominal, and could only accrue in the event of two contingencies—the railway not paying a moderate dividend, and the Turkish Government failing to fulfil its part of the contract.

18. Only under the above circumstances could Her Majesty's Government be called upon to make any contribution, and it will be seen by reference to Sir J. Macneill's Report, that the existing traffic upon that portion of the route of the proposed railway is sufficient in his judgment to yield a dividend of 8 per cent. on the capital required.

19. The East India Company might fairly be expected to share the responsibility of the counter guarantee, in the same way as they have already contributed to the subsidy to the European and Indian Junction Telegraph Company, as the establishment of the proposed route appears to be of vital importance for securing the good government and peaceable possession of India.

20. The experienced and distinguished gentlemen with whom I had the honour of being associated in waiting upon your Lordship, on the 22nd instant, are well aware that the question of the Government guaranteeing interest on an industrial undertaking is not free from difficulty, and this difficulty would be increased if, on the present occasion, the granting of the guarantee might hereafter be quoted as a precedent for similar demands.

21. The pecuniary support of Government is on the present occasion sought, not on industrial or commercial considerations, but on account of the political importance of the railway to the empire at large; and it is to be remembered that whatever assistance the Government may render to the Euphrates Valley Railway, can never be quoted as a precedent for the furtherance of any similar undertaking, for no similar undertaking can possibly be brought forward, as the route proposed is at once the shortest and the easiest between England and India, the whole length of the valley of the Euphrates is so free from impediment, that it would seem as if Providence had specially ordained it to be the great highway of nations between the East and the West.

22. I beg to call your Lordship's attention to the accompanying memorandum by Sir Justin Sheil, on the political advantages that might fairly be expected to accrue to England by the proposed Euphrates Valley Railway being in the hands of Englishmen, and to the annexed report of the evidence in the committee of the House of Commons on the European and Indian Junction Telegraph Company, to the effect that no danger is to be apprehended to the construction of either a telegraph or a railway from the Arabs on the banks of the Euphrates and Tigris.

23. In confiding to the consideration of Her Majesty's Government

what is believed to be the most important work, viewed in all its bearings, that was ever submitted to any Government, I must state the general conviction that the Euphrates route will most assuredly pass into other hands if England declines the task.

24. I beg again to express, on behalf of the deputation, their grateful sense of your Lordship's consideration and courtesy.

I have the honour, &c.,

W. P. ANDREW, *Chairman.*

The Right Hon. Viscount Palmerston, K.G.

Report of the Select Committee of the House of Commons, on the Euphrates Valley Railway, dated 22nd July, 1872. Extracts.*

THE SELECT COMMITTEE appointed to Examine and Report upon the whole subject of Railway Communication between the *Mediterranean*, the *Black Sea* and the *Persian Gulf*, have considered the matters to them referred, and have agreed to the following Report:—

Your Committee have to report that, in compliance with the directions of your Honourable House, they have taken evidence upon the whole subject of railway communication between the Mediterranean, the Black Sea and the Persian Gulf.

They find that at the present time no such communication exists, nor is any plan for establishing it in course of execution, though it has been stated to them that the Turkish Government has it in contemplation to extend the line of railway now in course of construction from Scutari towards Bagdad, thereby connecting Constantinople and the Black Sea with the Valley of the Tigris, whence the line might at a future time be continued to the Persian Gulf. *The Russian system of railways is nearly completed as far as Tiflis, and may shortly be expected to reach Reched on the Russo-Persian frontier. It is surmised that this system also might at a future time be extended to the Gulf, which would thus be brought into communication with the Black Sea at Poti.* This is, however, as yet, mere matter of speculation.

It has seemed to them (the Committee) that they would most properly discharge their functions by confining their attention to the question of establishing a route to the Persian Gulf from some port on the Mediterranean, to which British ships could at all times have easy and uncontrolled access, and which would be likely to be available, whenever required, for

* The Committee was composed of the following members:—Sir Stafford Northcote, Bart.; Viscount Sandon; Sir George Jenkinson, Bart.; Hon. Fred. Walpole; Mr. Eastwick; Mr. Baillie Cochrane; Mr. Laird; Mr. Grant Duff; Hon. Arthur Kinnaird; Mr. Brassey; Sir Charles Wingfield; Mr. Henry Robert Brand; Mr. M'Arthur; Mr. Dyce Nicol; Mr. Kirkman Hodgson. This Committee was appointed on the motion of Sir George Jenkinson.—W. P. A.

the transmission of troops and mails, as well as passengers and goods, to India.

Upon this point they have not only taken the evidence of a number of official and non-official witnesses, but have also obtained, through the kindness of the Secretary of State for Foreign Affairs, a series of reports from certain of Her Majesty's consuls, who were considered by his lordship to be the best qualified to furnish valuable information on the subject. These reports, which are highly interesting, will be found in the Appendix.

The evidence which your Committee have taken, and to which much more might have been added, has satisfied them that there is no insuperable obstacle in the way of the construction of a railway from some suitable port in the Mediterranean to some other suitable port at or near the head of the Persian Gulf; that there is more than one port which might be selected at either end of the line; that there are several practicable routes; that there would be no difficulty in procuring the necessary supply of labour and of materials for constructing a railway; and that there need be no apprehension of its being exposed to injury by natives, either during the process of its construction or after it shall have been completed. They find, too, that there is reason to expect the sanction, if not the active concurrence, of the Turkish Government, in any well-conceived project that may be presented to them.

So far as the information they have obtained goes, they are disposed to prefer Alexandretta to Tripoli as the point of departure, even for a line down the right bank of the Euphrates; while, should a line down the Tigris be preferred, or should it be thought desirable to connect the new line with the projected Turkish system, there can be no doubt of the superiority of the former terminus.

As regards the terminus on the Persian Gulf, your Committee are decidedly of opinion that it would be better to carry the line to some point where it might be brought into communication with the steam-vessels which are now under Government subvention to carry the mails, and which ply from the Indian ports to Bussorah, than to continue it along the coast to Kurrachee by a very expensive and probably unremunerative route. Of the particular ports which have been mentioned, they are inclined to prefer the port of Grane; but upon this point, as well as upon the selection of a port on the Mediterranean, they think that a local inquiry, conducted by competent scientific authorities, with a special reference to the purpose in view, would be desirable.

Passing from the question of the termini to that of the route itself, your Committee find that the arguments in favour of, and against, the Euphrates and the Tigris routes respectively, may be thus stated:—

The Euphrates route is considerably the shorter, would be the cheaper to make; and, assuming an equal rate of speed, would afford the quicker passage for persons, troops, or mails passing between England and India. The Tigris route might attract the larger amount of traffic, and would connect itself better with the projected Turkish system.

Among the witnesses whose evidence tends most strongly to support the policy of incurring the cost or risk of a national guarantee, your Committee may mention Viscount Stratford de Redcliffe, Lord Strathnairn, Sir H. Bartle Frere, Sir Donald Macleod. Mr. Laing, Colonel Sir H. Green, Colonel Malcolm Green, Captain Tyler, R.E., Mr. W. Gifford Palgrave, &c.

Among those who suggest considerations tending to throw doubt on the propriety of such an expenditure, your Committee would call attention to the evidence of Lord Sandhurst, Sir H. Rawlinson, Major Champain, &c.

Your Committee have not obtained full information as to the cost of any of the lines which have been proposed; but they think it probable that the sum of £10,000,000 would be amply sufficient to cover the expense of the shortest route, at all events.

What then are the advantages which the country might expect to gain from this possible expenditure? They are principally those to be derived from the more rapid transmission of mails, and from the possession of an alternative and more rapid route for the conveyance of troops; and from the great commercial advantages, both to India and England, which the opening up of the route would confer.

The amount of time that might be saved in the transmission of mails from England to Bombay is variously estimated by different witnesses, some placing it at four days, others as high as seven or eight days; but it must of course materially depend upon, first, the length of the railway, and secondly, the rate of speed at which the trains can travel, which again depends partly upon the gauge to be adopted, and thus the question is resolved into one of cost. Captain Tyler, R.E., who has gone carefully into the question, states the saving of distance by the Euphrates route from London *viâ* Brindisi and Scanderoon to Bombay, as compared with that *viâ* Brindisi, Alexandria and Suez, at 723 miles, and estimates the saving of time at 92 hours. The adoption of Kurrachee as the point of debarkation instead of Bombay, would of course materially enhance the saving, and during the season of the monsoon the gain would be increased by avoiding the Indian Ocean.

But nearly all the witnesses concur as to the importance of having a second or alternative route available in case of the first being impeded,* or

* It has already been mentioned that in Sir Garnet Wolseley's opinion "the largest ironclads could not pass by the canal, and it was evident that it would be the *easiest matter in the world* to stop the traffic on that canal. It might be done by a few barges, by one good large torpedo, by a vessel laden with dynamite or powder and taken to certain positions in the canal, where they would do enough damage to stop the canal for a year."—W.P.A.

in case of an emergency arising, which might call for the rapid dispatch of troops, especially if they were wanted in the north-west of India.

The importance of the proposed route by way of the Persian Gulf would of course be materially enhanced, especially as regards the conveyance of troops, by the completion of the works now in progress at the harbour of Kurrachee, and of the Indus Valley, and the Lahore and Peshawur Railways. Your Committee have therefore taken the evidence of Mr. Thornton, the Secretary to the Public Works Department at the India Office, and of Mr. Parkes, the consulting engineer to the Secretary of State for India for the harbour at Kurrachee, who have spoken most favourably of the works now in progress there. Your Committee gather from the evidence of these gentlemen that the harbour, which is already available for the landing of troops and mails, will in the course of two more years be capable of receiving the large Indian troop-ships. THEY ARE NOT AWARE OF THE PERIOD WITHIN WHICH THE SYSTEM OF RAILWAYS CONNECTING KURRACHEE WITH PESHAWUR MAY BE EXPECTED TO BE COMPLETED; BUT WHENEVER THIS SHALL HAVE BEEN DONE, THERE CAN BE NO DOUBT THAT A ROUTE BY WAY OF THE PERSIAN GULF AND KURRACHEE WILL AFFORD MEANS OF COMMUNICATION BETWEEN ENGLAND AND THE PUNJAUB, AND NORTH-WEST FRONTIER OF BRITISH INDIA, SUPERIOR TO THOSE AFFORDED BY THE WAY OF SUEZ AND BOMBAY.*

Speaking generally, your Committee are of opinion that the two routes by the Red Sea and by the Persian Gulf, might be maintained and used simultaneously; that at certain seasons and for certain purposes the advantage would lie with the one, and at other seasons and for other purposes it would lie with the other; that it may fairly be expected that in process of time traffic enough for the support of both would develope itself, but that this result must not be expected too soon; THAT THE POLITICAL AND COMMERCIAL ADVANTAGES OF ESTABLISHING A SECOND ROUTE WOULD AT ANY TIME BE CONSIDERABLE, AND MIGHT, UNDER POSSIBLE CIRCUMSTANCES, BE EXCEEDINGLY GREAT; AND THAT IT WOULD BE WORTH THE WHILE OF THE ENGLISH GOVERNMENT TO MAKE AN EFFORT TO SECURE THEM, CONSIDERING THE MODERATE PECUNIARY RISK WHICH THEY WOULD INCUR. THEY BELIEVE THAT THIS MAY BEST BE DONE BY OPENING COMMUNICATIONS WITH THE GOVERNMENT OF TURKEY IN THE SENSE INDICATED BY THE SEMI-OFFICIAL CORRESPONDENCE TO WHICH THEY HAVE ALREADY DRAWN ATTENTION.

July 22nd, 1872.

* *Vide* pp. 369 and 379 of this Appendix.

From the Under Secretary of State for India to W. P. Andrew, Esq., Chairman of the Scinde, Punjaub, and Delhi Railway Company, regarding the approaching completion of the Indus Valley State Railway.

INDIA OFFICE, 15*th March*, 1877.

SIR,—With reference to the correspondence noted in the margin,* I am directed by the Marquis of Salisbury to acquaint you for the information of the Scinde, Punjaub, and Dehli Railway Board, that his Lordship has received a letter from the Government of India relative to the progress of the Indus Valley State Railway, from which the following is an extract:—

* Letters from Mr. Andrew to Under Secretary of State for India, dated 14th December, 1876, (No. 896); and 10th January, 1877, (No. 905). Letters from Under Secretary of State for India, to Mr. Andrew, dated 2nd and 31st January, 1877.

"The section of the line from Mooltan to Chunni Ghate, and thence by a temporary surface line to a point on the Sutlej below its junction with the Chenab has now been opened for goods traffic, and thus is saved the difficult navigation in the Chenab, thereby adding some 20 to 30 per cent. to the carrying power of the Flotilla in correspondence with the Scinde, Punjaub, and Dehli Railway. The passage over the Sutlej at Bahawulpore is effected by a temporary bridge in the dry season, and by ferry in the rains."

It is estimated that, with the exception of the bridges over the Sutlej and the Indus, the line throughout will be finished by the end of the present year, viz., the Section from Kotri to Sukkur by June, and that from Chunni Ghote to Kotri by December.

I am, Sir,

Your obedient Servant,

Signed LOUIS MALLET.

INDEX.

B.

C.

D.

E.

U.

V.

W.

LIST OF WORKS PUBLISHED BY THE AUTHOR.

THE INDUS AND ITS PROVINCES.

Their Political and Commercial Importance. Illustrated by Statistical Tables and Maps. 8vo. 10s. 6d.

MEMOIR OF THE EUPHRATES VALLEY ROUTE TO INDIA.

With Official Correspondence and Maps. Dedicated to the Earl of Clarendon, K.G. 8vo. 10s. 6d.

THE SCINDE RAILWAY.

In Relation to the Euphrates Valley and other Routes to India.

With Illustrative Maps, Statistical Tables, &c., from Official Sources. 8vo. 10s. 6d.

LETTER TO VISCOUNT PALMERSTON, K.G, ON THE POLITICAL IMPORTANCE OF THE EUPHRATES VALLEY RAILWAY.

With Reports by General CHESNEY and Mr. JOHN MACNEILL, and Memorandum by Sir JUSTEN SHEIL, K.C.B.

THE EUPHRATES VALLEY ROUTE TO INDIA.

A Paper read before the British Association at Brighton in 1872. With Map and Appendix.

THE EUPHRATES VALLEY ROUTE TO INDIA IN CONNECTION WITH THE CENTRAL ASIAN QUESTION.

A Lecture delivered at the Royal United Service Institution, Lord STRATHNAIRN, G.C.B., G.C.S.I., in the Chair.

ON THE COMPLETION OF THE RAILWAY SYSTEM OF THE VALLEY OF THE INDUS.

A Letter to the Duke of ARGYLE, K.T., Secretary of State for India.

INDIAN RAILWAYS AND THEIR PROBABLE RESULTS.

By an Old Indian Postmaster. Third Edition, 1848. Maps. 8vo 10s. 6d.

LETTERS REPUBLISHED FROM THE "TIMES" ON TELEGRAPHIC COMMUNICATION WITH INDIA.